Migration of the Ukrainian Population: Economic, Institutional and Sociocultural Factors

Yuriy Bilan

]u[

ubiquity press
London

Published by
Ubiquity Press Ltd.
6 Windmill Street
London W1T 2JB
www.ubiquitypress.com

First published 2017

Cover design by Amber MacKay
Cover image is licensed under CC0 Public Domain and sourced
from Pixabay.com / Unsplash

Printed in the UK by Lightning Source Ltd.
Print and digital versions typeset by Siliconchips Services Ltd.

ISBN (Paperback): 978-1-909188-99-0
ISBN (PDF): 978-1-909188-96-9
ISBN (EPUB): 978-1-909188-97-6
ISBN (Mobi): 978-1-909188-98-3

DOI: https://doi.org/10.5334/bbg

The full text of this book has been peer-reviewed to ensure high academic
standards. For full review policies, see http://www.ubiquitypress.com/

Suggested citation:
Bilan, Y 2017 *Migration of the Ukrainian Population: Economic, Institutional and Sociocultural Factors*. London: Ubiquity Press. DOI: https://
doi.org/10.5334/bbg. License: CC-BY 4.0

To read the free, open access version of this
book online, visit https://doi.org/10.5334/bbg
or scan this QR code with your mobile device:

Contents

Acknowledgements

The author would like to thank the European Commission for its support of the EU FP6 projects Marie Curie Action, Transfer of Knowledge, Development Scheme "Development in competitiveness of labor market" and FP7-SSH-2009-A Small or medium-scale focused research project "EUMAGINE – Imagining Europe from the outside". The author would also like to thank the project coordinators, prof. Tomasz Bernat and prof. Christiane Timmerman.

Special thanks goes to my dearest family.

Reviewers

Introduction

Today Ukraine is seen by many as one of the least stable and pre-
dictable neighbours of the European Union. Possible scenarios for
Ukraine's further development as a country are very diverse – from
the collapse as such, as described by Huntington (1993) in his narrative on the so-called "torn countries" to rather optimistic proph-
ecies on rapid growth, similar to the South-East Asian "tigers"
Taiwan and Singapore, which are known for their significant and
rapid economic achievements, leapfrogging from being agrarian
and highly corrupted neofeudal countries to high-tech and postindustrial economies, living now happily under free market.

   Even though there have been indeed several episodes of quality
economic growth in the contemporary history of Ukraine, a lot

How to cite this book chapter:
Bilan, Y 2017 *Migration of the Ukrainian Population: Economic, Institutional
   and Sociocultural Factors.* Pp. vii–xxi. London: Ubiquity Press. DOI:
   https://doi.org/10.5334/bbg.a. License: CC-BY 4.0

of time and resources since Ukraine's independence back in 1991 have been wasted. Instead of following exactly, step by step, the already developed reforms programme, Ukraine's political elite was often balancing between populism and primitive egoism, and this has lead to the creation of a rather hybrid national economic model. This model is now being overloaded by an enormously huge and at the same time low-efficient officialdom, millions of public servants and the same millions of public benefit holders, while public servants at all levels are mostly devouring their shadow rents. Meanwhile, the political system in the country is more of a fragile and immature, not a fully functioning democracy.

New hopes and opportunities suddenly showed up in Ukraine in late 2013–early 2014, being the natural consequences of the political and socioeconomic crisis in the country. Speaking generally, early signs and preconditions for this wide social split in which Ukrainian society found itself at the very end of 2013 had been formed over many years. This split reached its peak in the situation of vital strategic choice for the country between external political vectors – European or Eurasian. This geopolitical dichotomy quickly became just another double game for Ukrainian politicians, and this double game had lingered for decades. It is noteworthy, however, that this state of the political elites managed to find its nourishing sources in the ambivalence of the mass consciousness of the Ukrainians. This ambivalence somehow combines features of paternalism and nostalgic feelings towards the "Soviet easy life" with its guaranteed employment, totally free healthcare and education on one side, with rather idealized (if not to say utopic) ideas about "flourishing Western democracies" on the other.

The Revolution of Dignity and further political developments in Ukraine made it quite clear that there is no place of geopolitical imitations anymore, and all further development of the country will depend not on diplomacy and oratory, but on real steps and changes.

At all previous stages of Ukraine's development, migration flows of population were always the key indicator, the litmus test for internal policies of frequently changing governments.

At the beginning of the 1990s, after the fall of the Iron Curtain, citizens of Ukraine got the opportunity for free movement, and not only within the socialistic camp. Since those times, the migration of Ukrainians has been always synchronized with the trends of country's socioeconomic development: periods of stabilization and growth always demonstrated positive migration balance, while periods of economic slowdown and/or political instability were always accompanied by growing external migration. In Ukraine, external migration is not a situational phenomenon, but a historical and traditional one: Ukrainian diaspora in the world totals several dozens of millions, among which there is quite a large number of those keeping constant contact with Ukraine, thus forming a sort of social network welcoming newcomers in host countries.

It is important to differentiate between stationary labour migration and other types of migration by their aims and forms. At the same time these differences are rather abstract, in real life and empirical research they will not be always that obvious. To the best of our knowledge, the share of Ukrainian citizens who leave the country and renounce citizenship at once is miniscule. Double citizenship is illegal in Ukraine, still, many migrants keep passports and citizenship even after naturalization in a host country. Therefore, in real sociological practice it would be extremely hard to measure the volume of stationary migration as such.

Absolute majority of external migrants belong to the economically active population. They perform paid labour in host countries and often send money back home; hypothetically, they can also return to Ukraine anytime. Thus, even artificial and not-always-accurate division by migration types would simplify the research procedures.

During spring and summer 2016, more and more frequent news concerning the liberalization of visa regime between Ukraine and the EU became the first sign implying that maybe the hard times of this EU's "uneasy neighbour" are over. However, Ukraine's way to a visa-free regime, with all of its legislation and institutional and economic changes, has not always been perfect. The military conflict on the East is still ongoing; April's Holland referendum result was not favourable for Ukraine; in addition to that, a range of corruption-related scandals and yet another Cabinet rotation delayed the formal decision on visas.

At the same time, the Association Agreement between Ukraine and the European Union has already formed an institutional and political framework for further gradual integration. The external economic activity of the country was among the first to feel the changes: EU-Ukraine export-import relations are moving fast, while sales turnover with Russia has decreased dramatically.

Significant changes took place in the mass consciousness as well. In the last two years, the ideas of joining the EU and NATO got thousands of new fans. And now Ukraine, in its public discussions, just like any other European country, has two camps – Eurooptimists and Eurosceptics. The Eurooptimists perceive visa regime liberalization as a good sign of the country's "homecoming". Eurosceptics, on the other hand, tend to emphasize the rather symbolic meaning of it, deprived of any real life value, since visa liberalization as such does not guarantee more employment opportunities and/or a longer stay in the EU. Additionally, considering the scale of the recent hryvnya devaluation, for the vast majority of the Ukrainians, European tourism is just a dream.

At the same time, visa liberalization gave rise to a range of new fears related to the EU migration risks. Today especially this issue is becoming more and more sensitive, considering the almost uncontrolled mass migration from the Middle East, and also the fact that starting from 2014 Ukrainians also started to apply for the refugee status much more frequently. The (half-)open doors to Europe led researchers to pose the following general questions: What is that combination of factors which force Ukrainians to migrate? Which of these factors are decisive, final ones? What is the hierarchy of these factors, and does this hierarchy change over time? Which social groups are the most inclined to make a migration decision? How do potential migrants imagine Europe to be? What do they expect from hosting societies? With what life goals are they coming to the European Union and what are they looking for there?

The subject matter of external migration in Ukraine is rather well developed in research (historic, demographic and statistical, economic and sociological), mostly due to the significant impact and volumes of this phenomenon in the country. Ukraine is a historic donor of migration flows, and the related corpus of studies has been formed since the middle of the twentieth century when the third wave of Ukrainian migration was about to slow down. Aside from Ukrainian authors – who for obvious reasons have always had an interest in this subject matter – foreign authors, first of all from Central Europe and Poland in particular, have joined these academic debates.

In general, scientific discourse on external migration from Ukraine have several distinctive features as follows: 1) ethnocentrism, the studies consider specifically external migration from Ukraine as migration of ethnical Ukrainians, disregarding ethnical minorities and providing no cross-national context as such; 2) disciplinary narrowness, external migration of the Ukrainians has been hardly ever studied in the interdisciplinary context; 3) alarmism and negativism in the descriptions of external migration, priority is always given to problems not prospects related to the phenomenon.

All of this has shaped the corresponding academic paradigm of migration studies on Ukraine. Naturally, such specific features did not contribute to adequate assessment and understanding of external migration from Ukraine. However, as it was well noted by Kuhn in his "Structure of scientific revolutions" (1962), the growth of scientific knowledge is happening as a result of struggle between competing scientific theories and paradigms, while revisionism is one of the most widely spread model of scientific activity.

These days we can observe the gradual change of the external migration research paradigm in Ukraine. This change has become possible due to many researchers, among which the international project EUMAGINE has its prominent role. This project from the very initial stage has been implemented as cross-national aiming at well grounded description of migration intentions, perceptions and practices in the societies which are traditional donors of migration flows to the EU Member States. Covering both socio-cultural and economic aspects, this project provides an opportunity to abandon the so-called methodological nationalism and to form the most advanced corpus of comparative knowledge on the factors behind migration to the EU (Bilan, 2015).

In the theoretical and methodological sense this research is a good example of wide interdisciplinary integration. The empirical material was gathered using quantitative and qualitative sociological methods, while the data obtained was interpreted using such culturological and economic concepts as: imagined geography, informal economy, institutional efficiency, private transfers etc.

Finally, the Ukrainian part of this project has managed to prove that negativist and alarmist approaches to external migration phenomenon are outdated and not adequate to realia[1]: at the levels of both mass and expert discourses, external migration is more and more often perceived as a potential life success strategy. And the very phenomenon of migration in Ukraine today is becoming more circular and highly dynamic, disruption of families and social contacts is observed less frequently. Moreover, one of sudden discoveries for both politicians and researchers became the fact that a large share of external migrants do not end up as miserable hunters for low-paid jobs or social allowance – many of them are successful innovators and agents of economic, cultural or even political change, both in hosting countries and at home.

The EUMAGINE project also turned out to be fruitful when it comes to a number of the related publications, which are still growing. The Ukrainian part of the project is covered, inter alia, by the following authors: B. Vollmer, F. Duvell, Y. Borshchevska, I. Lapshyna, S. Vdovtsova, among others. Namely, F. Duvell (2014) has been concentrating on the phenomenon of highly paid professionals' migration and the correlation between this phenomenon and the socioeconomic development of sending countries. Duvell emphasizes that the very idea of "brain drain" is already outdated since it does not take into account that today's migration processes

---

[1] This vision is also supported by Prof. Ella Libanova, who also mentions that"there are absolutely no grounds to conclude that families of migrants risk poverty more than other, risk to be social excluded" (Libanova, 2011, p. 24).

tend to be more seasonal, circular and temporary. Therefore, academic discourse on brain drain develops into the new concepts of "brain circulation" and "brain gain" as advantages and achievements which a sending country may get as a result. However, as it is well noted by the same author, in public, media and academic discourse, negativism in relation to external migration from Ukraine still does not cease to be dominating.

B. Vollmer, in his monograph "Ukrainian Migration and the European Union – Dynamics, Subjectivity, and Politics" (2016), somehow goes beyond traditional academic discourse borders, and along with the analysis of external migration from Ukraine in its historic perspective, structural determinants of external migration at the current stage, perceived corruption as being the central push factor, he also suggests a wide range of methodological and sociocultural reflections concerning subjectivity of migration decision – meaning the level of independence in the decision to leave and the ability to implement this decision.

In spite of the variety in theoretical and methodological approaches applied, methods and tools, and disciplinary polyphony as such, there are still certain gaps in scientific knowledge on external migration from Ukraine. First of all, such a gap is observed due to the total absence of integrative interdisciplinary studies which would use the potential of sciences' orchestra to its fullest in order to form the complete understanding of external migration as a truly multiaspect phenomenon.

The study presented here is actually an attempt to fill in this gap by means of combining sociological, econometric and statistical analyses. The study also covers rather understudied aspects of the external migration phenomenon: the dynamics of mass, expert and public media discourses concerning external migration; the role of post-imperial cultural dependences in the formation of migration intentions and geographical perceptions of Ukrainian citizens; the role of religion and confession in external migration processes; the roles of political instability, corruption and conflict on the East of the country stimulating migration intentions; mathematical modelling of the system of both micro- and macroeconomic, institutional and sociocultural factors of external migration since the beginning of the fourth wave through today.

Theoretical grounds

Back in the 1970s, one of the leading social notionalists of today, R. Inglehart, introduced the notion of progressing postmaterialization into scientific use and circulation, implying the value shift which had taken place after the World War II in many countries, first of all, in those which are called developed now. This value shift made these countries move from industrial development to the postindustrial stage in their development (Inglehart, 1977). Since then the dynamics of economic, political and sociocultural processes has increased dramatically. Global information space, mass culture, highly developed communications and transport infrastructure has turned our world into a "global village", as well noted by McLuhan (1962). Postmateralization of values, easing of national borders and strengthening sociocultural integration in today's world, on one hand, lead to certain changes in motivation behind human behaviour. On the other hand, they also require a brand-new scientific optics to be applied. The once-popular model of homo economicus is now being treated as limited, if not to say archaic. It treats humans as consumers in a supermarket who are driven by rational choice, and today in all fields (economic, cultural or political) such an explanation would not be valid anymore. The same is observed for many other classical concepts and notions. In sociology these would be social roles, group affiliations and identity. Liquid modernity, as termed by Z. Bauman, makes social structures, values, norms and the whole system of interpersonal communication also liquid, changing all the time. Besides, sociological only approaches to the analysis of external migration factors would require shifting some attention to the institutional dimension as well. In this context, attention would be paid to the actions of governments and political elites, forming migration regimes, signing international agreements, setting barriers or providing opportunities for external migration. Other subjects bearing the "right for nomination", as stated by P. Bourdieu, deserve similar attention – in particular, those who set the agenda, describing external migration as the good and the bad, presenting it as a problem, a threat, or on the opposite – as a potentially positive life strategy.

Understanding traditional subject matters of economic science, like the factors of migration, require today the integrated scientific methods since only their integration would enable covering all aspects and levels of this complex phenomenon. One of such integrative method is neoinstitutionalism which combines the institutional organizational dimension with its own political, legal and economic logic of functioning with the dimension of mass, group and individual consciousness predetermined by various psychological, social and cultural factors. From the neoinstitutionalism grounds, external migration can be interpreted as a comparatively autonomous fragment of social space, with its rather stable structures of perception and action, which are revealed through institutionalized or informal rules: starting from migration regimes which are set according to international agreements, specific rules of employment centres, registration offices, customs etc. and ending with informal perception structures and actions, which are then rooted in individual, group and mass consciousness through social and moral norms, traditions and codes of conduct, patterns of social networks formation and functioning, social discourse, and specifically, imagined geography.

The structure of the book

The first chapter, titled "Material and Non-material Factors of External Labour Migration in Their Theoretical Aspect", analyzes the scientific discourse on external migration according to the classical, neoclassical and structural theories. It emphasizes that till now most research on external migration from Ukraine is rather one-sided, carried out within rather tight frames of economics, or demography, or sociology, while system analysis of this phenomenon is still missing. Secondly, most of these research works are essentially ethnocentric; that is, they consider the experience of Ukrainian migrants only, without any comparison with other donor countries in terms of influence factors. The prospects of the use of a neoinstitutional approach as applied to external migration are considered in its combination with sociological elements.

The second chapter, "Factors of External Labour Migration of the Ukrainians in History and Today", considers the peculiarities of external migration from Ukraine in its three waves: 1) the last quarter of the nineteenth century till the beginning of World War I; 2) in between the two world wars; 3) after World War II. Using the methodology described above and a large corpus of sources in this chapter we try to reconstruct institutional, socioeconomic and discursive factors forcing the Ukrainians to migrate.

Concerning the contemporary, fourth wave of external labour migration from Ukraine, the socioeconomic dynamics of the development of Ukrainian society is analyzed for the period of the country's independence. These dynamics are considered in correlation with the external migration dynamics. Within the fourth wave of external migration from Ukraine, we can already track down two distinctive periods which differ from each other by both socioeconomic and discursive factors forcing emigration. In the 1990s the typical combination of push factors included: economic crisis, growing unemployment and inflation, currency depreciation and, on the other side, high social anxiety, demoralization and social pessimism. At this stage the key motivation factors for external migration were rather tangible, and they mostly concern "getting by" as such. From the beginning of the new century to the explosion of the global financial crisis, socioeconomic and discursive factors were already radically different: in this period of time Ukraine was demonstrating rather good growth indicators, the welfare level was objectively going up, and Ukranian citizens' subjective perception of life was also improving. Therefore, at this stage along with material motivation for external migration there was also mixed motivation, with some postmaterial values included. While the first period can be called the "escape from misery", the second one was already "searching for better life", in which this search for higher life quality was seen, for example, through starting one's own business.

The third chapter, "Empirical Research on the Factors of External Labour Migration from Ukraine at the Current Stage", analyzes the current sociological research on the factors behind labour migration from Ukraine. It considers in detail the theoretical and methodological grounds of the EUMAGINE project, its design, both its quantitative and qualitative sociological data on the discursive factors behind external migration in the mass consciousness of the population in four macroregions of Ukraine, as well as the migration intentions and migration experience of the Ukrainians in the context of other donor countries for external migration to European countries.

It is demonstrated that in Ukrainian respondents' perception of their own country and of the countries for potential migration, we can clearly observe the negative stereotyping of Ukrainians' own country and the positive stereotyping of Europe. In their view, Ukraine's scores on institutional efficiency and social infrastructure are very low, while education and healthcare in European countries are evaluated as affordable and of good quality. The Ukrainians tend to negatively evaluate and do not trust Ukrainian politicians, while their European colleagues are highly evaluated. One of the most painful problems the respondents see in Ukraine is corruption; however, they reject their own personal experience with it. They rate the level of corruption in the imagined countries of Europe as low, or "close to zero".

In the context of positive stereotyping of Europe, regional features are very important. People from Western and Central Ukraine tend to have more of positive stereotyping about European countries than those living on the opposite side of the country, very far from the EU border. The general ideas about Europe are very much idealized. In Ukrainian minds Europe exists as a discursive structure, as an image of an ideal society, and this image is built by the principle of mirror reflection: what is so bad and inefficient at home simply must be perfect in Europe. And as our quantitative research shows, there is a significant correlation between such ideas about Europe and migration intentions. This discursive structure becomes one of the important pull factors.

Peculiarities of media discourse are also considered in this chapter. Significant differences are observed between public authorities, experts and mass media discourse. First of all, these discourses differ by topics: mass discourse on external migration has strong resemblance with tabloids, with all these dramatic life stories, scandals etc. Mass media discourse is concentrated on the problems from external migration. At the same, all three studied discourses demonstrate the general decrease in the emphasis on problems of external migration from Ukraine. Once-popular topics of human trafficking and sexual exploitation are off stage today. The same concerns the illegal emigration of the Ukrainians.

The subchapter on mathematical modelling of the external migration factors demonstrates that during the fourth wave, the system of migration factors is changing. These changes are naturally determined by the corresponding socioeconomic, sociocultural and institutional changes in Ukraine itself during the period in question. By means of regression analysis two models are built to describe the importance of certain external migration factors at two stages of the post-Soviet development of Ukraine (1991–2002, the stage of deep crisis; and 2003–2013, the stage of stabilization and relative welfare). At the first stage, important factors were related to the labour market and employment, since this was the period of long-term delays with salary payments and overall the period of the lowest life quality in Ukraine. At the second stage the key factors behind external migration became the index of poverty and several institutional factors related to efficient governing, people's impact on political and administrative changes, overcoming corruption. The picture of the population's demands and visions then became more complex. This change can be called the shift from materialistic factors in external migration to mixed ones (materialistic but also post-materialistic).

In the fourth chapter, "System Analysis of External Labour Migration of Ukrainian Population at the Fourth Stage", the system of external migration factors is constructed on the basis of regression analysis. It concerns macro- and microeconomic factors (just like in many other studies) but also institutional and sociocultural factors. The dynamics of migration factors is analyzed for two periods – 1992–2002 and 2003–2013. Significant differences in factors for these two periods are determined. During the first period the key factors behind external migration were related to the peculiarities of the labour market and employment, while during the second period of the fourth wave external migration was determined by a mix of economic (materialistic) and institutional (post-materialistic) factors.

Therefore, the aim of this monograph is to present its readers with a wide-scale interdisciplinary study on the factors of external migration from Ukraine in its historic retrospective and at the current stage, as well as to model the system of factors related to migration behaviour of the Ukrainians, taking into account the wide range of socioeconomic, sociocultural and institutional dimensions with a special emphasis on the European vector of external migration from Ukraine.

CHAPTER 1

Material and Non-material Factors of External Labour Migration in Their Theoretical Aspect

1.1 Classical, neoclassical and structural theories of external labour migration and their bottlenecks

Migration is inseparable from any human community function-ing and it accompanies humanity throughout its history, mutating all the time and becoming either a marginal factor, or the decisive factor of social development. Migration as such is a complex soci-oeconomic and culturally predetermined phenomenon, which is rather unpredictable and ambiguous in its consequences, since a range of various factors is affecting it at the same time.

These days research on migratory processes is getting more and more important due to intensification of social interactions which

How to cite this book chapter:
Bilan, Y 2017 *Migration of the Ukrainian Population: Economic, Institutional and Sociocultural Factors.* Pp. 1–44. London: Ubiquity Press. DOI: https://doi.org/10.5334/bbg.b. License: CC-BY 4.0

now often disregard national borders and are becoming global. The same applies to the research too, globalizing the research provides new opportunities to use different statistical and sociological approaches and data and makes it possible to perform comparative analysis in new dimensions. Thus, today in many humanities and economic disciplines new, more specialized subdisciplines arise to study cross-border migration. A good example is limology (from the Latin "limes" – border, limit). Such interdisciplinary synthesis is very much determined by the interest of public and political circles in thorough studies of migration processes and the possibilities for their further forecasting.

The most topical trends of today's global development create preconditions for academic revision of international migration. These include, inter alia: the dismantling of the global bipolar system, the consequences of which are still influencing many countries; gradual formation of the global labour market, which partially eases migration regimes in many countries; constant attempts to find a reasonable balance between migration policy and national policy, which is a rather sensitive problem for both sending and hosting countries.

In the historic perspective, countries have been demonstrating rather diverse approaches to regulation of migration processes. Some approaches are restrictive, when migration is seen as a threat to local labour market or even to state security. In such a case public authorities try to control, limit or even stop migration as such. In more open models of migration policy, authorities encourage and stimulate external migration. In each specific case migration should be considered, applying a wide range of research disciplines and constructing integrated methodological approaches. From the standing point of public authorities, the focus must be on regulation of migration flows, and then on integration and adaptation of migration communities, on interaction between migrants and hosting societies and the growing role of sociocultural factors in international migration. All of this clearly demonstrates the need for a brand-new vision and new public policy created and supported by experts in the field who can assess and forecast both opportunities and threats from external migration.

Before we turn to the specifics of academic discourse on external migration, we need to settle on the key notions used in our study. From the statistical viewpoint, a *migrant* is a person changing his/her place of residence due to relocation to a different country. According to the recommendation of the UN Statistical Commission (1998), a migrant is "anybody who is changing the country of usual residence". The research object in this study is external migration, which we understand as voluntary or forced, repeated or one time, legal or illegal crossing of a border of a sovereign (at least formally speaking) political unit; and this crossing becomes the precondition for the following interrelated processes of economic and sociocultural nature. In this study specifically we are interested in labour migration; however, we are not trying to narrow down this term. Migration is a complex and multiaspect phenomenon, and we do not want to narrow it to the only dimension of human functioning. A migrant's key intention may be getting a university education or getting married abroad, but at the same time he/she is performing paid or unpaid work in a host country, regularly or from time to time. In the case of repeated migration the key goal of such travel may also change.

External migration is a study object for many sciences, like statistics, geography, demography, law, sociology etc. However, the largest corpus of studies on migration obviously belongs to economics. The central notions used in economics to study migration are: demand and proposition at labour markets of donor and hosting countries; workforce flows; professional and qualificational structure of the workforce.

The contribution of economics in migration studies would be hard to underestimate; however, it also has its limitations. Economic analyses of migration focus mostly on voluntary labour migration with a range of specific, purely economic factors. Many other factors are left ignored, namely, forced migration, migration determined by cultural and/or social factors, migration intentions and planning, specifics of migrants' adaptation to a new sociocultural environment, non-economic consequences of migration (including changed social status, shift in values, change in behavioral patterns etc.). Let us consider the key stages in academic discourse on external migration in its historic perspective.

The origins of external migration studies can be traced down to the eighteenth century and Adam Smith. Being a liberal thinker, Smith formulated the so-called mercantilist approach to external migration (Engl. "merchant" – trader), according to which unrestrained international movement of the workforce promotes economic growth and reduces poverty. The priority in this context is given to attracting foreigners with specific qualifications and limitations on emigration of own citizens.

In the second half of the nineteenth century the classical theory of migration was formed. Its origins are connected with the name of E. G. Ravenstein, who introduced the "laws of migration" and explained how migration determinants are divided into pull and push factors. After him, such authors as E. Lee, S. Eberg and W. A. Lewis studied the functions of external migration for both sending and hosting societies. Particular attention was placed on how external migration is balancing labour markets in both sending and hosting countries. Any economy, despite the level of the country's economic developments, has its subsistence sector and capitalist sector. The former is the traditional source of labour resources for the latter which is usually much more profitable. Opponents of the classical approach found its weak points in the overestimation of the role of homo economicus, while ignoring the non-economic factors of migration behaviour and the dysfunctions which may potentially be caused by external migration.

Criticism of the classical approach in external migration studies has logically led to the formation of neoclassical approach, which dates back to the end of the twentieth century and is associated with the names of D. S. Massey, A. Palloni, J. Durand etc. According to the neoclassical approach, migration is based on individual calculations of benefits and losses. During such calculations an individual takes into account the opportunity to get a new working place, and in the case of illegal emigration, chances to avoid deportation. Also, attention is paid to such factors as cost of travel, savings to be spent while looking for a new job, stress related to cultural changes, loss of well-established social contacts etc. Literature has demonstrated a wide range of criticism of neoclassical macro- and microapproaches. This criticism concerns both methodological grounds of the neoclassical approach as such, and also its local aspects. Most of this criticism is turned against the central idea behind both classical and neoclassical theories: migration as a mechanism of balancing and positive changes. At that, critics turn to the dysfunctional consequences of external migration, including primarily brain drain (Boucher et al., 2005).

This brain drain is caused by a range of objective reasons. As noted by B. Jałowiecki, J. Hryniewicz, A. Mync, motives for brain drain obviously come from the difference between the potentials of the more developed countries and those, putting it mildly, which are on their way. Emigrants are attracted to

Western countries by high wages, better working conditions, stability and political freedom, and also by the opportunity to get education for their children in better universities. In recent years, among the most frequent reasons behind migration are ethnical wars and lack of political stability in many countries worldwide (Jałowiecki et al., 1994, p. 7).

The major threat from external migration is that in cases when emigrating people are mostly well-qualified and educated, those are left behind simply are not able to keep the productivity of country's economic activity at a decent level. This interpretation of migration threats is often present in political and everyday discourse; however, scientific analysis clearly demonstrates that it is not that simple: in some cases positive changes happen too (the so-called brain gain instead of brain drain). Reverse migration can have significant positive consequences for sending countries; however, those would be rather long-term.

Interestingly, this political concern about the negative consequences of emigration in practice translates, for example, into the so-called "tax on brain drain", which is supposed to compensate for a country's previous investment in one's education and professional training (Bhagwati, 1976). In a much lighter form this is translated into the creation of a high-profit economic sector which prepares and recruits for working abroad. For example, such newly industrialized countries as Hong Kong, Korea, Singapore or Taiwan establish companies which prepare professionals in high demand abroad and then provide their own labour resources, thus getting both direct and indirect profit (including remittances later sent by these migrant workers back to their families) (Angsuthanasombat, 2008).

The destroying influence from the brain drain is overestimated as such and today definitely has the signs of politically inspired alarmism. Besides, as it was very well noted by Angsuthanasombat (2008, p. 103), brain drain from emigration is causing much less staff losses in science and higher education as compared to specializations' changes inside the country.

All in all, functions of migration as described by the neoclassicists are not always visible in real life. For example, migration is not always correlated with economic growth, and even when this growth is indeed observed, it may be not enough to turn migration in the opposite direction. Thus, in a longer perspective we may not observe levelling in development; however, there is some sort of balance restoration between capital and labour resources (Goss et al., 1995).

Concerning financial transfers from labour migration to the countries of origin, this may be negated by the following: First, migrants' savings sent home are not really invested in economic development of their home countries (for example, capital development or creation of new work places). They are mostly used on consumption, and thus, stimulate inflation only. This especially concerns the cases when emigrants come from poor families and later "sponsor" those who have large consumption needs. Speaking in wider institutional terms, transfers from emigrants are sources for less-efficient economic systems, because they are aimed at households which would further spend them on improving their own material and financial status, but not on development or capital accumulation. Thus, migrants' financial transfers are supporting the economic system but do not cause innovations. Moreover, incoming into rather closed, very much corrupted and rent-seeking economy, these resources get involved in the financial circulation channels which basically only reserve pathologies of the economic system. Secondly, even though most of migrant-sending countries usually have rather high levels of unemployment, those who become migrants are very seldom unemployed before their decision to migrate (Bustamante, 1979; Zazueta et al., 1982). This means that external migration does not help solve the unemployment problem, in fact, it aggravates it. Thirdly, the Philippines' experience, as described by the above authors, clearly demonstrates that even years of rather intensive external migration do not bring in the desired growth of salaries inside the country. Besides, there are no grounds to assume that external migrants from the Philippines, after getting new qualifications and external knowledge, have returned home and enriched their national economy, simply because the vast majority of them have been involved in low-paid and low-qualified work in hosting countries (and this usually leads to losing some professional skills, rather than to their accumulation or enrichment).

Besides the already described gaps in neoclassical approaches, there are also difficulties with explaining the reverse migration in cases when migrants do not reach the level of wages and/or welfare they were expecting (or sometimes there is a difference, but it is a reverse one, favouring the sending country).

There exists a false but frequent assumption that most migration flows come from the poorest countries. If this was true, the migration leaders would have been the countries of Sub-Saharan Africa, and also Bangladesh and Haiti, as well noted by Portes (1983). However, the actual macrolevel situation analysis clearly demonstrates that the largest "suppliers" of migration are not the poorest countries of the world, but those the level of welfare in which is about the world's average, the so-called middle income countries, like Mexico, Morocco, Turkey or the already mentioned Philippines. In these and other countries the most important push factor is not as much poverty, but inequality (Morrison, 1982, p. 8). Therefore, in our analysis we can surely include the notion of subjective deprivation, meaning the mass perception of unfair social distribution of resources and values. This phenomenon has both psychological and social elements and is most definitely far beyond the model of homo economicus.

The criticised theories also do not consider the institution-normative aspect of the subject matter. The neoclassical theory (and the system of push and pull factors as such) does not take into account that individuals do not determine the migration policy of states, while this factor often determines the migration decision the most. It is not for the migrant to decide whether he/she gets the legal status of migrant or must remain in shadow, but for the state and migration regime in it. At the same time a migrant can take into account the specific features of this regime in a potential hosting country, also considering difficulties while crossing the border, deportation risks and other factors which might influence the migration decision.

And overall, the solely economic model of migration is very much criticised by many researchers, since in it we see only a person of no consequence who is using a calculator to account for benefits and advantages from migration to various places (Bohning, 1978, p. 10). Also, as noted by Fevre (1984), numerous sociological studies demonstrated that many people are simply not ready to make a migration decision, and even under the worst possible economic conditions they do not make it. The major reason for it is that people are not always rational in this important choice and consider much wider range of factors, many of which are not economic at all.

In order to overcome the limitations of the neoclassical model J. Harris and M. Todaro offer a somewhat modified interpretation of it, according to which individuals are making migration decisions basing not on the objective knowledge about the current state of the markets and their chance to improve their own well-being, but coming from certain perceptions and expectations which are obviously not objective at all (Harris et al., 1970). More specifically, instead of the notion of "difference in incomes" in this context we should operate with the notion of "the expected difference in incomes" (Todaro, 1976). However, even with all these modifications taken into account, the neoclassical theory of migration is still being criticised as one-sided and oversimplified, reduced to the economic dimension only. Instead of "static" understanding of self-balancing labour markets in sending and hosting countries, external migration should be treated as a choice, often not rational and rather contradictory (Kearney, 1986).

Considering the theories of external migration in their chronological order, the next should be the structural approach represented primarily by the world-system theory. Its key difference from the theory of push and pull factors is that the former emphasizes the voluntary nature of humans' movement, while the latter concentrates on the role of large organizations (corporations and states) in the formation of migration flows.

The theories of migration combined under the title "structural approach" focus on macrosocial processes which result in inequalities and limitations on the life chances of individuals. The structural approach explains migration as a consequence from the exploitative relations between sending and hosting countries. The most well known theories within this approach are those related to neo-Marxism – the world-system theory and the theory of underdevelopment by A.G. Frank. The predecessor of the world-system analysis was French historian F. Braudel who actually introduced the very notion of world-system, understanding it as a regional self-sufficient and autonomous economic system,

the world inside[2]. Sending and hosting societies are components of the same world-economy system which is comparatively
autonomous from the rest of the world, having at the same time
economic, sociocultural and institutional similarity and correlation within. The most explicit and obvious example of this world-
system approach is external migration from former colonies to
their former metropolicies. In the course of world-system analysis development during the 1990s the theory of international
migration system was formulated by Kritz (1992). This system is
formed by migration flows between two or more countries that
exchange migrants. Such a system rests upon the system of historic, political, economic and cultural connections.

For example, labour migration from Morocco to France is preconditioned by a rather complex set of relations and dependencies which include: sociocultural features (the Moors know
French language and are comparatively familiar with French
culture, and this eases their adaptation in French society); structural and institutional factors (social networks of already settled
Moor immigrants in France; numerous French-Moroccan joint
enterprises which mostly combine French capital with Moroccan
labour force); political factors (many government agreements and
comparatively favourable migration regime). All of these factors
have been gradually formed during the decades of French colonial rule in Morocco. The same interpretation can be also applied
to the Ukrainians who opt to migrate to the Russian Federation

---

[2] In Braudel's interpretation world-economies existed since ancient time
(Phoenisia, Carthage, Rome, India, China, the Islamic world) and they have
a range of common features: territorial limits in their stability (the borders of world-economies are changing very seldom and very slowly); each
world-economy has its center, usually a capitalistic city (in European history those were Venice in 1380–1500, Antwerp in 1500–1550, Genoa in
1560–1610, Amsterdam during 1610–1815, London during 1815–1929,
and finally New York became such a world-economy in 1929).

(especially to Moscow, the former mother city). Therefore, the world-system approach shifts the emphasis from the level of individual decisions and actions, to the objective facts which create conditions important for labour migration.

The world-system has certain structural zones (the narrow centre, semi-peripheries and peripheries). The periphery is essentially archaic and underdeveloped, and this makes it an easy catch for exploitation by others. The most attractive destinations for migration flows from former colonies (or putting it in more neutral terms, dependent territories) are the centres of world-economies, their cores. These are always metropolis cities, which are dynamic, rich in resources, culturally diverse and comparatively liberal.

At the same time the countries of periphery are involved in the complicated process of "development of underdevelopment", the participation in which only worsens the situation inside the sending country, while migration of valuable human resources deepens the dependency. Migration flows enlarge when the key features of the involved territories reveal themselves more (the periphery demonstrates its underdevelopment, while the core shows high rates of development) and also when specific political or economic acts influence the situation. For example, subjects working from the core (the state itself or large business) may try to attract the most valuable resources by means of setting convenient migration regimes for them.

Most of today's sociologists agree with this interpretation, including M. Burawoy who thinks that the countries of the former socialistic camp (countries "of the second world" using the terminology of the Cold War period) obtain the features of the third-world countries, that is, they demonstrate higher dependencies and more explicit underdevelopment. Interestingly, this concerns both the dependency from the former core of the Soviet Union as well as from the comparative new core inside the European Union (when it comes to Central European countries) (Burawoy, 1999).

Thus, international migration is the consequence of the capitalistic formation of the market in developing countries, while global economy's intrusion in the periphery regions usually catalyzes migration processes in them. Capitalistic investments provoke changes, and changes lead to population mobility in the periphery. Years of close relations between the core and the periphery shape stable material, cultural, language, administrative, transport and communication connections, and this naturally leads to the establishment of transnational markets and transnational cultural systems. Within the world-system theory, the phenomenon of cultural dependence is treated as a marginal one; this is explained in detail by Polish authors, among others (Fiut, 2003; Cavanagh, 2003; Korek, 2007). The key factor of international migration is first of all the structure of global economy, not differences in wages or gaps in employment structure (Massey et al., 1993).

The considered above approaches (both functional and structural) do not take into account that each action has its own balance of agency as defined by the free will of an individual and certain limitations on it (sociocultural, institutional, economic, legal and other "corridors" which set the limit on our behaviour in terms of the most and the least possible variants of it). While functional approach is overestimating the agency role, the structural approach overemphasizes the constraints' role.

Now we can turn to the specifics of the contemporary stage of research on external migration. These specifics concern not theories or methodologies, but the very choice of research object, methods and design of future research. In particular, contemporary research on external migration treats it mostly from the standing point of hosting (receiving) states and considers first of all their demands and requirements for optimization of migration policy, taking into account both real and perceived (imagined) threats (national security threats, human trafficking, illegal migration, saturation of the labour market which disadvantages citizens in their employment opportunities, problems related to cultural adaptation, law abidance or identity of newcomers etc.). Researchers often leave out of scope the aspect of sending countries as such as well as complex migration trajectories in which an individual travels in a serial manner, thus getting involved in social, proprietal and political relations on both sides. Such manner of migration, with its unique sociocultural, economic and political features, is known now as "transnationalism" (Schiller, 1992).

The widely acceptable way to solve the problem of the one-sidedness of the research is to perform cross-national studies, which rebuke ethnocentrism and provide a wider view on both positions – that of a sending country and that of a receiving one.

Obviously, such a research strategy is closely related to the most recent challenges, as cross-national studies are also cross-cultural in their nature, and this is even more challenging in terms of methods and tools used (Jowell, 1998). As noted by R. Jowell, there are two almost opposite answers to the question on adequacy in cross-national research, and these would be: 1) the maximum quality approach according to which the research design, its methods and tools are maximally adapted to the context in question; however, in this case the comparison would be difficult to perform; 2) the consistent quality approach according to which research design, its methods and tools are not adapted at all and are left unchanged; however, this increases the risk that true local specificity would be left behind the scenes.

Obviously, both of these approaches have significant bottle-necks, and our task here is to find the middle way between them, so as not to lose the quality of the research while keeping it truly cross-national.

The following critical point can be applied to all non-sociological models of migration behaviour: a truly comprehensive, all-dimensional research on external migration must take into account that migrants, non-migrants and potential migrants are the representatives of various social and demographic groups, bearing important features, such as gender, age, confession, cultural and/or ethical identity, all of which significantly determine both the migration behaviour of individuals and the barriers to migration.

Thirdly, in non-sociological research, as a rule, mass perceptions, including motivations, aims and values are left out of scope. All of these factors are especially important in today's world where communications' development, logistics and transport technologies and mass culture create both the desire and the opportunity to emigrate. Motivations, discourses and the symbolic side of our sociocultural reality in a wider sense are often left ignored. While the sociocultural aspect of any migration process can be understood first of all through such notions as the "migration project" and "geographical imaginations" etc.

Finally, in the studies on migration the general shift is on the side of economic factors analysis, and those do not actually explain migration, but merely describe it. Statistics on wages or quality of life in both sending and receiving countries are part of basic descriptive research. There is an obvious gap between studies on migration and the analysis of the related social changes, and this gap needs to be bridged. Moreover, there is hardly any really long-term research on migration which would reveal the major trends and explain what social innovations may follow from the "waves of migration".

1.2 Institutional aspect of studying external labour migration: the research potential of neoinstitutionalism

There is a range of integrative approaches which are aimed at overcoming the limitations of structural and functional models. In particular, these are the economic approach, the migration systems approach, the network approach and the neoinstitutional approach. Besides those, significant disciplinary specifics are observed in the research on external migration. In this subchapter we will concentrate on the essence of the theories mentioned above, their critics and opportunities to form some of sort of metatheory which would enable systemic, all-sided conceptualization of external migration.

The new economic approach is refocusing research from individuals and their personal decisions on the level of households. As noted by E. Jaźwińska, an approach which represents a household as a whole is somehow reducing the role of lesser units in decision-making, but at the same time it allows for a better understanding of the conditions in which these decisions are made (Jaźwińska, 2007, p. 16).

Considering households in the conditions of the so-called subsistence economies, the key motive behind households' behaviour is minimization of losses and risks (Stark, 1991). In poor households the income level is low and also changing. Thus, during certain long-term periods (sometimes longer than one generation) certain rather specific socioeconomic strategies for survival are being formed (Collins et al., 2009).

Households are able to manage their risks by means of own resources. Households as units of production and consumption, unlike autonomous individuals, are the true units for analysis in migration processes research. And the difference between wages' level is not the key decisive factor for migration here: households often have other more powerful stimuli to engage in external migration, even in cases when the difference in wage levels is not significant. One of the most important predictors of households' migration behaviour is the socioeconomic state of the environment in which a households exists. And the better the household looks against the general backgrounds (neighbours, for example) – the less intentions it will have to migrate. Thus, it would be logical to assume that high migration indicators are observed not in the poorest societies but in the societies with significant differentiation in life quality levels (Stark, 1991).

Poor households can borrow from friends and relatives, thus building a certain network of rather stable relations based on mutual help and non-economic resources exchange, investing in the so-called economy of favours. They can also try to increase their incomes by means of finding alternative jobs with better pay, or start their own business, or invent other ways to increase their overall welfare status. External migration is in any case considered along with a range of alternative options.

Migration as a form of investment in human capital has been rather metaphorically described by M. Clemens and T. Ogden in their article "Migration as a Strategy for Household Finance: A Research Agenda on Remittances, Payments, and Development":

"What is the human capital of a Russian professional ballerina? Her human capital is much more than the classes she has taken … Her earning potential is also lower if she has rarely performed publicly, if she knows no ballet directors, if she is obese, or if she lives in Krasnoyarsk, Siberia. That is, her income is directly affected by her knowledge, experience, connections, physical condition, and location – all traits of her person, and all changeable. She can improve all of these traits … to raise the value of her time and labour next year. One of the best investments she could make in her human capital would be to pay for changing her location – to Novosibirsk or Moscow. In fact, without that investment in changing her location, her investments in other personal attributes might be nearly worthless" (Clemens et al., 2014).

From this viewpoint, external migration is seen as a household strategy, a form of investing in human capital, aimed at diversification of incomes, and at the same time minimization of unemployment risks, changing (unfavourably) economic environment etc.

A new economic approach indeed has shifted the emphasis in research (for example, on such issues as whether households use transfers from abroad on investment; whether households form a dependency from such aid; what could be the optimal tax on such remittances etc.), but still, this approach was not able to overcome the limitations of classical and neoclassical approaches. In particular, this theory does not take into account the influence of migration institutes, the related social networks, the role of intermediaries etc.

The next approach in question is the theory of social networks. Transnational social networks increase the probability of external migration, mostly because they reduce the costs and the time for obtaining necessary information, and they also decrease the risks related to relocation.

The network approach emphasizes that external migration is predetermined by the migration at the preliminary stage; that is, it has the signs of autoregression process (the indicators of which in a given moment of time depend on the previous indicators linearly).

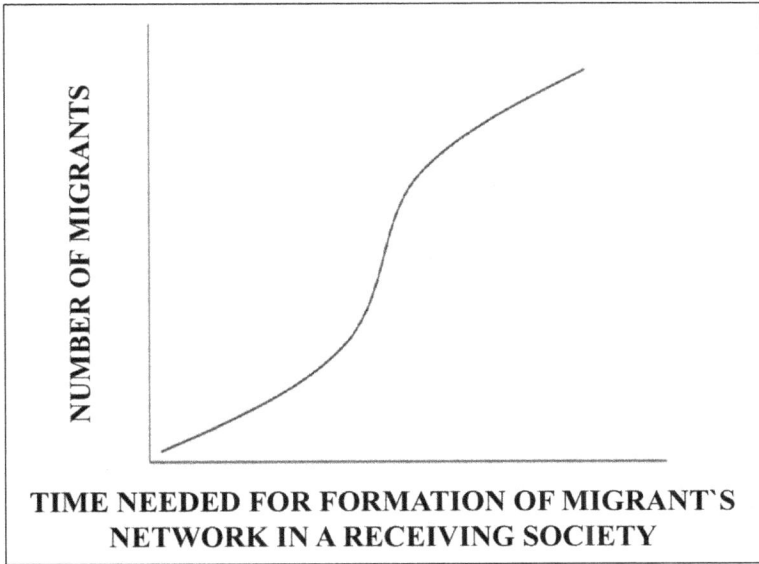

TIME NEEDED FOR FORMATION OF MIGRANT'S NETWORK IN A RECEIVING SOCIETY

Figure 1: The influence of social networks on external migration dynamics.
Source: Reichlova, 2004

Primary migration is caused by various reasons, like difference in wages, labour market conditions etc. Thus, the first migrants usually have very high costs of relocation due to lack of information and many uncertainties. For the next wave of migration the costs are already lower because there already exist certain networks of relatives and acquaintances in the new country. And this situation may be progressing up to the point when nearly anybody in a sending country who has the desire to emigrate can actually do so comparatively easily.

Such social networks form the capital of behavioural origin which would further reduce losses and prevent unnecessary spending, thus optimizing income at early stages already

(Massey et al., 1993, p. 448). Social networks (which are being formed by former and current migrants, their families and sometimes also local friends) represent an important resource with the help of which migrants can find a place to live, a job, necessary information, psychological support etc. With the growing size and density of social networks, losses and risks related to relocation are decreasing – and thus, the probability of migration is increasing. Therefore, availability of social networks in a receiving country becomes an additional factor of external migration, and this factor is always an encouraging one (Boyd, 1989).

Former migrants which today are residing in the receiving country are the best information source for newcoming and potential migrants in terms of all possible benefits and losses, best practices and problems experienced. Sometimes they also provide direct financial support, help finding a job and assist during the adaptation period in other ways (Arango, 2000). Potentially, every new wave of migrants would become the supporting one for the next one to come. In this way, a chain of interrelated repeated events and actions is formed. Once started, migration is reproducing itself. The key advantage of the migration networks theory is that it explains migration between countries in the most general manner, whatever were the reasons for the first wave of migration. The very presence of the migrants' community in a receiving location already creates preconditions for continuing migration.

The theory of migration networks is able to explain different volumes of migration to the countries which are equally attractive in economic terms, and also the cases when intensive migration is observed despite quite restrictive migration rules (including the legal mechanism of family reunification) (Arango, 2000).

The bottleneck of this theory is that it does not consider economic factors as such and thus, is unable to explain the reasons behind the very first wave of migration. Also, the weak side of this theory is the neglect of sociocultural context around the migrants' community. Namely, in literature on the subject there is a phenomenon described as "downward levelling pressure". This sort of pressure occurs when migrants' community in a receiving country exists at a rather low level of the social stratification system. This can be caused by a range of reasons, including formal and informal discrimination of this particular ethnical community; failures to adapt to the existing labour market requirements etc. In such a situation the migrants' community becomes a rather closed system with its own subsistence economy, and the relational resources inside the community compensate for the lack of economic resources. In such communities families usually consist of several generations living together, located in one, ghetto-like, area; small and medium businesses in these areas are family- and ethnic-based. Informal structures in these areas also have distinctive ethnical features, and this concerns both support institutes and criminal circles. Zero-interest personal loans "inside one's own circle" are widely spread in such communities, as well as intensive exchanges of services and non-economic resources. Marriages are arranged inside the same ethnic minority group.

In such a situation, a bright representative of the community who is able to move forward in the social hierarchy (get better education, better job, higher overall status) ceases to be the native element of this community. The reason is that usually the successful member of such community will be overloaded by numerous requests from the least succesful members of community (lend money, help with employment or business contacts, share experience etc.). At the same time the community applies this "downward levelling pressure" on its brighter representative, demanding a share in the newly acquired resources. This pressure makes anybody who managed to reach a certain level of success in life leave his or her community. These community members are forced to cut short their friends and family connections, or at least reduce the intensity of such contacts (along with the related obligations). They usually move from the ghetto and try to build their own social networks based on personal contacts but not on the requirement of resource redistribution in favour of the most needy.

The migration systems approach is applicable to all international structures of both macro- and microlevels which have some sort of exchange in resources, capital and people. Macrolevel components of migration system include: political structures which set migration regimes; structures of economic domination and dependency; cultural and language structures and other structures manifested through network connections (Fawcet, 1987). This theory emphasizes the importance of pull factors in highly developed economies (including primarily the demand for foreign workforce and the corresponding targeted recruitment by both enterprises and public institutions).

Within the migration systems approach lies the theory of the dual market which explains external migration through macroeconomic specifics of labour markets in receiving societies (Piore, 1979). In the countries with high level of welfare there always exists some shortage of workforce for unpopular, low-paying jobs, which do not require specific qualifications but may sometimes be unsafe. Thus, these markets perceive migrants as a necessary element of the total workforce (Arango, 2000; Cohen, 2017). In such a situation migrants are actually stabilizing the labour market in a receiving country. This problem cannot be solved in any other way, since the only way to attract local residents to such work is to increase the pay, and this would not be economically feasible due to potential inflation growth (Massey et al., 1993).

This situation can be described by means of a mathematical model which takes into account the qualitative features of labour resources. According to this model, labour resources supplied by migration flows into a receiving country can be of two types – qualified and unskilled. When we consider a situation in which the receiving country is getting both types of new labour resources and they influence the wage level, we need to take into account the limitations on the lower margin of wages set by trade unions or local legislation. The model is based on the hypothesis that in the labour market filled with an unskilled workforce, the level of wages is set by monopolistic trade unions and it is higher than the equilibrium level, Wu. Wages in the unskilled workforce market can be reduced due to pressure coming from the proposition of extra workforce, that is, emigrants. In the labour market of the qualified workforce, wages are at the market level, with no artificial intrusion of trade unions. The effects of the unskilled workforce migrating to a country are demonstrated in Figure 2, while the effects of the qualified migrants' inflow is presented in Figure 3. Figure 2 shows that migrants without specific skills substitute local unskilled labour force, and thus, along with qualified residents, form the total labour resource of the society. The key effect of this situation would be that the curve of proposition in the unskilled workforce market is moving from Ls1 to Ls2. This would force trade unions to agree on lower wages from Wu1 to Wu2, since otherwise unskilled residents would have to face mass poverty because employees would prefer non-residents (the same unskilled workers ready for lower pay). Then the employment rate would go up from L1 to L2 since both types of workforce (unskilled and qualified) supplement each other. Growing employment of unskilled workers would lead to a similar trend for qualified workers, and therefore, the curve D1 would move to

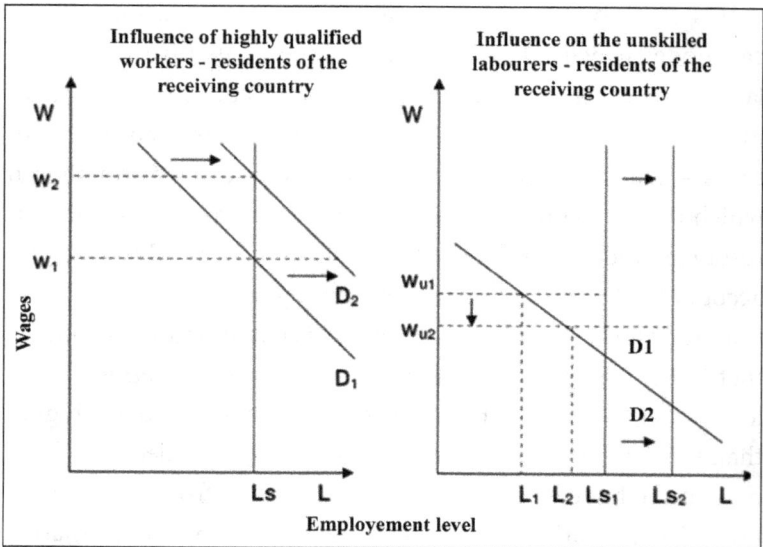

Figure 2: Model of economic effects from unskilled workforce proposition growth resulting from external migration.
Source: (Bauer et al., 1999).

D2. Since the labour market of the unskilled workforce is competitive and the proposition on it did not change, the current situation would lead to higher demand for qualified workers and their wages' growth, from W1 to W2 level (Bauer et al., 1999).

In the case when, due to the immigration process, the receiving labour market is experiencing the growing proposition of qualified new workers, there is the growth in qualified workforce proposition, from Ls1 to Ls2. This will lead to a new point of equilibrium being at E2, and the growth of demand of the qualified workforce market would lead to the similar demand growth at the market of unskilled workforce from D1 to D2. Since wages of the unskilled workforce are higher than the market ones, the employment rate would drop from L1 to L2. The growth of unskilled

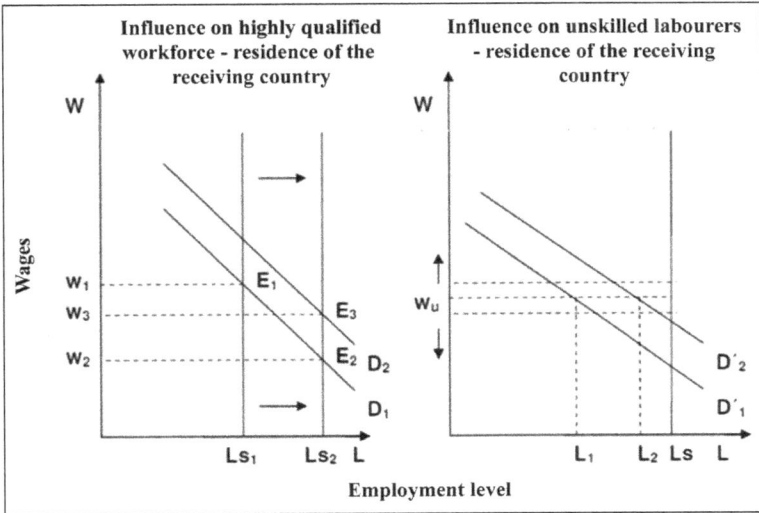

Figure 3: Model of economic effects from qualified workforce proposition growth resulting from external migration.
Source: (Bauer et al., 1999).

workforce employment would lead to higher demand for qualified workers (the curve of demand for qualified workers would move from D1 to D2), thus, the new point of equilibrium would be at E3. In this model, economic effects from external migration for the receiving country are not unambiguous. Positive effects dominate; however, in certain regions, for sectors of certain categories of workers, external migration may still decrease wages or may lead to jobs being cut (Boeri et al., 2001).

The major drawback of the migration systems approach is that institutional factors, migration regimes, political activity and the like come forward, while individual and small groups' effects are almost totally neglected. The latter are considered only as passive participants in the migration process.

One of the integrative approaches which aims to combine the most essential features of the considered theories is the theory of cumulative causation. Cumulative causation is a complex interconnection of social phenomena due to which system reproduction takes place by means of functions being performed by its components. This notion to some extent corresponds to the notion of autopoiesis, introduced by Niklas Luhmann. In his interpretation autopoiesis stands for such organization of the elements in a system (social system, for example) under which its components are the consequences of this system functioning (Luhmann, 1995).

The theory of cumulative causation states that each act of migration changes the social context in the frames of which further migration of more people becomes more probable. Within this theory the following socioeconomic factors of migration are considered: income distribution; land resource distribution; organization of agriculture works; regional distribution of human capital and the social value of labour. Eventually migration flows are getting stable and an opportunity to determine the international system of migration appears.

One of the most prospective theoretical and methodological directions which can positively impact the conceptualization of external migration is neoinstitutionalism. This research vision is rather heterogeneous in representation, for example, both H. White (1981), the representative of the new economic theory, and P. Di Maggio (1988), the representative of sociocultural approach to studying organizations are considered to be neoinstitutionalists.

Explaining rather wide representativeness of this direction, N. Fligstein defines the subject of neoinstitutional theories as: determining the regularities in functioning of social realia fields and in complexes of social practices which regulate the functioning of these fields (Fligstein, 2001). It is worth noting here that these fields are constituting in the situation of already available social practices and structures. The above-mentioned notions of "practices and structures" are used in a rather flexible manner. Thus, practices can be collective actions according to a set pattern – as in emigrating, looking for a job in a new place etc. Or, for example, typical verbal and/or cognitive practices of knowledge and attitudes distribution concerning external migration. A good illustration of the latter is the existence of cognitive frameworks which help individuals in their assessment of current situation and what is to be done (or not). This interpretation of structures in neoinstitutionalism is very similar to P. Bourdieu's idea of "habitus".

Accordingly, we can interpret external migration as one of comparatively autonomous fragments of social reality, formed by stable structures of perception and actions which manifest themselves on the level of institutionalized and informal rules: from legal frameworks of government agreements and national legislation on external migration through more specific rules of employment offices' functioning, passport registration offices and customs offices up to informal structures of perception and action which reveal themselves on the group level, on the level of social groups and society in general (moral norms, traditions and habits, codes of conducts, patterns in social networks' formation and functioning, social discourse as such etc.).

We fully agree with D. North, who stated that informal practices and structures are the most stable and socially supported ones (and thus, also the most socially reproduced). They quickly spread within and beyond social networks, while a majority of them are actually formed based not on group interests but on personal ones, and thus, from time to time they can stimulate illegal activity

(North, 1990). For example, this includes fraud for getting a visa, transporting prohibited products, illegal employment, violation of visa conditions, negligence at work etc. Such models of action are reproducing themselves in time and thus, become sort of cultural heritage for a certain part of society, constituting the sociocultural grounds for socioeconomic and political underdevelopment.

Variety in the neoinstitutionalism vision also reveals itself in the research scope on external migration. Analyzing the corresponding academic discourse we can differentiate two key directions of neoinstitutionalism in the external migration research: one direction is concentrated on the organizational aspects of social systems functioning; another one covers mostly symbolic (value and normative) structures.

The subject field of the first direction (which can be called here formal neoinstitutionalism) includes the regularities of organizational and legal mechanisms which influence the migration processes; the target orientation on optimization of formal institutes' design. The second direction is more sociologized, more attention being paid to sociocultural dimension of rules, structures and practices (and this direction can be called constructivist neoinstitutionalism).

Within the first direction, it is worth paying attention to the research of institutional factors which generate migration flows. This direction is concentrated on institutional design, for example, on the mechanism of rotating presidency (Tallberg, 2006) or on the procedure of co-decision (Farrell, 2007). In particular, F. W. Scharpf, in the middle of the 1980s, was already grounding the idea that the system of institutes in the EU creates the so-called trap of common decisions, in which the institutional design of the Union weighs more than the political will of its separate components – political or social ones (Scharpf, 2014). From the neoinstitutionalism standing point, the evolution of liberal democracy has been considered as being embedded in the activities of international organizations, in agreements and contracts, all of which lead to setting certain institutional frameworks with the intention to expand personal rights, including the right for free movement and freedom of residence. For example, Y.N. Soysal emphasizes that the popularity and global spread of ideas of human rights puts certain pressures on governments and thus makes them provide equal rights to citizens and non-citizens (Soysal, 1994). A few authors also note that the migration policies of Western established democracies demonstrate the so-called embedded liberalism which is a specific feature of nearly all policies in these countries in the period after World War II (Jacobson, 1996; Hollifield, 1998). Discourse concentrated around human rights is very popular today – on the levels of democratic governments and their citizens, and as applied to migrants too. This discourse is operating with rather specific terminology in discussing the related issues. In particular, within it there is no place for populist statements appealing to ethnic solidarity and homogeneity (at least in discussions about ethnical majority groups). Institutionalism in this context concentrates on such institutes, values, norms and practices which guarantee reproduction of this embedded democracy in various spheres of societal life, including external migration. In the historic perspective this can be seen as a trajectory which creates a corridor of new opportunities for societies (Steinmo et al., 1992).

Apart from the analysis on the societal level this direction also covers more local research. For example, on the level of firms and organization, both non-profit and for-profit, which arise to satisfy the needs of past, current and potential migrants. Part of such organizations are completely legal, other are shadow ones (Massey et al., 1993).

This direction has been criticized mostly because along with studying the complexities of bureaucratic mechanisms of decision-making "in the offices" (that is, along with formalized and top-down impact on migration processes), there is also a necessity to pay attention to down-top processes and informal structures, to mass consciousness in both sending and receiving countries, to public discourse and media reflections on external migration etc.

It is worth noting here that such division (formal and construc-tivist neoinstitutionalism) is very much schematic, though it can be useful in terms of scientific discourse codification. Obviously, there is a whole range of softer variants, in between the first and the second directions. In the second variant the researchers rep-resenting it can go beyond organizational analysis and constitu-tional right, as does, for example Moravcsik (2000), who applies R. Putham's metaphor of the prisoner's dilemma to demonstrate the influence of trade preferences on institutional design.

In general, neoinstitutionalism as such originates from the attempts to overcome the excessive attention to homo economi-cus, which exists only as an ideal type of human, and at the same time, in order to reveal the rooting of economic actions in social ones (Granovetter, 1999) and wider – in sociocultural structures. And at the same time neoinstitutionalism serves to avoid the spread of economic factors' dominance in explaining those fields of social reality the very existence of which are defined by non-economic structures (Zafirovski, 1999). The new generation of researchers appears to concentrate more on individual and col-lective actors, not on formal organization, and at the same time, to use qualitative, interpretative methods more widely (Favell et al., 2010).

The sociological variant of neoinstitutionalism (or as above, constructivist neoinstitutionalism) has been also criticized. The

major emphasis from the critics is on the dangers of anthropo-
morphizing identity, practices, values and norms, understanding their essence as the key features of the society, community or
social group. According to this position, we could, for example,
state: "the Ukrainians have European values, thus, Ukraine's place
is in the European Union". However, the homespun truth of real
life is that there is also a powerful intermediary involved (maybe
even the most powerful one in this particular context) that promotes values, norms, practices and identities in the political-
institutional dimension. This is the political elite, interest groups,
national government and supragovernmental structures[3].

For the analysis of the phenomena of mass consciousness and
practices (such as migrational ones) the simple, oversociologized
scheme would require further corrections and detailed provisions,
and in particular, more attention to the institutional dimension.
Mass consciousness, for example, arises not quite naturally – it is
partially formed with certain purposes (especially on its upper,
rational level). Therefore, when we consider public sentiment and
public opinion, we would need to concentrate our attention on
the central "interpreters of knowledge" which have "the symbolic
rower" to nominate (Bourdieu, 1989), which set the agenda and

---

[3] In this context we need to remember the important feature of political
systems, or more accurately political regimes and elites – the level of their
responsiveness (the ability to correspond to population demands, to be
sensitive to the changing requests of citizens). This level of responsiveness
of the public bodies determines whether the actions of the mass consciousness and the political elite are moving in the same direction. This is not always the case, as e.g. it was during the mass protests in Ukraine in late 2013
through the beginning of 2014: political destabilization was caused by un-
precedentedly massive protest movement supporting Ukraine's course on
Eurointegration, while the government was planning to abandon this idea.
This is a perfect illustration of a low level of public power responsiveness.
In such a case, separate research on institutional situations and on the
mass consciousness would have completely irrelevant results.

priorities in it, approve the list and the composition of central players, topics, alternatives, problems and prospects. This first of all means media and media representation.

Media representation means the power to set the meaning of social relations, to represent one's interests and discuss them publicly (Jensen, 1990). Media coexists along with other "producers of meaning" in their various modalities: from conflicting and conquered to equal and well-balanced in case of harmonious social development. In a situation of a high level of civil society development, media is a comparatively autonomous producer and retranslator of interests for all influential actors, such as the state, political parties, international corporations, ethnical and religious communities, the third sector etc. In the chapters that follow we will consider the influence of both formal and informal structures and institutes which may determine the nature and the course of migration processes, including state policy, media representation, features of mass consciousness etc.

The neoinstitutional approach, on one hand, is still focused on institutional and bureaucratic (political) realia which determine migration processes. On the other hand, it also concentrates on the multiple levels of discourses, values, practices and norms which also influence migration processes on the individual level, group level or on the level of the whole society (including population, political elite, media, experts etc.)

1.3 Sociological theories in the research on external labour migration

The sociological theories within external migration research turn researchers' attention to important issues which are out of scope in many other disciplines, namely: the issue of sociocultural adaptations and changing identity of migrants; social and psychological barriers and consequences from migrants' adaptation to new sociocultural environment; possible dysfunctions related to migration, like social exclusions and discrimination; isolation of newcomers in the receiving societies etc. Other topics covered by the sociological theories within external migration studies may also include mixed transnational families, sociocultural changes in societies brought in by the returning migrants once they get back to their original societies (the so-called returners, as noted by Ivankova-Stetsiuk (2012)); problems specific for migrants families, specifically, the problem of social orphanhood and forced active aging of the grandparents who are left behind to look for children, while their parents are working abroad etc. Overall, sociology interprets external migration as, first of all, a sociocultural phenomenon that means changes in the social, cultural and personal life of migrants and their communities, as well as for various other representatives of institutes in the receiving societies (Volodko, 2011). Aside from very specific topics, which cannot be covered by any other discipline, sociology can be involved in the research of those aspects in external migration which are traditionally within the economic science subject field. For example, sociological verification may require the following hypotheses which concern the factors of migration behaviour of "non-economic character": growing migration numbers are observed for those countries in which human rights and self-fulfilment are among the state priorities. This is applicable to those receiving societies where the postmaterialistic nature of the whole system of values essentially promotes self-actualization, efficient functioning of institutes and a higher sense of the existential security of the population.

People who experience labour migration usually have more progressive, advanced views, especially in terms of postmaterialistic values and gender models. People with the experience of labour migration are more inclined to start their own business, and they also have more innovative minds. They do not expect much from the social protection system and do not demonstrate paternalistic behaviour (however, there might be political exceptions to this, since sometimes people with the experience of staying in the countries with established democracies tend to be proactive in political life; they highly value their political rights and freedoms). People with experience in labour migration are also more socially active; they often participate in various volunteer and charity projects. Overall, people who experience labour migration have higher expectations in terms of life achievements and prospects.

It is noteworthy that, when we talk about sociological research on external migration, we mean, first of all, the use of sociological methodologies, theory, categories and tools etc. Secondly, all these sociological methods, tools and instruments are used to process the results of empirical research (more details on this in the subchapter 3.1.).

In this chapter we will consider the contribution of sociology into the theoretical and methodological aspects of external migration studies. The flows of migrants directed to Western Europe and the USA since the early twentieth century caused the appearance of rather large communities of non-autochthonous population, with their quite specific social values and norms, different cultural competencies and distinct behaviour models, in the receiving countries. Thus, the receiving countries had to face the problem of these communities' integration. The specific feature of this socially tense situation was a new phenomenon of ethnocultural segregation in large cities. The first generation of emigrants were usually able to occupy very specific (mostly low or mid-level) niches at local labour markets and thus had a very special rank on the overall social structure of the receiving societies. They were mostly involved into unqualified or low-qualified labour which was not considered to be prestigious for the local population. Thus, these very groups of migration also faced the largest risks related to unemployment in case of economic downturn in the receiving economies. Obviously, under such conditions a new object field has been formed which soon became the focus of many sociologists' attention. The central questions of this arising discourse were related to the social factors of migration behaviour and migrants' adaptation to the new environment, their integration into the receiving societies.

The origins of sociological research on external migration date back to 1918 – the year when W.I. Thomas and F. Znaniecki published their study "The Polish peasant in Europe and America" which analyzed the letters of Polish migrants to America addressed to their relatives back in Poland (Thomas et al., 1918). Another representative of the Chicago school, R. Park was working on the theory of migrants' assimilation, also known as the theory of the race relations cycle. This theory had a rather significant impact on the further development of this research school overall (Park 1950 [1913]). According to Park's concept, there exist four stages of assimilation, and all migrants are going through these stages in any receiving society. The first stage is establishing contact, getting familiar. It is followed by a conflict or competition, then an attempt of accommodation. In case all these attempts turn out to be unsuccessful for an emigrant, he or she has nothing left but to assimilate in the receiving society. Interestingly, neither Park nor his follower E. W. Burgess differentiated between ethnical minorities and migrant communities originating from European countries, considering them as similar social groups. We can agree on this similarity, because, for example, African Americans and Polish migrants, studied by Thomas & Znaniecki (1918), both moved from rural agrarian areas to city ghettos; thus, their social situations were indeed nearly identical.

The next big contribution into sociological research of external migration became the work of J. S. Lindberg (1930) on social networks of Swedish migrants to the USA and also, the auto-ethnographic research by L. Adamic (1932). Also important was the ethnographic-sociological study by W. Whyte titled "Street corner society" in which he studied the life of Italian community in Chicago, its internal structure and hierarchy (Whyte, 1943).

One of the classical sociological studies on emigrants in receiving societies belongs to W.L. Warner and was titled "The Social System of American Ethnic Groups" (published in 1945 at Yale). This book was very much criticized for its rather ultra-right and conservative discourse and vision of the ethnocultural policies in the receiving countries. The author took the stand that migrants simply must assimilate in the American society due to its universal laws and its open system of social mobility. Further, the author also stated that migrants would have to leave their own values and perceptions, which are second-rate to the receiving society, and fully adopt the new culture.

In contrast, a much more flexible position was the generation theory of assimilation by H.G. Duncan. According to Duncan, migrants enter the life in the receiving societies gradually, generation by generation. The first generation is responsible for the economic entry and had only formal signs of belonging to a receiving society. This means economic and social integration only, while the emotional component and life values, just as before, are determined by the group to which this migrant still belongs. The second generation is responsible for emotional and psychological entry. This generation is already able to overcome emotional and psychological barriers which previously were insurmountable for their parents due to education, professional skills etc. This second generation of migrants intakes the values of the new society, but at the same time they are still the carriers of the culture belonging to the first generation, their parents. Only the third generation of migrants is fully ready to grasp the life values of the receiving society and thus assimilate. The important element of this theory is that it differentiates between various types of assimilation and integration, namely, economic, social and cultural ones.

Also valuable in the context of sociological research of migration is the theory of three phases in the process of migration by S. Eisenstadt (1954). This author studied the migrants incoming to Israel during the 1950s, and in this research he divided the migration process into three phases from the standpoint of migrant's socio-psychological condition.

The first phase is the formation of migration motivation. Eisenstadt wrote that at this phase there arises and quickly develops the feeling of uncertainty and inadequacy of life circumstances for a potential migrant. The author emphasizes that the very fact of migration for a migrant himself become the only way to improve one's life situation, and not only economically, but also psychologically and socioculturally.

The second phase is relocation as such, movement to a new place of residence. A migrant changes not only his or her place in space, but also gets brand-new social and cultural surroundings. This relocation is accompanied by the process of desocialization: most of previously attributed life skills, in a new place, become low-priority. There, this feeling of uncertainty already formed during the first phase often gets only stronger. Besides, other negative socio-psychological reactions arise: fear of the future, uncertainty about tomorrow etc. Thus, the migrant faces the need to resocialize, that is, to master new social norms and rules, necessary in the receiving society.

The third phase is entering the receiving society. Eisenstadt initially used the term "assimilation" for that matter; however, later in the text he switches to "absorption". According to Eisenstadt, this phase covers three aspects: 1) institutionalization of daily social roles and daily social life of migrants by means of learning the language, adjusting to new social norms etc.; 2) adaptation to the requirements of the receiving society, and in turn, receiving society's adaptation so that to accept the migrant; 3) finally, we can talk about migrant's integration into the receiving society when the migrant loses his or her previous ethnical and cultural identity.

Furthermore detailed description of migrants' assimilation in the receiving societies was suggested by M.M. Gordon (1964) in his famous "Assimilation in American Life: the Role of Race, Religion and National Origins". In this work the author introduced seven types of assimilation: acculturation (adopting norms, values and way of life in the receiving society); structural assimilation (engagement in the local society's institutes); marital assimilation and identification assimilation (when there arises the sense of unity with the receiving society, but not with the society of origin), and then behaviour reception assimilation, attitude reception assimilation and finally civic assimilation.

Gordon also paid attention to such phenomena as xenophobia and discrimination of persons and groups due to their foreign origin. His research and observations mostly concern migrants in the USA during the 1960s, and he came to the conclusion that belonging to a particular ethnical group very much determines career and overall life opportunities, and to describe this feature and its influence on life chances of an individual he introduced the notion of "ethnoclass".

M.M. Gordon viewed the process of assimilation as being composed of certain stages. Migrants' entry to the new society starts with cultural assimilation, the aim of which is to attract migrants to the core values of the receiving society. Structural assimilation means joining the most important institutional structures of the society. The assimilation process ends with cross-ethnical marriages, when migrants lose their ethical identity.

A number of later sociological studies on the migrants' adaptation to receiving societies actively use the notion of social capital. In particular, the authors apply it while considering the differences in children's upbringing in different communities of migrants and how this upbringing determines the life chances of younger generations (Hirshman, Wong, 1986, pp. 1–37). In particular, they came to the conclusion that children coming from the families of Asian migrants have significantly higher levels of education achievements than, for example, the children from Latin American families of migrants.

In the same regard, Portes and Rumbaut (2001) came to the conclusion that nationality or ethnicity may be a powerful predictor of the successful adaptation of migrants. The same authors also outlined three types of resources which migrant communities may use for this matter. The first one includes various state programs (this resource is, of course, first of all applicable and accessible for refugees). In some cases there exist the so-called programs of positive discrimination of such communities, providing their members with convenient opportunities to get better education and thus later achieve a higher social status. The second type of resource is intergroup integration and solidarity of migrant community. Within the separate groups of migrants, especially when they are economically diversified, there are the relationships that provide mutual help and the so-called social elevator as well as ethnical entrepreneurship (Brettell, Altstadt 2007 pp. 383–397).

The above-mentioned Portes and Rumbaur, in their book *Legacies: The Story of the Immigrant Second Generation*, also described the phenomenon of downward social mobility within migrant communities. The authors stated that migrants' adaptation in receiving societies should be viewed with special attention to which segment of the receiving society these migrants are being "built in", since there are certain risks related to marginalization and ethnic criminality. Also, within the complex processes of assimilation and adaptation, the personal features of migrants as well as specific features of migrants' communities and the selected features of receiving communities are important.

One of the mostly intensively developed directions in sociological research on emigration issues focuses on cultural dependencies and supranational hierarchies of cultural and political loyalties. Numerous studies have demonstrated that common colonial past which, inter alia, leads to similarities in education systems as well as to language and cultural hegemony of the leading nations on the territories of their ex-colonies may become a truly powerful predictor of migration flows' division (Behdad, 1994; Blunt, 2007).

Overall, American researchers have demonstrated to be highly productive in sociological research of migration, which is rather self-explanatory, considering the very history of the United States.

The European school of external migration research differs from the American one significantly, first of all, by the general context which determines the subject field. The European school in sociological research of migration had its truly solid studies, with application of qualitative methods, providing classification of migration types and determining its patterns. In particular, it was the European school which introduced the notion "ethnical migration" as then applied to the Germans, Turks, Greeks and also various groups from the post-Soviet territories and the Balkans. The typology which differentiates between pendulum migration, cross-border commuting and transit migration is popular today; it was first used in a European case study by Duvell (2006).

German researchers have provided a significant contribution to the sociological research of migration. One of the most fundamental studies of the latest decades created by German research- ers under the leadership of J. Alt was titled "Life in the world of shadows" ("Leben in der Schattenwelt" in original) and it con- cerned the problems of illegal migration (Alt, 2003).

The contribution of sociology in the research of interaction between the hosting society and migrants and the adaptation of migrants to new environments is also solid. Modalities of such interaction may include: assimilation (the process which leads to identifying oneself with a new group, which is usually accompa- nied with the gradual loss of elements from one's own original culture and attributing new features from the hosting society); acculturation (the process of cultures' interaction in which the receiving culture accepts the elements from the donor culture); isolationism (this type of interaction is specific for conflicting parties; in it certain ethnocultural distance is formed and limita- tion of cultural contacts is observed).

One of the most important contemporary concepts to explain regarding the migration processes is the theory of transnational- ism, originating in Europe in the 1990s. Its essence lays in the statement that there are no diasporas or ethnic groups anymore, at least not in the meaning we used to attribute to them. With the development of technologies and lowering of air ticket prices, cheaper and better-connected phone calls, and especially with the development of Internet technologies, relatives' relocation to other countries does not mean the full end of connections with the sending society anymore. As a result, today it is pointless to consider diasporas, rather we can talk about transnational networks and communities. Therefore, a new term is introduced, which is more adequate in its description of the new properties of today's migration – transmigrant.

Transmigrants are the people whose life activity is tightly connected with their country of origin but also with the receiving society. Having both, transmigrants are developing economic, institutional, cultural and interpersonal relations between the countries (Click Schiller, Basch, Szanton Blanc, 1995 pp. 48–63). Transmigrants may move between the two countries, thus engaging in circular migration, or they may stay on the territory of a receiving society but communicating only with the country of origin, actively using today's means of communication. Transmigrants can be physically already in a new country, but at the same time their engagement and interest in the events back in the origin country is too high, thus, they in fact never cease to be the active members of their previous community. Accordingly, the theory of transnationalism emphasized that such a migrant is not fully detached from the country of origin and thus is forced to assimilate and to adapt to a receiving society. This migrant can be treated as the bearer of two identities, two political loyalties, as a participant of economic relations in two countries at the same time (Baubock, 2003).

In order to illustrate the peculiarities of the sociological approach to the analysis of migration processes at the theoretical and methodological levels let us consider an illustration – the theory of migration as a response to professional stigma. The theory of migration as response to professional stigma considers the motivations behind migration decisions with the emphasis on migration as a means to avoid social humiliation. Social humiliation as stated by C. S. Fan and O. Stark is felt when others who are important to the individual people think he or she is doing something unworthy. In this case migration enables this individual to avoid social humiliation, and under such circumstances migration will happen even if the economic benefits from it are not significant. And if those benefits are significant, then the individual gets even more stimuli to relocate. C. S. Fan and O. Stark, interestingly, provide the example of Ukraine, where in the early 1990s ship-building companies in the city of Mykolaiv did not have demand for engineers, but welders were in high demand. Engineers who lost their jobs massively became welders but not in their own companies, where they used to work as engineers. They were shifting companies to avoid social humiliation due to the despicable change from white-collar to blue-collar work (Fan et al., 2011).

The conceptual difference between experienced stigma and perceived one is important here. Perceived stigma comes from real or imagined stigmatization, while experienced stigma is an objective case of discrimination (Jacoby, 1994). This difference is rather similar to the one between subjective and objective discrimination.

B. Link and J. Phelan have presented the internal structure of the stigmatization process as a range of stages which on the operational level can be recorded as social facts (Link et al., 2001). The five stages of components of stigmatization include: 1) labelling – people identify and symbolically mark the difference related to prestige, "normality", level of pay, working conditions etc.; 2) stereotyping – labelled individuals are attributed similar features of the whole category, for example, profession[4]; 3) separation – distancing from labelled individuals, dissociation of "they" from "us"; 4) "loss of status" – labelled individual are somehow "devalued" in the attitude; and 5) discrimination – systemic disapproval and exclusion.

Thus, external migration can be interpreted as a way to avoid stigmatization: firstly, one can have a "not cool" profession, but this would be not at home, somewhere far away, where nobody knows him or her; secondly, low social status of the profession would be compensated by comparatively high pay (this especially concerns migration from poor countries to richer ones, with significant difference in wages for similar jobs) (Link et al., 2001).

The factor of social stigma is an important addition to the summary of non-economic factors of external migration.

---

[4] A good example here would be numerous media presentations of the stereotype of migrant works from Central Asia in Russian newspapers, Moscow ones especially. There is even the term "emigrant criminality" – when without any statistical or legal proof high rate of criminality is related to migrants. However, in certain cases, similar to ethnical organized crime, ethnical origin can be indeed an influential predictor for engagement in illegal activity.

CHAPTER 2

Factors of External Labour Migration of the Ukrainians in History and Today

2.1 Historic retrospective of the factors in external migration of the Ukrainians

Intensive processes of external migration from Ukraine during the whole twentieth century have lead to the creation and active development of one of the world's largest diasporas. The largest shares of it reside today in Russia (over 4 million), the USA (2 million), Canada (1 million) and Kazakhstan (around 900 thousand) (Diaspora yak chynnyk…, 2008). Researchers outline four waves of external migration from the territory of Ukraine, each having its specific features due to different historic and political contexts and

How to cite this book chapter:
Bilan, Y 2017 *Migration of the Ukrainian Population: Economic, Institutional and Sociocultural Factors.* Pp. 45–139. London: Ubiquity Press. DOI: https://doi.org/10.5334/bbg.c. License: CC-BY 4.0

diverse migration factors. We would like to explore these waves of external migration using, wherever possible, the analytical pattern suggested by Polish sociologist P. Sztompka in his study "Sociology: Analysis of Society" (Sztompka, 2002). According to Sztompka, social practices are being formed by two groups of factors – institutional and discursive. Besides these two dimensions, which are a constant focus of sociology, it is also necessary to remember the economic dimension of external migration.

Social practices we consider here are external migrations of the Ukrainians during the whole twentieth century and today, in the new century already. The related institutional realia include institutional, political, legal and organizational features of sending and receiving societies; the discursive realia include perceptions, commitments and values of migrants which actually provoke them to leave the territory of Ukraine.

We base our research mostly on Ukrainian historiographic sources since they have studied migration from Ukraine most thoroughly, with much attention to each migration wave. It is noteworthy that Ukrainian historiography, in its analysis of migration processes, is deeply ethnocentric. Such processes as Jewish emigration from Ukraine and the forced migration (basically deportation) of the Pols and Crimean Tatars are left totally out of research scope. These topics have their corpus of historical works, but they are considered as separate phenomena, not in the general context of external migration from Ukraine during the twentieth century.

Interestingly, one of the least considered aspects of external migration from Ukraine in its historical retrospective is the estimation of external migrants' numbers as such. Contradictions in such estimations are caused primarily by the fact that in all official documents and reports in the receiving countries these migrants were identified by the country of origin. However, during the three (of four) waves of external migration from what is today the territory of Ukraine, migrants – though they were ethnically Ukrainian – were often affiliated with Russians, Austrians, Slovaks or Pols. Besides, we need to remember that in the early twentieth century the ethnonym "Ukrainian" was not widely spread as such, and was hardly ever used in official documents. Obviously, this was one of the negative factors of influence on preservation of Ukrainian ethnocultural identity.

Let us consider external migration wave by wave paying special attention to its institutional and discursive factors. The first wave of Ukrainian external migration covers the period of 1870–1914. The receiving countries in those times were the USA (since 1877), Brazil (since the 1880s), Canada (since 1891) and also Siberia (after the first Russian revolution, 1905–1907). Additional directions, insignificant in volumes though, during the first wave were Argentina, Australia and New Zealand (Veryga, 1996).

Halychyna, Bukovyna and Zakarpattya in those times were the least developed agrarian Austrian provinces. Ninety percent of their total population were engaged in agricultural works only; 80% of all Halychyna peasants had lands plots smaller than 5 hectares (in Bukovyna such plots amounted to 85% of the total, and in Zakarpattya, up to 73%). In the Eastern part of Halychyna only 5% of all peasants had plots over 10 hectares, in Bukovyna, also 5%, and in Zakarpattya, 10%. About 70 thousand rural households did not have land at all. Lack of land and extreme poverty were the key features of the Ukrainian regions under Austria those days, while their agrarian population constituted about 1.2 million people (Kacharaba, 1995).

Traditionally, Soviet historiography described Austria-Hungarian policy in relation to Western Ukrainian lands as the one aiming to conserve its agrarian status of raw supplier only, a permanent appendage to more developed provinces of the Empire. Western Ukraine in those days was the source of cheap raw materials, first of all; however, certain industries were still developing in this region, namely, wood processing, food industries and also oil extraction. There is a widespread idea, constantly repeated in literature, that the technological development of Western Ukraine was artificially hindered by the metropolis. However, in our opinion it was not just an evil plan of Austria-Hungarians, but more about the poor resources of the region as such and the constant conflicts of the regional elites for their use, since this periphery of the Empire was always financed by the leftover principle, thus leaving no chances for innovations of any sort.

This way or another, within the borders of Austria-Hungarian Empire, the economic system had both segments – the capitalistic one and the so-called subsistence economy, as described by the neoclassical theory of external migration. At the same time that economic system also had certain barriers which hindered the mobility of labour force. Thus, in many cases external migration turned out to be the only way possible to not only increase one's welfare level but merely to survive.

Industrialization on Western Ukrainian lands developed rather slowly but still the share of population engaged in industrial production gradually increased. This new working class was multinational from the very beginning. The Ukrainians in this new sector constituted only a minority, mostly due to a low level of necessary skills and qualifications. The majority of industrial workers in the regions were Pols, Germans, Hungarians, Romanians and Czechs (Petriv, 1993).

The elements of political discrimination and marginalization were added on the top of all the social and economic hardships of Ukrainian population at the periphery. For example, Western Ukrainians had very limited representation in the Austro-Hungarian parliament due to the specific curial election system. At the beginning of the twentieth century in Eastern Halychyna only 7% of the general population were able to vote, while in Bukovyna this number was even lower – only 4.9%. Thus, wherever in Austria one parliament member was representing 40 thousand people, in Bukovina one PM was representing 65 thousand of the population, and in Eastern Halychyna, 94 thousand. The situation remained like this till 1907 when general elections by the curial principle were introduced; however, certain inequalities in ethnical and social class representation remained (Chornovol, 2002).

Already during the first wave of external migration from Ukraine we can clearly observe two very distinct migration vectors – Euroatlantic and Eurasian. This was predetermined by Ukrainian lands' inclusion in two different political orbits, or two different world-systems, in the terminology of F. Braudel, A. G. Frank and I. M. Wallerstein.

The most thoroughly studied segment of the first migration wave is Canada and the USA directions, during 1891–1901 about 80 thousand Ukrainians emigrated there from Eastern Halychyna only. During 1901–1911 224 thousand more Ukrainians relocated in the same direction. Such a massive flow was provoked not only by the push factors described above. There were also pull factors contributing to that. First of all, these receiving countries had targeted governmental programs encouraging immigration. Canada, for example, founded a special migration syndicate at the very end of the nineteenth century which sent groups of recruiters to Western Ukraine. In 1872 the liberal government of Canada headed by J. A. MacDonald approved the law according to which any male of full legal age entering the country could pay ten dollars and get a plot of land up to 65 hectares in size. In Canada the Ukrainians settled mostly on the virgin lands of Manitoba, Saskatchewan and Alberta, where Ukrainian hunger for land could be entirely satisfied. Besides, apart from 65 hectares for only ten dollars, one extra hectare cost slightly more than two dollars which was a hilarious price even for those times. However, the mandatory condition for getting the land was also constructing a house on it, which would cost no less than 300 dollars additionally. The mandatory term of stay on this newly acquired land was three years; during this period, the settlers were supposed to spend at least 6 months on grubbing and plowing, so that by the end of the third year at least 14 hectares would be cultivated. If these conditions were not fulfilled, the immigrants lost their right to the land. There was, of course, a range of benefits and preferences for these newly-minted Canadian farmers; however, if an immigrant did not invest enough efforts in his land during the first six years, the plot was reverted to the state (Gutsal, 2005).

At those times the key news distributors about the benefits of emigration to Canada were the agents of shipping and railways companies who were hoping to profit from migrants' travels. These agents usually got about 2–5 dollars for each immigrant to Canada (Kacharaba, 2002).

The average Ukrainian emigrant of those days was a young man from Eastern Halychyna, Bukovyna or Zakarpattya, he was illiterate and did not have any specific qualifications but was ready for any low-paid job. However, the names of the first Ukrainian migrants to the New World became known in a very different setting. One of the first Ukrainians in the USA was Atypiy Goncharenko, the former monk of Kyiv-Pechersk Lavra who had to escape the country because he was followed by the Czar authorities for his active participation in the anti-serfdom movement. He came to the USA back in 1865 to later become the publisher of the *Alaska Herald*, a newspaper with certain influence on American social life (Varvartsev, 1996, p. 116).

Overall, clergy and public figures participated quite actively in Ukrainian diasporas, in many, founding news places and documenting its activities in particular. In 1885, Rev. Volyanskyi organized the first Ukrainian fellowship of solidarity in America. At that time it had only several dozen members, and its primary aim was to compensate funeral losses to the families of deceased migrants.

The economic life of Ukrainian migrants in the New World was mostly within the borders of the subsistence economy; that is, it was concentrated on labour intensification under the conditions of rather limited resources, with some support within Ukrainian migrant communities. Entrepreneurship with all of its risks was new for the Ukrainians, and thus, quite a rare case in the community. There were many reasons for this: low level of cultural competences in the new sociocultural environment; undereducation and absence of qualifications; poor knowledge of English; certain distance from the receiving society which was not quite ready to integrate with the newcomers. In general, among the first-wave migrants who came before 1914, the share of those who spoke English (at least to some extent) was 40.8%, however, among the Ukrainians their share was much lower. The level of literacy was one of the lowest among all ethnical groups in Canada (Grabovych, 1992).

During this period the institutionalization of Ukrainian diasporas in the receiving countries took place. Already then Ukrainian diasporas had their institutional structures, with financial and cultural infrastructure, with its own public and even political life.

The initial intention of the majority of Ukrainian migrants was to earn money and then return home. However, eventually advantages and benefits of the New World persuaded many to stay for good. The history of Ivan Pylypiv is quite illustrative in this sense. Once a peasant from the village Nebyliv in the Sub-carpathians, in 1891 he arrived at the Canadian port Quebec and then moved to Manitoba. After his first harvest in a new place, Pylypiv returned home for his family and told many his success story[5]. At the end of his life Pylypiv already had 324(!) hectares of arable lands, which was definitely a fantastic career for a Western Ukrainian peasant who at home could have had 2–3 hectares at best. Interestingly, during his rather short trip back home, Pylypiv was such a successful propagandist of migration to Canada, that the local authorities had to intrude. At that time Austria-Hungary was already realizing the related risks, and passport procedures for peasants very soon got much more complicated.

The first Ukrainian migrants in Canada lived on a standalone basis. This was not only because they did not speak the language and were trying to "restore Ukraine" in a new place. This happened due to their place in the new social hierarchy – at the very bottom of it. For the next waves of immigrants, the situation was already different (at least for part of them): they had better education overall and certain professional skills too, and this allowed them integrate in Canadian society more freely, moving up the social ladder but keeping elements of their Ukrainian identity at the same time.

Meanwhile, the inclusive character of the Canadian political system allowed the Ukrainians to politically integrate into the

---

[5] This clearly shows that during the first migration wave already the so-called multiplicate effect occurred, when one migrant was first followed by his close family, and gradually the whole settlement migrated

new society, keeping away bad memories about national and religious discrimination in Austria-Hungary. In 1912 the representative of Ukrainian community Teodor Stafanyk was elected to the municipal council in Winnipeg. In 1913 two more Ukrainians were elected to the provincial level parliaments – T. Forlei in Manitoba and A. Shandro in Alberta.

Other Western directions in the first wave of Ukrainian migration were Argentina and Brazil. Despite the limited sources available, we still know basic statistics on these directions too. The massive relocation of the Ukrainians to these countries started in the 1890s, and during the first three years (1895–1897) 20 thousand Ukrainians migrated to Brazil; a majority of them settled in Parana. During the next ten years 7–8 thousand more Ukrainians moved to this country, and then again 20 thousand until 1914. Thus, at the beginning of World War I in Europe, the Ukrainian colony in Brazil was already as large as 45 thousand people.

As for Argentina, we know the exact date when the mass immigration of the Ukrainians began – August, 27, 1897, when the first 12 Ukrainian families arrived in Buenos Aires. In 1914 around 15 thousand Ukrainian migrants lived in Argentina (Vasylyk, 1982).

The opposite direction in external migration from the territory of today's Ukraine was the Eurasian one. The Ukrainians living then in the territories belonging politically to the Russian Empire were also oppressed, the same as in Austria-Hungary. The abolition of serfdom in 1861 led to the situation when numerous Ukrainians of the peasant class were left without land, and this logically increased their mass migration to the other side of the Ural Mountains. South Siberia was the most preferred location because lands plots were distributed there for further grain farming. Migration in this direction became massive after the Siberia railway was constructed (1891–1905). During the period from 1987 till 1916 around 900 thousand people moved from Ukraine to distant regions of the Russian Empire (Siberia, Kazakhstan, Far East). The largest Ukrainian community was in Tomsk guberniya ("province" equivalent in Russian); about 100 thousand Ukrainians lived there. The second largest was in Omsk guberniya. Many new settlements on these territories got typical Ukrainian names (which are still used now) – Poltavka, Odeske, Maryanivka, Ukrainka etc. During the whole first wave of migration (1850–1916) almost 490 thousand people moved to the lands of Far East; of them about 56% were originally from Ukraine. However, other sources state that during the twenty years before World War I over 2 million Ukrainians relocated to the Far East (Veryga, 2002).

Thus, we can state that institutional push factors that forced the Ukrainians to emigrate were the following: economic underdevelopment of Western Ukraine under Austria-Hungary, lack of land plots, heavy tax load, and high percentage rates on credit, political and social discrimination. In this regard, famous Ukrainian-Canadian historian M. Marunchak wrote: "Social and political pressure which was forming in Ukraine during several centuries created a situation when the owners of this land, this country, which is called 'the breadbasket of Ukraine', were forced to leave their own land, and as one Ukrainian lyricist wrote, 'go over the hills and far away'. Obviously, political and social pressure left its imprint on the consciousness of those leaving the country for better economic and political conditions" (Marunchak, 1991, p. 17–18). In the discursive dimension V. Chopovskyi describes the push factors in the following way: "The press of those days paid attention to the gloomy connection between poverty and emigration. Poor peasants were forced to emigrate by their material needs. High taxes, lack of lands, and most of all – lack of jobs.

No factories – thus, no work... Emigration is the escape from a powerful enemy" (Chopovskyi, 2011).

In the meantime the institutional pull factors were represented first of all by the activities of numerous emigration agencies, created by both governments and large businesses of the receiving countries. In Western Ukraine, the Austria-Hungary government only began to restrain the activities of such organizations at the beginning of the twentieth century, when their destructive demographic and economic impacts were already too obvious.

As for the discursive dimension we can assume that rumours about the countries across the ocean were spread by those who had more inclination to migration behaviour: those were neighbouring Pols, Slovaks or Hungarians, who started their external migration earlier than the Ukrainians. Such information was spread through letters and they also returned for the families. There is evidence that the first Ukrainians moved to Canada having heard rumours only or having read personal letters from that country (for example, Pylypiv, mentioned earlier, heard about the advantages of emigration to Canada from school teachers and also from the relatives of some German settlers who already were in Canada). Therefore, we can state that even long before rapid development of global communications, mass imaginations of the advantages of emigration and its potential directions were quickly spread through personal communications, including those with recruiters, and this stimulated the migration processes of the first wave.

The chaos of World War I and the extremely complicated period between the wars had tragic large-scale consequences for Ukraine. Millions of human lives, sacrifices to the communist gods of industrialization and collectivization, establishment of the totalitarian regime (which lasted, as we know, for many decades, until the 1990s) – this was the horrible price Ukraine paid during that period. Not surprisingly, migration in that period was the relocation of those people who today would have been called "the creative class".

The second wave of external migration of the Ukrainians covered the whole period between the world wars and was caused by a complex combination of social, economic and political reasons. For this wave, obviously, the push factors dominated and fully explained the migration behaviour.

After the end of World War I, migration potential fed on the ruins of both monarchies – Austria-Hungarian and Russian – and more specifically, in the countries which arose from these monarchies. In 1918 Poland was restored, inheriting Eastern Halychyna from Austria-Hungary, and also Western Volyn and Western Polissya from Russia. Mass mobilization, increasing quantities of refugees from both sides, frequent ethnical deportations, political oppression – these were the reasons behind the migration intentions of this period in history.

A part of the migrating Ukrainians did not agree with the Soviet authority and ideology due to the Soviet terror against large and medium farm owners, merchants, clergy and intelligentsia. A large chunk of the second wave migration was formed from the liberation movement participants: the supporters of Simon Petlura, or Hetman Skoropadskiy, or Central Rada, or the Western Ukrainian People's Republic.

At the same time, emigrants of this wave were much more educated; these were professionals in many fields, researchers, economists, writers etc. The latter were especially prominent; many of them later became famous in Poland, Czech Republic and Slovakia, Austria, Romania, Bulgaria, France, USA or Canada – these were the receiving countries of the second wave.

Apart from the obvious social differences from the first-wave movers (higher literacy rate and better education, first of all), another key change was that the second wave settled mostly in cities. They did not form closed ghetto-like communities; many of them had enough education and skills for a good start in a new place. There were also a lot of activists among the migrants of the second wave, and this was the reason for the strengthening of organizational structure of the diasporas, with numerous clubs, cooperatives, newspapers etc. to appear very soon.

Remigration was also one of the features of the second wave, just like with the first one. However, during the second wave it did not have any economic reasoning, nor the aim to recruit further. The key reason for remigration was actually quite sad and naïve at the same time: many believed in the idea of the Soviet Union and were hoping for a fresh start there, under changed conditions. Probably, the most famous case of such remigration was the story of the former President of the Ukrainian People's Republic Mykhailo Hrushevskyi, who returned to the Soviet Union in 1924 to be politically followed later on, accused in nationalism and die ten years later under unclear circumstances after a surgery on an anthrax-related small carbuncle. The vast majority of those who returned to Ukraine during the 1930s died in concentration camps or were politically oppressed in some other way as "the enemies of the state".

As for the Ukrainians in the territories of the restored Polska Rzeczpospolita, several researchers state that during the 1920–1930s, the government of Poland was actively stimulating the external migration of the Ukrainians, mostly because the latter were seen as a threat to national security. The potential advantages of Ukrainian emigration for Poland were many: getting rid of excessive workforce in the country; intensified sea ports' performance; promotion of passenger fleet development; additional opportunities for foreign trade development; avoiding social tensions between social and ethnic groups inside the country (Kacharaba, 2002).

The migration policy of the Polish government between the two world wars was developing in the context of its ethnonational policy aimed at strengthening the national components in all regions in favour of the Pols and encouraging Ukrainian and Jewish emigration to Brazil, Argentina and Palestine (Kacharaba, 2003, p. 416). With such aims, a range of migration affairs offices were created in Western Ukraine, namely, the Commissariat for Emigration Administration (1920), the Administration for Labour Intermediation and Emigrants Support (1921) and the Navy and Colonial League (1924) (Stending, 1935, p. 13–15).

These organizations were so successful that already in 1938 the countries of Latin America, first of all, Brazil and Argentina, had to turn to immigration limitations – from Europe overall and from Poland specifically. However, this did not stop Poland from encouraging emigration of minorities further on, since the Pols continued to see emigration as the key to harmonization of social relations. In 1939 the State Secretary M. Arciszewski affirmed that "it is necessary to continue developing overseas emigration, and especially emigration of national minorities" (Kolodziej, 1982).

Since the Soviet migration regime was totally closed, even such powerful institutional push factors as the repressive policy of the Bolsheviks government (the so-called "red terror" (Bilokin, 1999)), collectivization and dekulakization (the campaign against individual farming), prohibition of peasants' mobility (in the Soviet Union peasants did not have the right to relocate independently from the assigned village until the 1960s), constants campaigns against the so-called "enemies of the state" etc. did not manage to cause mass emigration from the country. Mass discourses on the inability to perceive and "digest" the policies and ideology of the new state are manifested in a great deal of details in numerous memoirs of political and cultural figures of those times (Petrov, 1959).

As for the institutional pull factors (related mostly to the activities of numerous organizations and institutions encouraging emigration using a range of positive stimuli), we can mention networks of emigrant organizations (for example, "Prometheism" established in 1926 to work with the Ukrainians, Georgians, Turkmens, Karels etc. in their joint fight for creation of independent states on the territories of the USSR). European governments also often used political emigration from the Soviet Union as a card in the game against Soviet regime.

The third wave of external migration from the territories of today's Ukraine was, similarly to the second one, caused primarily by political reasons. It started at the end of World War II. The vast majority in this generation of migrants were the so-called DPs – the displaced persons in French, German or British zones of temporary occupation. These were former slaves (*ostarbeiters*) and/or prisoners from concentration camps who were left in the territories under the Allies' control once the war was over. These were also the guerrillas who fought against the Soviet Army, Nazi collaborators and/or participants of the national freedom movements, who knew that Stalin camps were waiting for them in the Soviet Union. These were the people who joined Ukrainian diasporas in Western Europe, the USA, Canada, Latin America, and also formed the new diaspora in Australia.

Once the war was over, the vast majority of them clearly refused to return to Ukrainian lands and settled down in Canada, the USA,

Great Britain, Australia, Brazil, Argentina and France. Quite a large share of these new emigrants travelled to the USA (80 thousand), fewer chose Great Britain (35 thousand) and Australia (20 thousand). Brazil was chosen as the destination point by 7 thousand people; Argentina, 6 thousand; France, 10 thousand. The political context of that period was favourable for the Ukrainians; they were seen as political refugees (Yevtukh et al., 2010).

Social trends of the second migration wave remained valid for the third one. Many of the newcomers were researchers, clergy and political and civil activists. They contributed a lot to the blossoming of political, cultural and religious life in Ukrainian diasporas. It is noteworthy that the third wave was very much politicized, for obvious reasons; however, the political orientation was not univocal – the political segments of the third wave migration were in constant confrontation, and this, of course, did not contribute to the sense of unity within the diaspora.

Later on, after those who left Soviet Ukraine straight after the war, there was also a minor wave of dissidents who occasionally managed to escape from the Stalin regime to the West. A separate group was formed by Ukrainian protestants (mainly Pentecostals with their families with multiple children) (Zakharov, 2003). These were included in the economic and political life of the receiving societies more freely and quickly due to the common religion factor.

The Western direction of Ukrainian external migration was not the only one. After World War II 100 thousand of the Ukrainians were sent to Siberia. Not all of them were political prisoners, though. Many were simply forced to relocate in the context of the state policy of creating a homogenous ethnocultural mix, which was supposed to serve as a foundation for the "nation of Soviet people".

The institutional push factors of the third wave are quite comparable with the same during the second wave. The key factor was the Stalinism threat, reinforced by the factors of after-war ruins and general social disorganization.

It would be wrong to state that the Soviet Union was trying to limit emigration. Officially, there was no emigration from the Soviet Union in the post-war years as such. Moreover, external affairs and intelligence offices of the Soviet Union were carrying out a lot of active secret work to return those citizens who "were lost in the West" during the war. Thus, in October 1944, the Repatriation Committee was founded, the aim of which was to return home those Soviet citizens who, for some reason, were relocated outside Soviet territories during the war. Its representatives, often accompanied by defence intelligence, were paying visits to many European countries, including Germany, which was then home for a quite numerous Ukrainian community (Danylenko, 2002). Most often such "returnings home" were forced ones, strongly resembling kidnapping.

The situation changed in 1947 when the International Relief Organization (IRO) was founded with the aim of taking care of and supporting the displaced persons. The IRO's activities were based on the agreements with new European authorities and their American allies, and in fact, the IRO became the diplomatic provider of legal and political protection for the displaced. Speaking strictly legally, all affairs related to displaced persons until 1949 were in the competence of the military occupation authorities of the Allies; however, both Canada and the USA already had civil organizations functioning in this field – the Support Fund for the Ukrainians of Canada and the United Ukrainian American Help Committee. These organizations helped those willing to leave Germany; they provided invitations for entry, explained what procedures and documents would be needed to do so etc. (Podobed, 2008).

A good example of how mass discourse explained the push factors of the third wave can be found in the pamphlet "Why I did not want to return to the USSR" (1946) written by Ukrainian writer Ivan Bagryanyi and translated very quickly into many European languages (Bagryanyi, 1946).

Among other works on Ukrainian emigration during and after the World War II we can mention the well-known I. Stebelskyi work "Ukrainian population migration after World War II" (1992) and O. Subtelnyi "Ukrainian political refugee: an historical overview" (1992).

Therefore, the first and all following historical waves of migration from Ukraine are very different in terms of both push and pull factors forcing Ukrainian population to go looking for a better place. The first migration wave from Ukraine can be described as relocation for land and for welfare. This wave is a good illustration of the importance of economic factors of migration and how migration decisions are made by the whole household (even in cases when only one person was moving abroad, it was so expensive that the whole family was gathering money for that). From the theoretical viewpoint, the first wave of Ukrainian external migration can be the best described by the neoclassical theory of migration, operating, in particular, under the notion of dual economy, which consists of the capitalist segment and the economy of subsistence.

In contrast, the second and third waves of migration from Ukraine were first of all forced and deeply political; they were least of all influenced by economic factors and household decision-making. These migration waves can be described as relocation in search of life and freedom. Such migration was not planned in advance; it was drastic, often under extreme circumstances.

It is curious to compare the first wave on one hand and the second and the third waves on the other, from both standing points – economic and sociological. Such a comparison reveals the specific features of institutional influences and the differences in migrants' mechanisms of adaptation to receiving societies, including the processes of ghettoization or, on the opposite, successful integration into the receiving society.

2.2 Socioeconomic factors of the fourth wave of external labour migration from Ukraine at its two stages: "escaping from misery" and "searching for better life"

During the Soviet Union times, Ukraine, like other Soviet republics, had a very closed migration regime. At that stage, the migration behaviour of all citizens was first of all determined by the institutional political factor. During the Soviet times there was no such phenomenon as labour emigration as such. In the late years of the Soviet rule, tourism spread, heading mostly to other countries of the Socialist camp. And in such rare occasions, the procedure of getting an international passport was extremely complicated as well as all other arrangements related to travelling outside the Union, and this stopped many from even thinking about it. Besides, any hint about travelling abroad immediately caught the attention of the Soviet secret services. There was a special list of documents to get an approval for travelling abroad and it included: a reference letter from the local branch of the Communist party (and it was supposed to be signed by the three top persons – the head of the enterprise, the secretary of the local trade union and the secretary of the local party branch); the so-called "objective data" – a detailed life story listing all places of work and residence; the statement of good health, including a detailed blood test; the written grounding of the travel aim; the invitation letter (in rare cases when the travel was private); the detailed calendar plan of travelling(!); and also, after the travel, the citizen had to write the travel report to be submitted to the controlling bodies.

After all these documents were ready, the potential traveller had to pay a visit to the local party unit to be instructed on proper Soviet behaviour abroad. Besides, there were also several categories of Soviet citizens which were banned from travelling abroad, mostly those working for the military sector and "politically unstable" citizens.

The fourth wave of external migration from Ukraine started in the second half of the 1980s, when first gradual democratization and later the Soviet split had liberalized the migration regime. Comparing this wave with the two previous ones, the fourth one can be called (relatively) voluntary; even though there were still rather powerful push factors, external migration was not seen as the only way to save life and freedom, as it was before.

Apart from more favourable institutional and political environments, the external migration from Ukraine was stimulated by the worsening economic conditions inside the country: the GDP drop was a dramatic one, by 60% from the end of 1980s till the mid 1990s. This was worse than during the Great Depression in the USA 60 years before. Additional contributing negative economic factors included: growing unemployment due to serious changes at the labour market; galloping inflation; concentration of money capital in big cities only and degradation of rural life; the loss of production potential (in fact, nearly total deindustrialization) etc.

The first migrants of the fourth wave were mostly the representatives of ethnic minorities which relocated under the programmes of family reunions, using the support of receiving countries. These were first of all Jews, Germans, Hungarians and Greeks. According to the state statistics, out of 95.4 thousand people leaving Ukraine in 1990, 92% moved to Israel (Vovkanych, 2004, p. 117). According to the data of Jewish organizations in the USA, in the period from 1989 to 1994 more than half of the legal immigrants from Ukraine were of Jewish origin. Later on, their share in the total migration flow was gradually decreasing: from 54% in 1994 to merely 8% in 2001.

Socioeconomic determinants of external migration from Ukraine at its fourth wave always have to be considered in the more general socioeconomic context of Ukrainian society – from the early 1990s till now, actually. There were two specific periods in this wave which were different in terms of socioeconomic context around the migration decision and also in terms of external migrants' motivations.

The first of these periods lasted from the beginning of 1990s and till the beginning of the new millennium. It was defined by the severe socioeconomic crisis, dramatic drop in the welfare level in the country, depreciation of nearly all savings due to inflation and also due to mass fraud with accounts within the Sberbank of the USSR (Bank of Savings). It is noteworthy that crisis phenomena in Ukrainian economy did not appear with the proclamation of country's independence (as it is often interpreted in certain politicized discourses) but long before that. The growth of the Soviet economy (of course, not the official one, but according to alternative calculations) was 6% during the 1950s, then 3% only during the 1960s, 2% for the 1970s and finally 1% in the 1980s (Popov, 2006). Reconstruction (now known as "Perestroika" in Russian) was initiated by the Soviet leaders in the mid 1980s as an attempt to save the country from the huge, unmanageable and self-destructing economic system, which was absorbing all possible resources, being oriented only on military production and totally ignoring the existence of the consumer sector as such.

The majority of the population in the late Soviet times were living with two key notions in mind – deficit and "blat" (a Russian slang word for cronyism, necessary connections). Deficit meant constant absence or very limited availability of consumer goods of any sort, while "blat" meant the opportunities to solve the problem of deficit through the intricate system of necessary connections. During the very last years of the Soviet Union even the most simple food products became deficit, including sausages, coffee, tea or sugar (Ledeneva, 1998). Ironically, having the largest agricultural potential in the world in terms of agricultural land size, the country was suffering from extremely low labour productivity, poorly developed logistics and disorientation in consumer preferences and needs. Unfortunately, the state authorities envisioned the ways to solve the socioeconomic problems only in the context of the established command system. One of the decrees of the Council of Ministers of the USSR, dated 1988, obligated all local authorities "to liquidate waiting lines and end up violations and abuse related to deficit products sales" (Postanovlenie Sovmina RSFSR…, 1988), while no specific economic measures were ever developed.

Thus, independent Ukraine inherited quite a heavy load of economic problems from the Soviet Union split. Sadly, Ukraine did not solve those problems but rather multiplied them. In the context of catastrophic socioeconomic problems, the liberalization of migration regime naturally led to a dramatic increase of emigration flows.

The first half of the 1990s was the period of recession for the Ukrainian economy, and this recession was only speeding up.

Overall, the recession lasted till 1999; however, in its last two years it was quite moderate. The gross product decreased significantly: its fall in 1992 was 16.5%, 14.2% in 1993, and even 23% in 1994. According to the official statistics of 1992–1993, the inflation index in Ukraine was ranging from 2100% to 10256% which was an unprecedented case considering that the country was not engaged in a war (Ganusyk, 2013, p. 47).

The radical transformation of the labour market led to the loss of millions of jobs. After the decades of traditional Soviet paternalism, people lost all guarantees regarding their job placement. Despite the numerous economic bottlenecks of socialism, the Soviet Union had a rather stable employment system which guaranteed many things, including: the first place of employment for all graduates, rigid standards on labour security, strict timing of working hours etc. The typical social package for any working Soviet citizen included free medical support, a once-a-year opportunity to use the Union-wide system of resorts and sanatoriums, guaranteed pension minimum etc. Under such a highly paternalistic system the employment rate in the country was almost 100%, employee turnover was nearly impossible and the difference in wages country-wide was not that significant. After decades of living "in an ivory tower of social protection" Ukrainian population was simply not ready for the changed socioeconomic conditions of the harsh 1990s.

It took quite some time to decrease the rate of social expectations on guaranteed jobs, long vacations, free-of-charge medical and education services, labour rights protected by default etc. And even till now, both in mass consciousness and in political discourse there is a certain place for sentiments about returning to the system of state socialism. Paternalistic habits are very stable, people get used to them too easily, and it will take some time to change this attitude (Susak, 2007).

Overall, in the post-Soviet and post-socialist countries there have been two radically different approaches to state management of the reforms. The first one involved the so-called "shock therapy", according to which in a short-term period of profound socioeconomic changes, all necessary elements of the free market economy were introduced at once, and this short-term shocking period was then followed by economic recovery. This approach was chosen by the majority of Central European countries from the former socialist camp, including Poland.

The second approach involved gradual and rather slow reforms, taking into account the current level of welfare and the public opinion. This approach was chosen by the majority of Central European postsocialist countries, including Poland, and also by Baltic countries. The second approach included gradual, rather slow reforms, taking into account the issue of welfare and life quality and also public opinion. These gradual reforms were, inter alia, carried out in Bulgaria and Romania. Both of these approaches could have been efficient, actually, if applied wisely; however, the case of Ukraine does not fall into any of them. After 1991, the year of Ukraine's independence declaration, the new political leadership did not manage to choose any consistent strategy for further development (Kovalskyi et al., 2012). To be more precise, the approaches to the process of reforms, their vision and their aims were changing all the time, in parallel with changes in the political environment. There is a range of reasons behind this situation, the key of them being the polarization of the political and ruling elite in the country: part of the politicians were thinking about the free market and European vector of the development; however, a significant share of the ruling class were still the representatives of the former Communist nomenklatura or people with rather leftist views, still oriented on establishing the socialist-like economic model and on a Eurasian vector of geopolitical integration.

Two key features of societal reform in Ukraine were on one hand, the neoliberal way, chosen just as it was by many developed Western countries, and on the other hand, the system of state socialism stayed. Lack of unity inside the political elite, dominance of pragmatic interests of certain business groups, constant pandering to populism and frequent political changes, all have led to the emergence of a hybrid economic and political system in Ukraine.

Similar processes were happening at the labour market and within labour policies which influenced accordingly the migration phenomena and intentions. Removal of nearly all state guarantees at the labour market led to massive precarization of labour in Ukraine. Changing regulation of Ukrainian labour market made it rather flexible, on one hand, but on the other, the whole load of risks and uncertainties was now on employees, not employers. As a result – just as in many Western societies, but many years before – a new social class emerged, the precariat (from the Latin word "precarium" – not stable, not trusted, threatening, the one which is in the state of uncertainty).

This term was introduced by G. Standing (2011), and according to Standing, precariat consists of those people who feel the lack of labour security; they are not sure that in case of workplace loss, they would be able to find a new one. This also concerns the lack of security at a workplace; lack of opportunities to improve qualifications and develop one's career further; lack of guaranteed income for a longer term; the fear to stand for one's position in a workplace; and the fear to communicate one's vision to an employer (Standing, 2011).

Labour migration from Ukraine is undoubtedly a precarious phenomenon. Legal, long-term and guaranteed employment under social security protection and with further opportunities for career growth is a very rare case for the Ukrainians working abroad. Overall, the dynamics of illegal employment of the Ukrainians abroad is relatively positive, at least if compared with the first half of the fourth migration wave.

During the first period of the fourth wave in external migration from Ukraine, human trafficking was a frequent phenomenon. Two major forms of human trafficking were females' trade for sexual services, and human trade for labour purposes. The typical situation with such trafficking was when a person left the country completely legally and voluntarily, but was later, when already abroad, forced into restriction and further labour exploitation. The number of the Ukrainians who became the victims of human trafficking during the 1990s, according to some estimations, may have been as many as 100 thousand people (Vasylyeva et al., 2012). The situation with illegal employment became much better after the so-called "migration amnesties" in a range of countries typical for Ukrainian labour migration (Italy, Spain, Portugal, Greece), after the new legislation was introduced extending the opportunities for legal employment of foreigners (in Poland). According to Ukrainian state statistics, in 2008 35.1% of labour migrants had work permits, 39.3% had temporary registration, while 25.6% of labour migrants did not have any official status abroad. The largest share of unregistered migrants from Ukraine resided that year in Poland – 56.2% (Ensuring…, 2012, p. 10).

This data is confirmed by similar information from the State Labour Inspection of Poland: in 2014 they checked around 15.5 thousand foreigners working in Poland, among whom 9.5 thousand were citizens of Ukraine. Among all working foreigners, 870 cases of illegal employment were detected, of which 777 concerned the Ukrainians (Mihranty..., 2015).

What is the share of precariat in the general structure of the society then? Many authors suggest their own criteria by which certain citizens can be attributed to this social group:

- Market criteria (unemployment, forced part-time character of the job, participation in seasonal work);
- Legal criteria (non-official employment; not determined legal status of stay in a country);
- Social and labour criteria (instability of work; flexible forms of work; overload and high technical risks);
- Social-psychological criteria (uncertainty about keeping the current job; social exclusion or stigmatization; uncertainty about the future);
- Economic criteria (low level of income as such) (Grishnova et al., 2014).

Using these criteria and the official data of the State Committee for Statistics and also the data from the International Labour Organization (Profil..., 2012) we can assume that the share of precariat in Ukraine is about 50% of the whole gainfully employed population.

An additional proof that precariat phenomenon was one of the push factors in external migration is the data obtained during the ESS, Round 6 (European Social Survey. Round 6 was carried out in 2012). The survey confirmed that the respondents who have the experience of unemployment also have much more experience with external migration, as compared to those who were never unemployed (ESS, Round 6, 2012). In the group of the respondents who declared the experience of labour migration during the last 10 years, the share of those who also had been unemployed is 56.5%, while in the group with no labour migration experience the share of those who were once unemployed was 41.7%.

For Ukraine, this trend would be similar, however, with certain clarifications. The specifics of the socioeconomic situation at Ukrainian labour market makes uncertain the status of not only precariat, but also those of salariat and professionals too. The phenomenon of poverty among the employed, delays of wages, high rate of inflation, frozen indexation of wages and general decrease of consumer spending – all of this makes the well being of the vast majority of all gainfully employed in Ukraine uncertain, despite the nominal status at the labour market (Mishchuk & Grishnova, 2015).

Precariat as a social group exists in most economic systems and at nearly all labour markets today due to the global shift in public administration to the side of neoliberalism. The problem of precariat among Ukrainian labour migrants remains quite serious; however, during the recent several years there has been a noticeable rebalancing in favour of legal employments (mostly due to "migration amnesties" and bilateral agreements of Ukraine with the migrant-receiving countries).

In Ukraine a large share of the population (according to our estimations, about 50% of the gainfully employed population in the country) experience precariatization. Under such conditions the absence of labour rights guarantees in Ukraine serves as the push factor, however, employment abroad is not considered as the way to get long-term legal employment and guaranteed social benefits. Labour migrants often agree to abandon their labour right only for the sake of higher incomes, albeit temporary ones.

All of the described socioeconomic, institutional and political preconditions have created a rather favourable context for the formation of migration intentions among a large share of the Ukrainians. Motivation of external migrants relocating during the first decade of the fourth wave can be called "escaping from misery", since most frequently their primary goal was not enrichment, but satisfaction of their basic needs. The first to appreciate the advantages of the migration regime liberalization on the background of socioeconomic collapse back at home were professionals with quite a high level of education and qualifications (Leontenko, 1999). Gradually, external migration became more and more common practice, expanding to other social stratas, including escapers from rural life and blue-collar labourers.

During 1995–1996 the Ukrainian economy experienced relative stabilization and even some sort of revival. The inflation went abruptly down, and the price growth rate demonstrated a decline – from 400% in 1992 to only 40% in 1996. The general economic situation had favourable effects on the salaries of all citizens; in the period from October 1994 to April 1997 the average salary grew more than fourfold (recalculated in the American dollar equivalent, this was from 22 to 90 USD) (Voronyanskyi, 2012).

Significant changes in migration intentions motivation took place during the second half of the fourth migration wave. The beginning of this period coincided with the beginning of the new millennium. It is worth noting that it was in also in 2000 when Ukraine had its first real growth recorded since the independence in 1991. The real GDP grew by 6% as compared to the increase by 0.4% back in 1999. The maximum level of GDP growth in Ukraine was recorded in 2003, and it was over 15%. In 2006 the GDP of Ukraine was 63% to the level of the year 1989, and in 2007 it was already 68%. That was the period of gradual improvement of the socioeconomic situation in Ukraine.

At the beginning of the 2000s the key reasons for external migration of the Ukrainian population were low wages, unemployment, the desire to improve life conditions, unsatisfactory workplace conditions etc. Therefore, during the second half of the fourth wave, external migration of the Ukrainians was motivated mostly by the desire to increase the general level of welfare, to solve the housing problem, to finance university education for children etc. The survey "External labour migration of Ukrainian population" carried out by the State Committee for Statistics and the Ukrainian centre for social reforms, under the support of the Open Ukraine Foundation and the representative offices of the International Organization for Migration and the International Bank for Reconstruction and Development in Ukraine, demonstrated that in the hierarchy of emigration motives the second most important place is occupied simply by salary, which is supposed to satisfy the basic needs – food, primary consumer goods (clothes etc.).

This finds its manifestation in the quantitative indicators of external migration. At the beginning of the 2000s the quantity of people leaving Ukraine was quite large, for example, in 2002 alone the emigration was 76.3 thousand people. However, according to the data of the State Committee for Statistics, in 2003, due to improving socioeconomic conditions, there was a decrease in the quantity of emigrants, and in 2005 their quantity was half on the previous number. The recorded minimum of Ukrainian emigrants of the fourth wave was in 2012 – 14.5 thousand. However, already in 2013 there was again recorded a growth of emigration which was, most probably, caused by the worsening socioeconomic conditions and also by the political turmoil at the end of that year.

Considering the most recent developments, we can assume that since the end of 2013 and through today we are experiencing

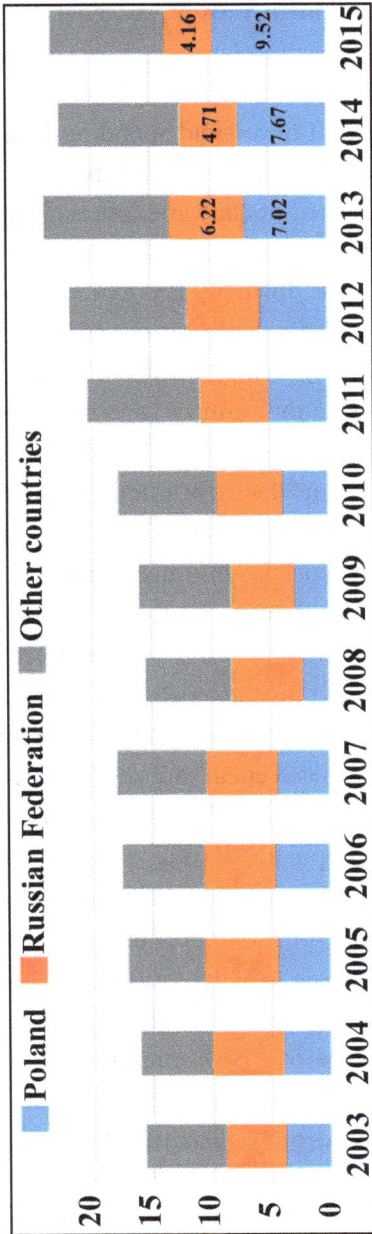

Figure 4: Number of state border crossings by Ukrainian citizens exiting Ukraine in 2003–2015, million times. *Source:* State Border Guard Service of Ukraine Наводиться за: Migration in Ukraine: facts and figures. 2016. Edited by Olena Malynovska IOM Ukraine. – p. 10.

the third period of the fourth wave in external migration from Ukraine which probably would later be called "the escape from political turmoil and war threats".

Data on the structure of household spending in Ukraine during the first half of the 2000s demonstrated the economic growth of the country which started in 2008 and lasted till the beginning of the world financial and economic crisis in 2009. Already in 2008 the GNP of Ukraine went down by almost 15%. However, during the first half of the 2000s the dynamics of household spending showed a gradually improving balance of food and non-food spending. As previously, in the country as a whole the key spending item was still food; however, its share in the total spending was gradually decreasing – from 70% in the middle of the 1990s to 50% in 2008. Along with the decreasing share of food spending, during 19999–2008 the share of spending on non-food products and on services was gradually increasing.

Economic growth, which started in Ukraine in 2000, sadly, had very little positive influence on the most vulnerable social groups. The rural population was still living under hardcore poverty, and the socioeconomic gap between urban and rural life was only enlarging. The specific feature of the Ukrainian economy is the poverty of the working population. Today, just as in the 1990s, the availability of a job does not mean better life conditions.

An important financial phenomenon in the Ukrainian economy during the second period of the fourth migration wave was (and still is) international remittances sent by Ukrainian labour migrants. The key feature of such remittances is that they are delivered mostly informally, via friends and/or relatives, and also through drivers employed on regular transits between Ukraine and the receiving countries. According to the World Bank study (2010), 40% of Ukrainian external migrants are using the help of friends or relatives to transfer financial funds to their families at home; 32% of them are using the services of a carrier (most probably the bus driver), and only 25% entrust their remittances to official companies which transfer funds internationally. The key reasons behind such distribution are low cost of transfer and also relative quickness. Ninety-eight percent of such transfers are done in USD, the average amount of one transfer is 200 dollars. As compared to other ethnical groups of labour migrants, the Ukrainians transfer home a comparatively small share of their incomes (around 7–9%) (World bank. Migration and Remittances Factbook, 2011). At the same time, the National Bank of Ukraine made an attempt to recalculate the actual volume of all private remittances to Ukraine from abroad, and their final conclusion was that only 13.7% of all personal money transfers from abroad come to Ukraine through informal channels (Remittances..., 2014).

Data on this can be seen in the table below. As the table shows, as of 2013, over one-third of all private remittances from abroad to Ukraine were from the Russian Federation, and the rest were from European countries, that is, belonging to the Euro-Atlantic vector in Ukrainian external migration. We can assume that since then the structure of these private remittances (as the overall structure of external economic activity of Ukraine) has changed by means of widening the Euro-Atlantic share and lowering the share of the Eurasian vector.

Overall, the dynamics of private remittances to Ukraine demonstrates its drastic increase since 2006, and the influence of the global financial crisis which started in 2008 was not so important.

Today in Ukraine there is a specific category of citizens for whom these remittances are the key means of survival (and in some cases, the only one). This phenomenon is especially

Table 1: Country division of private remittances to Ukraine using official channels, 2013.

Country	Volume, million USD	%
TOTAL *Including:*	7377	100
Russian Federation	2703.7	36.2
USA	642.5	9.3
Germany	417.6	6.2
Greece	335.0	5.2
Great Britain	304.7	4.5
Cyprus	244.9	3.7
Italy	325.4	5.3
...	...	...
Poland	34.0	0.9

Source: data of the National Bank of Ukraine.

important for those regions which have both high unemployment rates and an international border; thus, naturally, these regions would have all preconditions for the well-established practice of external labour migration. These are the Transcarpathian region, Ternopil, Lviv, Ivano-Frankivsks oblasts and also for Eastern Ukrainian regions which, in terms of external migration, are oriented in the Eurasian direction. During the periods of worsening economic situation in the country, these private transfers from abroad are mostly spent on the consumer needs of households, but when the general economic situation gets better, they can also be spent on real estate, transport vehicles, university tuition fees and also on starting one's own business (Varetska, 2005, p. 35). This regularity has also been detected by Ukrainian researcher Ella Libanova, and she also noted: "while the poorest households forced by their economic

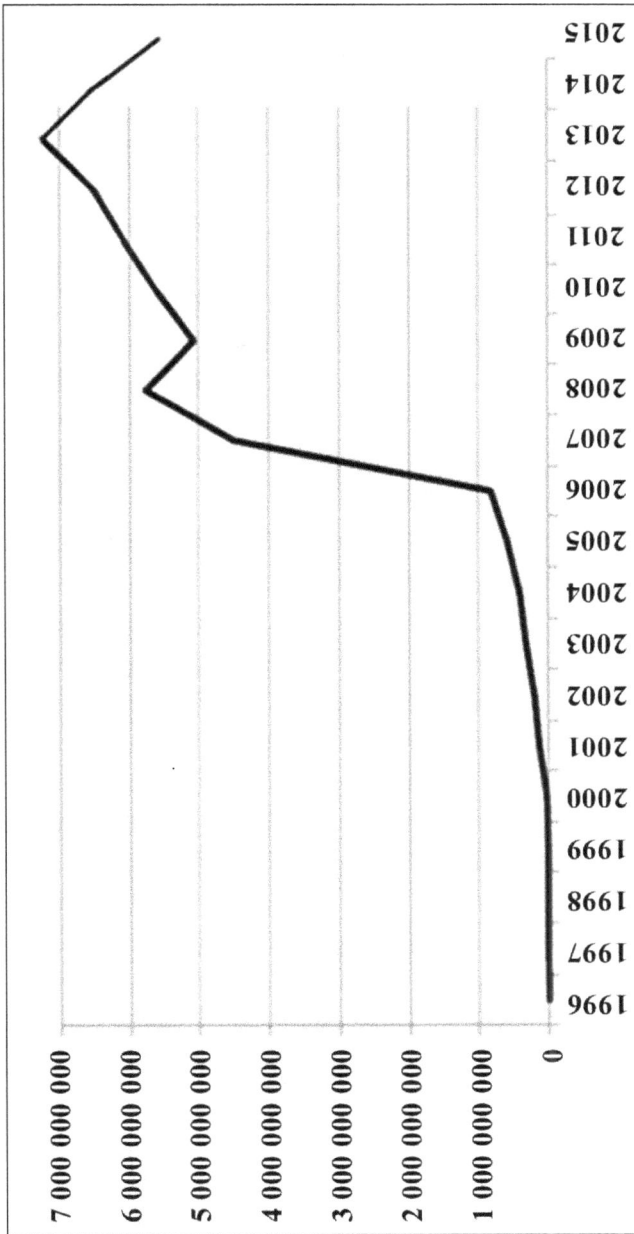

Figure 5: The dynamics of private remittances to Ukraine, in USD.
Source: World Bank and National Bank of Ukraine data.

troubles spend the obtained funds on consumption or medical services, those which are better-to-do, often invest these funds. First of all, this can be investment in real estate construction... the second option is education for family members... and the third one is starting own business" (Libanova, 2011, p. 17).

In 2012 Czech researcher B. Weyskrabova also wrote that: "The process of transformation after the collapse of the Soviet Union cannot be probably declared as finished. The country is still fighting high unemployment, slow economic development and high inflation. Overall development of the country is hampered particularly by political environment and situation of dependency on Russian energy sources and struggles for power" (Weyskrabová, 2012, p. 43).

The recent events in the social and political life of Ukraine have given the country new hopes, in particular, those related to speeding up reforms. Namely, the EU-Ukraine Association Agreement was signed; the free trade zone was introduced; the state policy on corruption fight and prevention has been significantly reinforced; also, important steps have been made in the direction of local self-government role's strengthening and business deregulation; in order to reduce the energy dependency on Russia certain measures have been taken on diversification of energy sources' use etc.

At the same time new challenges arise creating new problems for the socioeconomic development of Ukraine. A significant part of economic potential has been lost in the result of the Crimea annexation and the military conflict in the Donbass region. These events also contributed to the large-scale flow of forced relocations. According to the data of the Cabinet of Ministers of Ukraine, as of March 2015 Ukraine had 1.1 million forced internal migrants, and this is a significant load on the system of social protection and on the labour market (Kilkist..., 2015). The general level of life quality got worse not only for those relocated but for the whole society: according to the most optimistic government numbers, inflation in 2015 was at the level of 54% while all salaries were frozen and pensions for those who keep working after the retirement age have even been reduced. Drastic depreciation of the national currency has led to significant loss of population savings' value and the consequent increase of the national poverty level.

Obviously, such a situation has created the conditions for additional growth of migration intentions and the consequent increase of external migration flow. One of the recorded consequences in this context is the increase in the number of Ukrainian citizens applying for asylum in other countries.

The number of asylum seekers from Ukraine in the EU in 2015 went over 22 thousand (this is 33% more than in the previous year and 20 times more than back in 2013). The largest number of asylum applications were registered in Italy, Germany, Spain and Poland.

Data available on separate national cases adds to this picture. Thus, from the beginning of 2014 through February, 18, 2015, 2318 Ukrainian citizens turned to Polish government for asylum requesting the refugee status (Verner, 2015). Poland is among the most popular destinations among potential refugees from Ukraine.

The dynamics of this indicator indeed testifies to the growing number of Ukrainian refugees to Poland, and by percentage, this growth is rather impressive. However, if we pay attention to the absolute numbers, it becomes clear that this phenomenon is not large enough to become alarmist about it, as many media are.

We also need to mention that the number of the Ukrainians in the overall flow of refugees in the European Union back in 2015

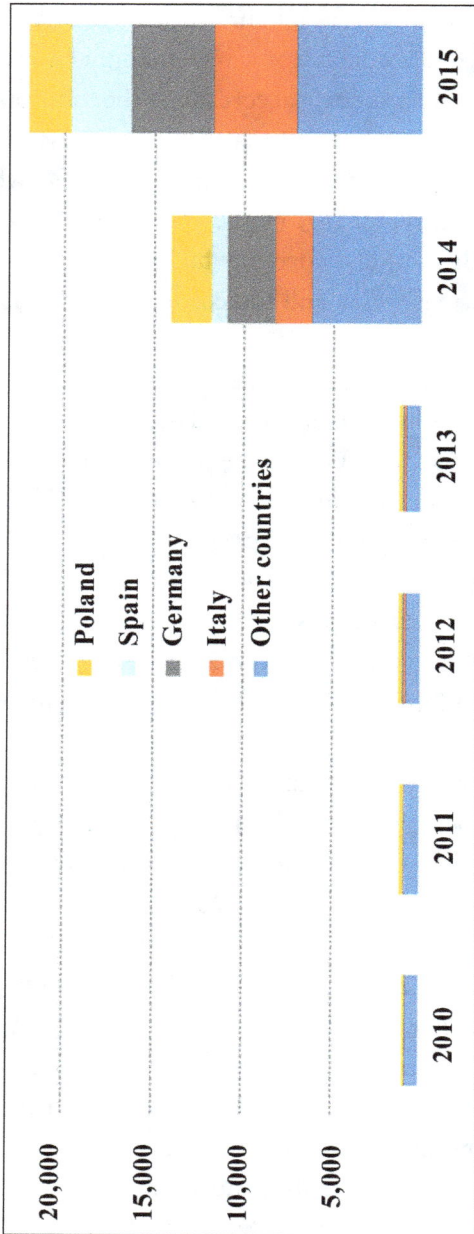

Figure 6: The number of applications for asylum submitted by citizens of Ukraine in the EU, 2010–2015. *Source:* Eurostat: Asylum and Managed Migration.

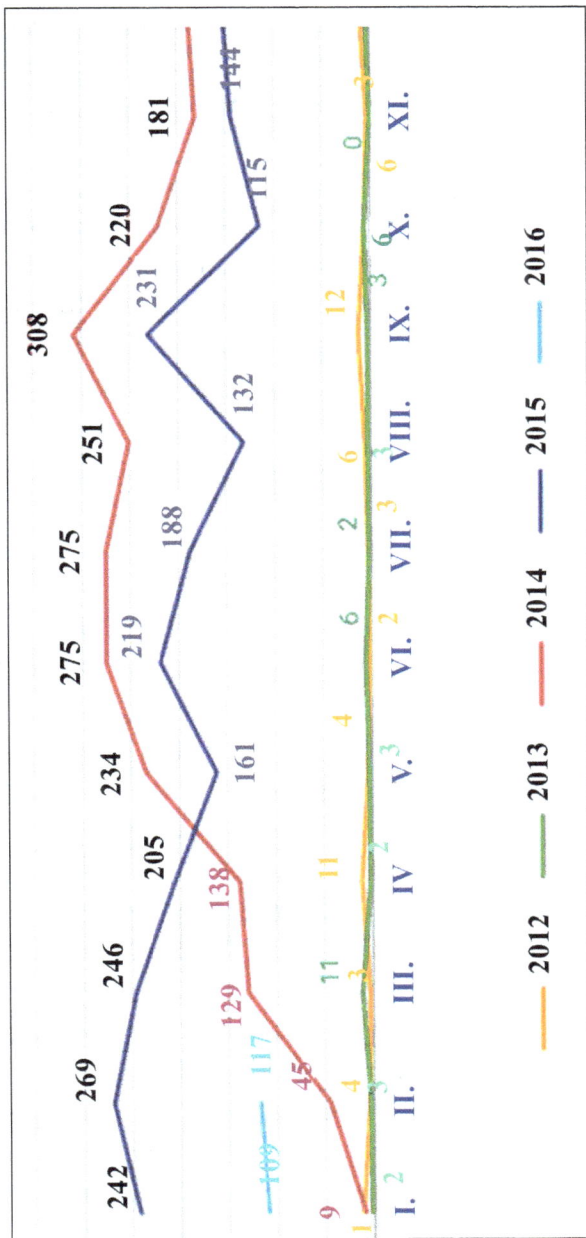

Figure 7: Number of Ukrainian citizens who applied for refugee status in Poland, by months, 2012–2016.
Source: Raport na temat..., 2016.

was only 1.7% of the total number. Moreover, even fewer of them actually got a positive response from European governments (in 2015, refugee status in the EU was obtained by 415 Ukrainian citizens) (Eurostat, 2017).

At the same time, not all popular destinations in external migration of the Ukrainians remained equally hospitable to them. The largest problem is with the Eastern direction of migration, Russian Federation specifically. Due to aggravation of Ukrainian-Russian relations in March 2015 the Ministry for Foreign Affairs of Ukraine recommended all Ukrainian citizens to "evaluate realistically the existing risks and threats and to estimate thoroughly the actual necessity to travel" to this neighbouring country. The same statement also mentioned that "recently there were frequent cases when the citizens of Ukraine were retained without an actual cause on the territory of Russian Federation, and Russian law enforcement authorities were treating them in a not humane way, demonstrating despicable behaviour and even using absolutely inappropriate methods of physical and psychological pressure, including tortures" (MZS poperedzhaye…, 2015). On its side, the Russian Federation introduced the restrictive migration rules for Ukrainian citizens (apart from those who reside in Crimea and Donbass). For those Ukrainian citizens who were still choosing Russia as a labour migration direction, the only option left, under these changed conditions, was temporary, seasonal work.

Ukraine also introduced a range of measures aimed to strengthen the control on the state border with the Russian Federation. In particular, Ukraine unilaterally cancelled the agreement on small transborder movement with Russia (Uryad rozryvaye…, 2015) and added the new requirement on passport control: now all citizens of the Russian Federation have to demonstrate international passports at the border (before they were able to cross the border using national passports). Considering that only 17% of Russian Federation citizens have international passports, this change will significantly reduce the migration flows between Russia and Ukraine. This is also confirmed by the data of the All-Russian survey by the reputable Russian sociological research centre "Levada centr" (Obshchestvennoye…, 2012, p. 172).

For obvious reasons the Russian direction of external migration from Ukraine quickly died out while liberalization of the migration regime with the EU, the second largest migration direction from Ukraine, which was so widely discussed, still did not happen.

Separate countries in the EU are issuing significantly larger quantities of visas for the Ukrainians these days though. For example, Poland in 2014 issued 15% more visas for Ukraine than back in 2013, the total quantity being 831 thousand visas, with a very low rejection rate of 2.66% (Polshcha torik…, 2015). However, such positive changes are not recorded formally and do not happen at the institutional level. As noted in this relation by the Minister for Foreign Affairs P. Klimkin: "European Union is concerned with the uncontrollable state border of Ukraine and the possibility that after the visa-waiver agreement the gunmen from the East can easily pass the EU border" (Klimkin…, 2015). This concern seems to be quite grounded considering the fact that as of today about 400 km of the Ukrainian-Russian border remains under the control of illegal armed groups.

Therefore, all socioeconomic push and pull factors for the fourth wave of external migration from Ukraine are both internal and external. The internal factors of external migration include:

- High unemployment rate under changing economic conditions, which is especially threatening in certain regions and sectors of national economy;

- Significant decline of the general welfare level, up to miserable, hardcore poverty in some regions, rural areas especially;
- Impossibility of having a salary high enough to improve life conditions: unattainability of buying an apartment or house, buying a car or starting one's own business, even for those citizens who are constantly working and getting a salary which is considered as average in the country;
- The so-called "envelope salaries", hidden wages, often without legal employment record; lack of or limited social protection of working population. Hidden wages also undermine the possibility for decent pension in the future and also increases the risks related to labour capacity loss. All of this stimulates Ukrainian population find alternative ways of saving;
- Radically lower levels of salaries in Ukraine than in any potential country for migration (in fact, qualified labour in Ukraine is often paid less than any non-qualified blue-collar labour in the receiving countries);
- Political instability and the Ukrainian-Russian military conflict on the East of the country, in which over 1 million people lost their homes and became forced internal refugees with a significantly decreased quality of life.
- External socioeconomic factors for migration from Ukraine include:
- The growing demand for low-qualified labour in the construction sector, agriculture, services in the majority of European countries because their residents refuse to perform such work due to low pay and/or low social status;

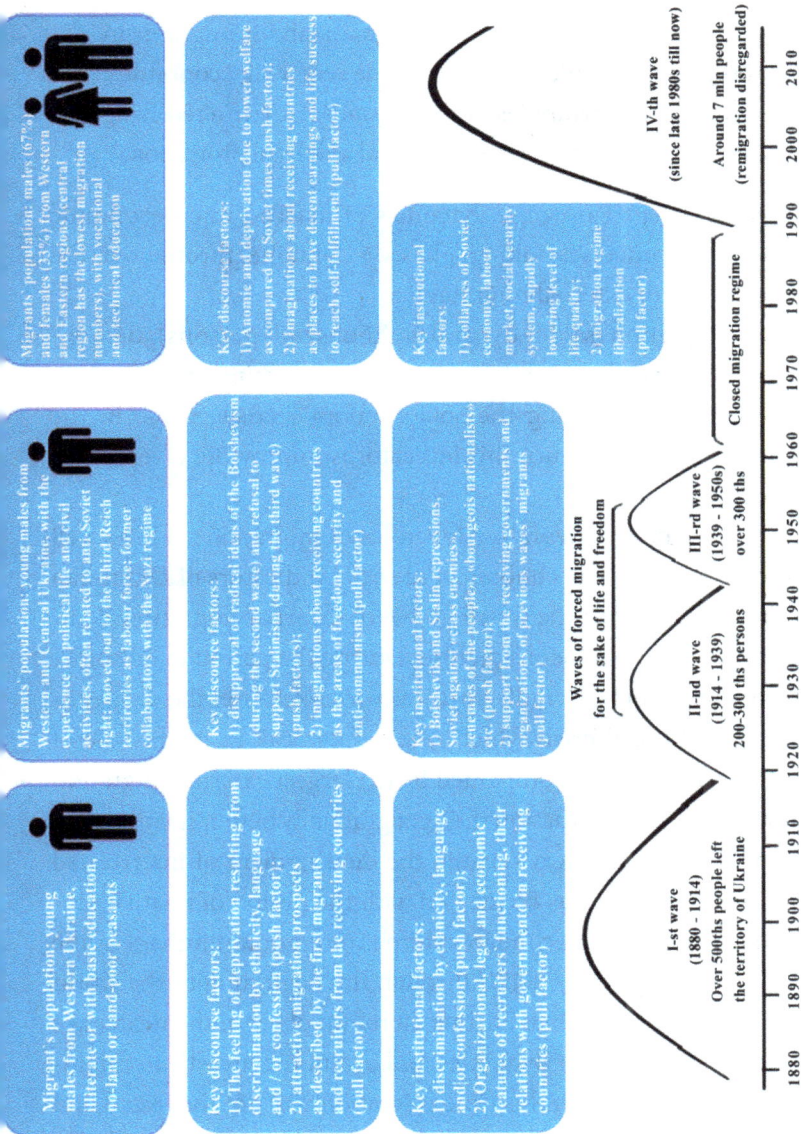

Figure 8: The overview of migration waves from Ukraine. *Source:* Author's own figure.

- Significantly higher salaries and much better work conditions than in Ukraine;
- Availability of demand for Ukrainian labour migrants in both legal and illegal sectors of the receiving economies;
- Potential opportunities to legalize one's status in a receiving society and thus get access to social and legal protection.

Let us consider now the dynamics of macro-, microeconomic and social processes taking place in Ukraine throughout the fourth wave of external migration.

The migration saldo dynamics (thousand persons) demonstrates the negative correlation between incoming and outgoing migration flows during the socioeconomic crisis, while in the year of economic upturn this indicator is improving. Overall, the dynamic is wavelike.

The presented data on the dynamics of migration saldo as well as on macro-, microeconomic and social indicators of Ukrainian society throughout the fourth wave of external migration demonstrates a rather obvious picture. During the period in question, the dynamics of most indicators was wavelike. After the deep economic and social crisis which reached its peak in the middle of the 1990s and was accompanied by the largest external migration from Ukraine, the situation then got gradually better, starting with the year 2000. The next stage in the development of interrelated dynamics of these was connected with the period of relative economic growth and decline in external migration numbers in the period from the early 2000s through the beginning of the world economic crisis in 2008. Furthermore, we observe the next stage of external migration dynamics and again, the growth in migration numbers, though this time migration was not that rapid and in absolute numbers it was much lower than back in the 1990s.

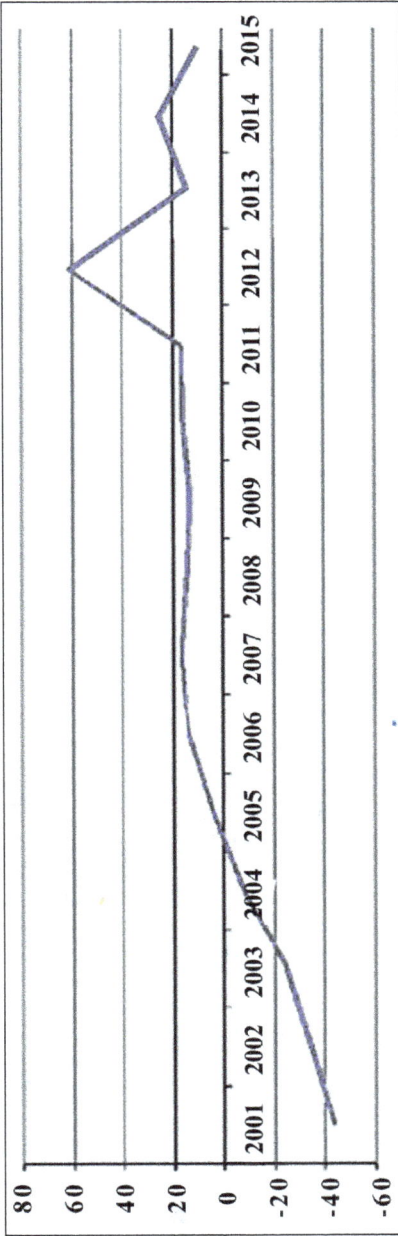

Figure 9: The migration saldo dynamics (thousand persons) during the fourth wave of external migration from Ukraine.
Source: State Service for Statistics of Ukraine.

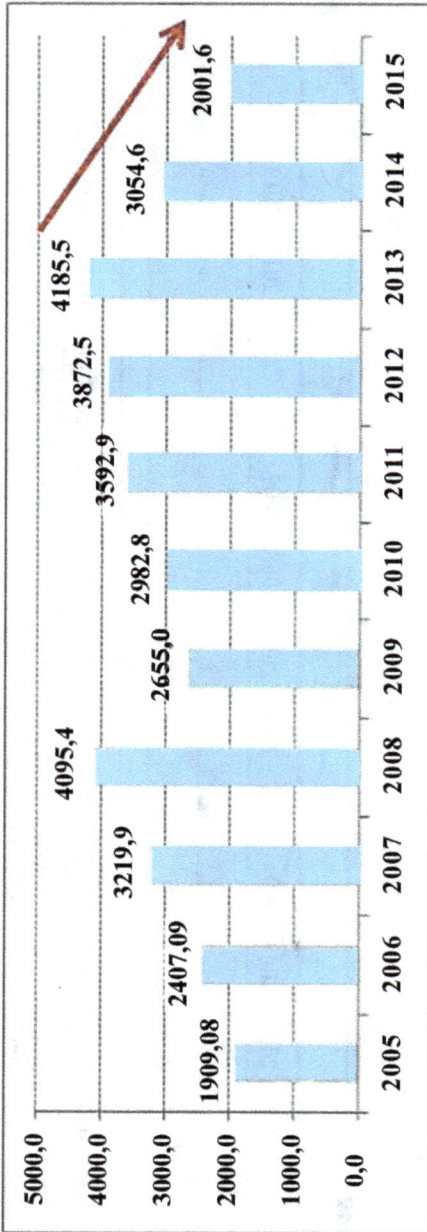

Figure 10: Dynamics of the Ukrainian economy GDP per-person dynamics, 2005–2015 (US dollars). *Source:* State Service for Statistics of Ukraine.

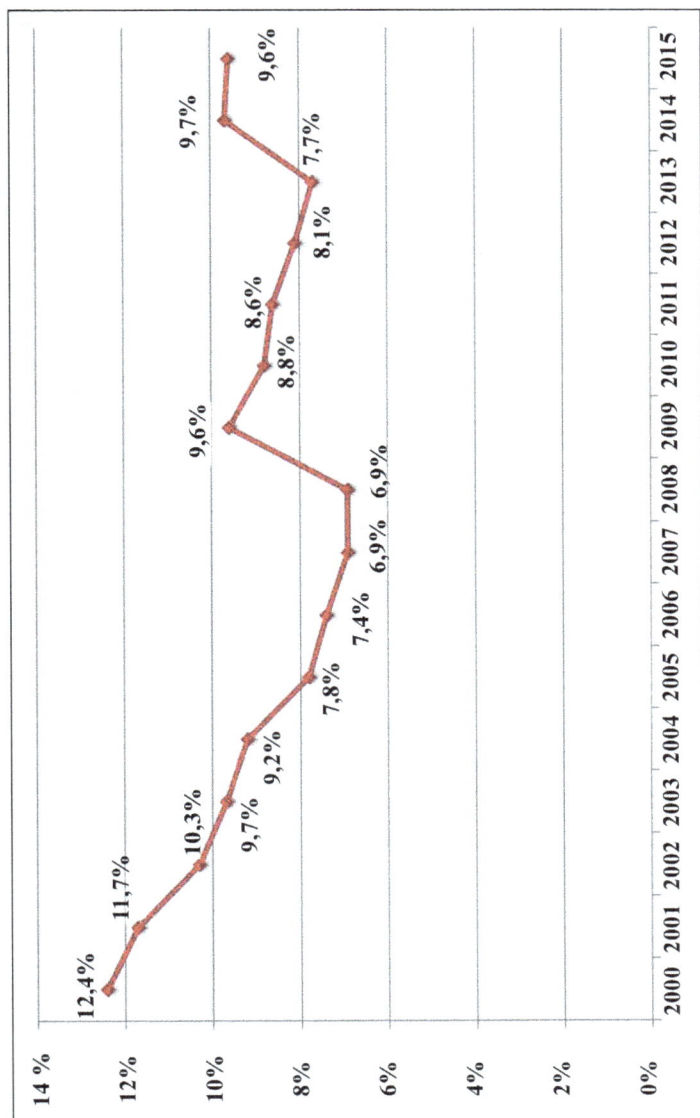

Figure 11: The dynamics of unemployment is wavelike in character and was improving in the first half of the 2000s but the world economic crisis worsened them.
Source: State Service for Statistics of Ukraine.

Table 2: The dynamics of social well-being indicators.

In your opinion, which of the following statements describe the current situation in the country the best?	1992	2000	2003	2006	2005	2010	2012	2013
It is not that bad, liveable life	4.1	4.4	17.9	13.4	11.7	9.3	9.2	11.1
Life is tough, but bearable	20.6	38.9	31.4	46.3	33.3	33.4	46.5	46.5
It is not possible to bear it any further	59.9	30.4	21.1	29.1	27.3	29.8	33.1	33.4
Hard to say	3.4	6.1	9.6	6.9	7.4	7.3	8.7	8.7
No answer	0.1	0.2	0.0	0.0	0.2	0.0	0.2	0.1

Source: The Institute of Sociology, National Academy of Sciences.

2.3 Discursive factors of external labour migration: media discourse on labour migration of Ukrainian population

Since migration processes in the contemporary history of Ukraine became more active with the Soviet Union split, all the related phenomena (including, first of all, the socioeconomic crisis) have their impact on mass perceptions and media representations of external migration. External migration, just like any other large-scale social phenomenon, has a rather ambiguous nature and unpredictable consequences, and thus, its social and media representations often fail to describe it fully, in all the aspects, concentrating only on its dysfunctional features.

In this subchapter we would like to concentrate on media representations of external migration in Ukrainian mass media, special attention will be dedicated to printed media. Obviously, today in a wide range of mass communication means printed sources are not the most dynamic and definitely not the most innovative one. However, under the conditions when Internet availability is still very much correlated to the level of socioeconomic welfare of a particular household, printed media in Ukraine remain rather egalitarian, that is accessible to many. Thus, printed media to some extent evidence the current perceptions, worries and intentions of the general population.

Here we will consider the results of the interpretative content analysis of several Ukrainian newspapers along with the visualization of these results[6]. The following newspapers have been

---

[6] In this particular case we prefer interpretative analysis to the quantitative one, since quantitative indicators which describe the contents of publications in certain newspapers would reflect mostly the editorial policy and vision of these newspapers, and only indirectly, the information space of the country. That's why our conclusions do not set rigid quantitative limits on media representation of external migration, but rather outline the key trends in it.

chosen for analysis: *Golos Ukrainy* ("The Voice of Ukraine") and *Uryadovyi kurier* ("The Government Herald") as the official media representations since these are the newspapers of the Verkhovna Rada of Ukraine and the Cabinet of Ministers of Ukraine accordingly; *Dzerkalo tyzhnya* ("The Weekly Mirror") and *Den* ("The Day") as Ukraine-wide analytical expert papers which often contain the media representations of various expert communities; and finally the newspapers *Vysokyi zamok* ("The High Castle"), *Express* and *Vesti* ("News") – the papers oriented on general reader and representing the most widely spread media representations on external migration (the latter of all the papers is published in Russian).

Let us start with a terminological note: writing about labour emigration from Ukraine, all of these newspapers really seldom use the notions "immigrant", "emigrant", "migrant" or "labour migrant". The most frequently used word is "zarobitchanyn". This word, in the academic thesaurus of the Ukrainian language, has two meanings. The first is: "one who moves for labour purposes, works on a daily or other timely basis". The second, which is more colloquial is: "one who works for money only, having purely self-serving interests". Thus, from the stylistic viewpoint, this word has explicitly negative connotations that can be also sometimes contemptuous, sometimes sympathizing.

After studying in detail the whole corpus of publications in the selected newspapers concerning our subject matter we can outline the key topics related to external migration coverage: 1) positive and negatives aspects of external migration; 2) selected biographical narratives, analysis of real life situations, causes and aims of migration, consequences from migration experience; 3) migration policy in potential receiving countries for external migrations from Ukraine (legislation and its changes, visa options, the issues of crossing the border); 4) criminal activity and migration (illegal migration, various fraud cases related to external migration). Some of these topics, especially those related to the history of external migration from Ukraine and describing the cross-cultural interaction of external migrants in destination countries sometimes have the marginal character.

Among the positive aspects of external migration the media usually mentions the following: new employment opportunities for the population from economically depressed regions; probability that money earned abroad would be further invested in small and medium business development in regions and/or for capital construction, but not just on family consumption. It is also often noted that, potentially, migration means less load on the state system of social protection: a large share of external migrants are potential unemployed, and if they stay in Ukraine, they would either occupy workplaces or apply for unemployment benefits.

Besides, migrants relieve the state from many other social obligations, since this social group is very dynamic, innovative, able and ready to learn, capable of quickly gaining experience borrowing from many technological, economic and business fields.

The experience of working abroad increases the life chances at both the individual and societal levels. Once migrants return home, they become the agents of changes: after the experience they gained they know very well how the real market economy works, what the employer-employee relations should be like, how institutions work in a more efficient way, what the communications standards are between the state and its citizens etc.

The articles which analyze the economic consequences from external migration usually concentrate on the macrolevel – the level of financial remittances and other impacts on the national economy. Individual success stories of migrants currently working abroad or those who already returned are seldom seen in media.

However, overall, negative aspects of external migration are covered in media representation in a much wider way. At the personal level the media usually mentions such negative feature as: problems in family life, distancing of partners up to divorces, poor communication with children, ruining family connections, lack of desire to return to Ukraine (the so-called Italian syndrome – lack of desire to be back in Ukraine due to inability to adapt after a long stay abroad) (Yeryomin, 2010). Also frequently mentioned is the phenomenon of social orphanage in relation to migrants' children who are left without the needed support and care, while the sent remittances actually only aggravate the problems instead of solving them (Uzarashvili, 2006). "They [the children of migrants] become uncontrolled, start smoking, drinking alcohol and using drugs" (*Express*, #139, 28–29.11.06); "They lose interest to studies, skip classes without a good cause, get aggressive" (*Express*, #139, 28–29.11.06). The children of migrants "usually stay at some relatives, for example, at grandparents', a brother, neighbours… Sometimes their labour can be used by their 'guardians' in farming, and nobody even assumes that this can be harmful for child's health" (*Express*, #139, 28–29.11.06).

In this way the perception is formed about migrants as "missing people", first of all, for their families, in which their presence is felt only financially, via remittances or occasional parcels.

There is also a widely spread media representation about the "wasted time" of migrants. And it is not about migrants' families only, in general, time spent abroad is perceived as "wasted", and in particular, in connection to employment history. This is mostly discussed in relation to female migrants of pre-retirement age (Farion, 2009; Voronovych, 2011). Another discussed topic is the absence of appropriate legal status of labour migrants and thus, their social and legal exposure. Also, according to this negativistic discourse, external migrants risk to lose qualification, since they are mostly working outside of their diploma profession, additionally, they risk becoming the victims of labour rights violations (Ukraiina stala…, 2013).

Concerning the level of social changes the negativistic discourse emphasizes the following aspects of external migration: the deepening dysfunctions in the demographic conditions (population ageing, outflow of population in the most economic active and reproductive age, depopulation of the economically depressed areas); wasted state investments in education of citizens according to certain professions (which are not used after or used in favour of a different country); "stripping" of the labour market – there is a range of vacancies which potentially would be taken by non-residents for which Ukraine is not the sending country but the receiving one; these would be mostly migrants from Central and South-Eastern Asia. These perceived threats have their economic, social and political manifestations (increasing xenophobia, outbursts of different diseases, formation of cross-national ghettos etc.).

According to the research carried out by the Institute of Sociology, National Academy of Sciences of Ukraine, the Ukrainian population has very high indicators of distancing from such ethnonational groups as the Arabs and the Afghans, and this, potentially, may create the preconditions for tensions in case external migrants belonging to these groups opt for vacancies in the Ukrainian labour market (Shestakovskyi, 2010).

Also, as noted by (Parkhomenko, 2012), there are other deformations in Ukrainian media presentation of the external migration phenomenon. For example, Ukrainian media workers do not always check the information that appears in foreign media; they simple translate it. Polish newspapers, for example, are often a source of information about Ukranian migrants violating various laws. However, even in such cases Ukrainian papers translate much more negativism in presenting the information they got from their Polish colleagues. Here we can assume that Ukrainian media are subject to certain alarmism as an element of editorial policy in relation to external migration.

In absolutely all analyzed printed media, negativism in relation to external migration significantly dominates over the presentation of positive aspects of migration, and this concerns both factual information and the emotional load on top of it. Moreover, newspapers oriented toward the general public tend to form the negative attitude toward labour migration as such, describing mostly the negative experience of migration, the cases when the Ukrainians became the victims of human trafficking, fraud etc. The motivation of migrants is usually presented as very much one-sided – as a complicated economic background, family troubles and/or other catalysts of such a "bad decision". Curiously, the guilty side in such interpretations is never a person, but "complicated times", "crisis", "the state" and also loss of job, delays in salary payments etc. As well noted by V. Volodko: "To describe labour migrants and their experience mostly pessimistic emotional expressions are used, such as 'deprived people', 'back-breaking work', 'pushed into the corner by unemployment'. Such metaphors are used frequently" (2007). Quoting just some of the newspapers: "Hemp as the best job Ivan can get!", "From street cleaner to a millionaire", "Breaking-back work of labourers" etc.

Media representations also somehow show a range of more and less "worthy" motivations for migration. External migration with purely economic motivation (when the migrant's family has serious financial problems) is perceived as more worthy, more valued than external migration for personal reasons (due to family breakup or plans to marry abroad).

Media presents the external migrant from Ukraine as a person for low-paid jobs and/or for such works which do not require any specific qualification (agriculture, construction, home services, looking after the elderly or the disabled).

The institutional mechanisms of migration processes regulation also have their media coverage. The most widely discussed topic is the migration and visa regimes with the EU and Russia. For example, the article titled "Euroorphanage, Ukrainian style" stresses the following: "The Ministry for Foreign Affairs has to take care of easing the border passing procedures, so that, most importantly, our migrants could come home more often. This would be possible if the visa procedures… would not have been so tiresome, if the Ukrainians would have had the visa-free regime…" (Ievrosyritstvo…, 2011). The presented above fragment of typical discourse contains the whole range of geopolitical and sociocultural imaginations up to more practical advice on how to get visas to different countries with the description of individual experiences (both successful and failed ones).

After the Agreement on Association was signed, Ukrainian media started demonstrating some sort of careful optimism concerning the prospects of visa regime liberalization. Several printed media were covering all the related agreements and negotiations. In November 2014 *Dzerkalo tyzhnya* published an article titled "Foreign Affairs promise visa free regime to all holders of biometric passports till 2015" which, inter alia, stated that already in January 2015 it would be possible to get biometric passports, and this would open the way to negotiations on visa-free regime with the countries of the Schengen zone (MZS obitsyaye…, 2014). Later that same month the same newspaper published one more article, but with a significantly more cautious title: "Abolition of visa regime with the EU: opportunities and risks for Ukraine. Why should we prepare for consequences already now" (Hajdutskyi, 2014).

Despite new hopes and relatively optimistic news on the West, the migration regime with Ukraine's Eastern neighbour still remains a big problem. At the end of 2014, after yet another escalation of the military conflict on the Donbass, the Russian government declared its intent to introduce a new system of work permits for Ukrainian migrants; previously, Ukrainian citizens were allowed to cross the border using their domestic passports, and now the general rules were applied to them and they had to get permits for work in Russia.

Media representations of "criminality and external migration" can be grouped by the following topical categories: 1) topics related to crimes while crossing the border (illegal crossing and contraband mostly); 2) criminal activity of foreigners in Ukraine, criminal activity of the Ukrainians and other foreign nationals in other countries (visa fraud, illegal employments, violations of labour and human rights by employers etc.); 3) human trafficking.

Visa fraud is mostly covered in media with the emphasis on the situations when potential migrants became the victims of predatory intermediaries or dishonest employees of embassies and consulates (Desiatky…, 2013). Other cases describe the situations when migrants and/or their families were threatened by criminals who wanted to profit on their account (Reketyry obkladaly, 2011). Representations describing unfair practices of potential migrants are very rare. There were several cases when known and quite reputable newspapers were publishing information which contained direct recommendations on migration fraud.

Probably the most frequent topics in the general public media are those related to constant humiliation of labour migrants abroad, their deprived status, poor life conditions, constant fear caused by the illegal status, in particular, fear of police (Herasymchuk, 2009).

In 2014 media news on the topic "migration and criminality" got a new modality. For example, the official newspaper of the Verkhovna Rada *Golos Ukrainy* published the following: "Tempted by high pay in Russia, you can join the terrorists in the military conflict zone..." (Rybalchenko, 2014). This article was using the data from the State Security Service of Ukraine to analyze the phenomenon of recruitment and training of gunmen among Ukrainian citizens, which are first trained and prepared in Russia and then sent back to Ukraine to fight on the Donbass on the separatists' side.

The increased intensity of external migration coverage by Ukrainian media is explained by the current political situation, and more specifically, by constant discussion about the geopolitical and cultural vector of the country's further development.

Ukrainian media representations of external migration contains certain implicit emphasis which forms a negative and rather biased attitude of the general population toward the phenomenon of external migration. The very notion of "gastarbeiter" which is widely used in relation to this social group implies that these people are "victims" of their complicated life conditions and they will definitely demonstrate the whole range of threats, risks and insecurities that are waiting for all migrants once they cross the border while their family life back in Ukraine is tearing apart.

External migration representations in general public newspapers have a mostly speculative nature; the conclusions are often based on rather fragmentary, out-of-context experience; research tools are not used for analytical purposes, and in those rare cases when experts are engaged, their contribution is very much simplified. Often the problematic side is emphasized just to attract the reader's attention. Objectivity is often sacrificed, and preference is given to laconic, rather metaphorical, exaggerated statements which sometimes have a nearly apocalyptic tone.

However, it is worth noting that emphasis in media discourse on external migration is shifting. New topics are now being covered, for example, the communities of migrants abroad, their institutionalization via formal organizations, manifestations of their civil and political activism abroad and at home (Bilan, 2014a). Very often these institutional forms of migrants' associations are affiliated with religious organizations. The Ukrainian Greek Catholic Church (UGCC) is probably the most active among them, since this confession group has the largest share of people with certain labour migration experience. Thus, back in 2013 *Dzerkalo tyzhnya* published an interview with H. Seleshuk, the head of the UGCC commission on migrants' affairs, and its title was: "Ukrainian migrants today put active pressure on our politicians" (Odynets, 2013).

We would like to analyze the peculiarities of media discourse on the highest level of its generalization, using visualization methods as applied to the results of content analysis, known as "concept cloud", or "tag cloud". On one hand, this method of discourse field description requires certain cultural competence skills to read the data correctly; on the other hand, we need to remember how rapidly changing and dynamic such raw data is – besides, it is actually constructed by both producer and consumer of the discourse. Thus, we think that in the context, quantity-oriented methods of empirical research are not completely trustworthy when it comes to media discourse on external migration. Below we present a comparison of the two relatively homogenous media discourses on external migration. As a means of visualization we use a content cloud, which enables a brief presentation of the central concept in the texts of large volumes and allows us to compare them. German researchers T. Melles and R. Jaron describe the methods of concept clouds and tag clouds as grouping of identical language units and constructions for further visualization of the central idea of the text based on the most frequently used language units, which are presented in larger fonts (the larger the font size – the more frequently this concept was used in the analysed text) (Melles et al., 2009).

Overall, there are significant differences in the discourses between official newspapers of public bodies and also specialized, expert newspapers on one side – and popular newspapers for general public on the other. These differences can be primarily explained by these newspapers' orientation toward certain target groups of their information products' consumption. Official governmental discourse is concentrated on political and legal information mainly; it also avoids expressing emotions and attitudes, and it is very careful in wording. Mass discourse is directly the opposite: it tends to have flamboyant headings and to use metaphors, and at the same time it is rather shallow in content; many complex phenomena are presented in an extremely simplified way.

The most significant difference between these two discourses is related to the "female topic" in external migration: in official and expert newspapers this issue is almost absent, while for mass newspapers it is one of the most popular topics. The situation with the topic of Ukrainian citizens' deaths abroad is similar: hardly mentioned in official newspapers, but very important in popular discourse.

Overall, popular media discourse on external migration is represented mostly by the topics related to female, children and family issues. Interestingly, the topic of human trafficking is rather underrepresented in mass discourse (however, migrants' involvement in sex services is mentioned rather often). On the other hand, popular newspapers favour "serious" social topics, like demographic consequences of migration and/or analysis of migration regimes in different countries.

It is noteworthy that during the whole studied period, all three types of media discourses (official, expert and mass) tend to shift the attention from the problems of external migration *from Ukraine* to the problems of illegal migration *to Ukraine* from the countries of Asia and Africa.

As we can see above, there are quite distinct differences between official, expert and mass media discourses concerning external migration. Official media discourse is concentrated on such issues as cooperation with the EU, common projects at borders and private remittances to Ukraine from abroad. Expert media discourse chooses the most important issue to be illegal migration. For mass media important discourse includes the topics related to migrants' daily life abroad, in particular, female experiences among Ukrainian migrants, criminality and sexual exploitation. For all three types of media discourses the of Russian vector in Ukrainian external migration is the leading one, along with the topic of European vector in migration.

Table 3: Visualization of official, expert and mass discourses in Ukrainian printed media.[7]

Type of discourse	Name (circulation volume a week, quantity of the analyzed publications)[8]	Visualization by means of concept clouds
Official (governmental) media discourse	*Golos Ukrainy* (150 thousand; 121 publications); *Uryadovyi kurier* (500 thousand; 415 publications)	remittances border **Russia** diaspora population protection human trafficking law passport **European Union**
Analytical-expert media discourse	*Dzerkalo tyzhnya* (57 thousand; 59 publications) *Den* (150 thousand; 59 publications)	border Poland European_Union foreigners **illegal_migrants** regime passport Citizenship **Russia** remittances Italy visa
Mass (popular) media discourse	*Vysokyi zamok* (500 thousand; 930 publications) *Express* (160 thousand; 382 publications) *Vesti* (over 2 million; 314 publications)	EU **Italy** Poland visa illegals border **death** road accident tax prostitution Czechia remittances Russia women

Source: Author`s own data.

---

[7] For this purpose the online service TagCrowd.com is used, created by D. Steinbock (Stanford University). Visualization covers the words which were present in the headings at least three times.

[8] We have analyzed the publications from January 2005 to April 2015, using those headings which contained the words "migrant" or "gastarbeiter" in their various grammar forms.

2.4 Institutional and legal regulation as a factor of impact on external labour migration during the fourth migration wave. The possibilities for its improvement

Within the general system of factors which determine migration behaviour, along with economic, sociocultural, political and other factors, there is the factor of institutional and legal regulation. This group of factors is usually denominated under the notion "migration regime". In a wider sense migration regimes are understood as the set of rather stable factors of economic, sociocultural, political and institutional nature that define the character of migration flows between sending and receiving societies. In more specified terms (like in this subchapter, for example) under migration regime we understand the set of legal and administrative means which regulate the status and the social protection of Ukrainian migrants in the receiving countries (Strielkowski et al., 2016).

Each migration regime has its history and its own specific and stable political, economic and cultural factors; thus, migration regimes may vary – from completely closed ones (like the militarized border along the Berlin Wall in Germany during the Cold War, or the 38th parallel dividing the peninsula into North and South Korea) up to completely open migration regimes (like the migration regime inside the Schengen group).

This aspect is very much understudied in external migration studies. One of a few authors to fill in this gap is D. Massey, who combined all his propositions in his theory of state influence on migration. In his work "A Missing Element in Migration Theories" D. Massey stresses the necessity for more theoretical attention to politicians, media experts and bureaucrats, who often act in their own interest and get certain advantages from social constructs and "crisis production" related to migrants, in the situations when in fact there is no crisis as such (Massey, 2015, p. 281). The author specifically points to those aspects of political and administrative activity and competing interests at bureaucratic, legislative and public arena which further define the scale of migration and the key features of migrants (Massey, 2015, p. 284).

The general logic of connecting political, administrative and public fields to migration regimes is the following: "in the periods of economic growth and expansion the permissive migration policy is applied, and in the time of decline – the restrictive one" (Massey, 2015). The key subjects for migration regime change are employees and employers. Thus, "in the time of economic growth the unemployment indicators go down, salaries go up and employers are lobbying to allow more labour migrants in the country, while in times of crisis the employees demand from their governments to decrease the scales of labour migration into the country" (Massey, 2015). At this, politicians and public servants are representing the interest of these two key economic subjects.

Another factor of the general socioeconomic environment is the total quantity of external migrants in a country: the larger this quantity is, the louder the demands for restrictions in the migration regime in order to weaken the migrants' inflow. There is an additional factor to that – the cultural distance between local population and external migrants. Massey (2015) also turns attention to the political-ideological and value dimensions: stronger conservatism in the society and greater conformism usually lead to restrictions in migration regimes, while the popularity of liberal ideas and values provoke more permissions in the migration regime.

While political and economic circumstances (factors) in the receiving economies which define the nature of a migration regime are very much changing, institutional factors tend to be much more stable, as noted by D. Massey. For example, such features of institutional efficiency or modality of institutes' functioning have rather deep historic roots, thus, are more stable. Here several features are combined together: efficiency of local (national) bureaucracy; rights protection as guaranteed by the constitution and citizens' equality before the law; historical traditions in relation to external migration. For example, in the countries of the Arabian Gulf there is very little tradition of external migration; the local political system (monarchy) is not competitive in its nature, and many legal aspects are extremely traditional, going against standard democratic practices and today's vision of human rights. Thus, rather restrictive local migration regimes comply ideologically and culturally to the state systems overall. In contrast, in traditionally liberal democracies radical restrictive political and administrative measures are hard to imagine, since they would be limited by human rights practice, presence of political competition and a long tradition of having external migration.

In Ukraine one of the most significant changes in the migration regime (which actually enabled the fourth wave of migration as such) happened in the late 1980s and was related to internal changes in the Soviet regime. That resulted in two key trends: first, the revival of migration flows from the periphery to more central territories, which was provoked by the economic dependency and also the increasing economic inequality under the new conditions of a hybrid economic system with its rather specific sociocultural, economic and sometimes personal relations; secondly, there was a revival of the migration flow in the Western, Euroatlantic direction, which was known from the previous migration waves and now was nourished by the presence and activities of diasporas and the related social networks.

At that time the Eurasian direction in external migration was not restricted at all; there were no legal or institutional barriers in it, plus there was a well-established tradition related to the decades of common Soviet history. While the Euroatlantic direction of the external migration of Ukrainians from the very beginning of the fourth wave was much more complicated, some researchers of that period even called the EU then "the Union of closed doors" (Tsapenko, 1998).

The migration systems of European countries started to obtain their current features after World War II when the quantity of the foreign population and the foreign labour force radically increased. Before the war European countries had been migration flows' donors only and used to have negative migration saldos, but during the two post-war decades they quickly became the recipients of migration flows, thus, their migration saldos became positive.

Labour migration to Europe straight after the war was unprecedented as such, and for European history especially. During the period of 1955–1974 the quantity of foreigners in Switzerland grew threefold, and twofold in France and Belgium (Yuskiv, 2009, p. 235).

This growth was caused by the targeted migration policy of European governments. A good example of such policy was the labour market regulation in Germany. In this country the government was managing migrants' recruitment from the very beginning, signing agreements with other countries. This policy in particular opened the door for large migration inflows from Turkey to Germany. During the 20 years of this policy the share of foreign workers in the German economy increased significantly: back in 1952 the German economy was using the labour of merely 50 thousand foreigners (0.4% of the country's total labour force), and in 1973 already 2.4 million foreigners were working in Germany. A significant contribution to the migration inflow to Germany was made by the policy of German repatriation from Eastern Europe. As a result, in 2000 Germany had the largest share of all European migrants, including 700 thousand unemployed (Okolski, 2004, pp. 215–216). One of the sources of migration inflows to Germany was the migration of Polish citizens of German origin. More specifically, those from the Opole voivodship, those who since 1993 got an opportunity for free employment not only in Germany, but elsewhere in the EU as long as they were able to verify their German origin and thus, German citizenship which (at least according to German legislation) was always theirs (Jończy, Rokita-Poskart, 2014).

During the two decades after World War II, migration to European countries was of a controlled nature and was mostly initiated by the governments of the receiving countries. However, in the 1970s, migration to Europe gradually became rather uncontrolled and unregulated. The major reason for this was the processes of family reunification in many migrant cases. Additionally, the inflow of refugees from the "third world" countries also increased.

Family reunification became an important source (and often the only legal one) of increasing numbers of migrants to Western European countries during 1970–1990. In Germany only in the middle of the 1970s the members of such reunited families formed the 90% share of all migrants (Yuskiv, 2009, p. 281). Diasporas and informal social networks of migrants eased the migration processes for hundred of illegal migrants, inter alia (Tsapenko, 2009, p. 54).

Temporary (as the governments and registration authorities saw it) labour migration turned out to be a completely different phenomenon leading to a range of new economic, political and cultural problems for the receiving societies. Migrants mostly aimed to settle in urbanized territories; thus, their presence in the society became much more visible, like all the related problems.

All these processes starting in Western and Northern Europe, have gradually shifted to the rest of the European continent, including the newest members of the EU in Central and Eastern Europe. As of 2006 the largest quantity of foreigners were working in Germany (3.528 million people), Spain (1.824 million people), Great Britain (824 thousand people) and Italy (802 thousand people).

Further, we will consider first of all, the theoretical grounding of the major migration policy models; secondly, we will analyze the development and the key features of the contemporary migration policies of the EU Country Members and that of the CIS (Commonwealth of Independent States) since these are the two key directions in external migration from Ukraine. And thirdly, we will describe the establishment and the specific features of the migration regime between Ukraine and the EU Members, and also between Ukraine and the CIS.

Researchers usually distinguish the following migration policy models: pluralistic, class model, realistic and neocorporatist. In its pluralistic model migration policy is considered as the process in which a certain group of subjects (entrepreneurs, religious organizations etc.) are trying to get certain benefits for themselves, disregarding the common interest (Freeman, 1979). According to the class models, migration policy is determined by group interests and is aimed at achieving the stability in relations of capital owners with the employed (Cohen, 1987). Realistic and corporatist models of migration policy take into consideration the acts of state as a political institute (geopolitical factors, power structures, influences from inside and outside of the political system, and also the influence of liberal norms established by the international legal regime). According to the corporatist models, the state is the intermediary between conflicting socioeconomic circles; however, it also acts in its own political interests (Hall, 1989). Another classification presents the models of policies not by their motives and aims, but according to their consequences, and thus, it distinguishes between restrictive and permissive models.

On the level of practical policies within the EU, initially two models dominated in external migration regulation; both were formed after World War II. According to Vidyakina (2008, p. 13), these were: the model by the International Labour Organization (ILO) and the model described in the framework of the General Agreement on Trade in Services (GATS). The former was applied from the beginning of the 1950s until the oil crisis of the 1970s and it was based on bilateral agreements concerning labour force attraction from the countries of Southern Europe and third countries, namely, Turkey and former colonies in Africa. External migration in those times was perceived in purely economic terms and was used as a mechanism for achieving the balance between demand and proposition at the labour market. Various humanitarian aspects of external migration (families' reunification, adaptation and integration of migrants in receiving societies) were totally disregarded in this model (Medved, 2003, p. 139; Gallardo et al., 2016, p. 245).

The latter model, which existed within the GATS framework, was based on regulation of migration flows by companies and states which are to cooperate economically. Just as with the ILO model, humanitarian and social aspects of migration were again ignored.

Considering the bottlenecks of these two models, early in the 1990s the EU offered a new model of joint regulation of international migration, according to the EU Agreement. This model guaranteed the freedom of movement for people and services within the borders of the European Union. However, the model was oriented mostly toward integration within the EU itself and did not cover third countries.

Today, concerning the citizens of third countries, the EU policies demonstrate three functional directions: 1) migration policy; 2) measures on incoming population integration; 3) counteracting the factors which induce external migration (Tsapenko, 2009, p. 191).

The process of joint migration policy development for the whole Eurounion was initiated back in 1986, with the creation of special groups consisting of the internal affairs ministers from the EU country members. This group was created to write out the agreements on external border control, visa unification, repatriation procedures for illegal migrants etc.

In 1992 the Maastricht Treaty was signed, and since then any citizen of any country member within the EU became a citizen of the EU, thus got the right for free movement and free choice of residence within the whole territory of the EU (Christiansen et al., 2012). Rules of crossing external borders and control over these borders, migration policy, including the conditions of entrance, length of stay, family reunification conditions, foreign employment, prevention of unsanctioned migration – according to this Treaty – became the issues of common interest to be settled on the intergovernmental level (Yuskiv, 2009, p. 309). Concerning the migration from third countries, this period became the time for wide intergovernmental debate. Most migration issues were left within the competence of separate countries. The Maastricht Treaty, inter alia, noted: the governments can take measures to control migration from third countries, in order to prevent criminality and contraband (Population and migration…, 1996). Those few decisions of the EU common institutions related to external migration were treated as recommendations only.

A vision of the common strategy of migration management in Europe was offered in 1998 by the Advisory Group of the European Commission. It was based on the following four principles: order (measures promoting migration aimed at maximizing opportunities and advantages for each migrant and the receiving societies); protection (guaranteeing migrants' rights and preventing unsolicited relocation of population); integration (creating such an environment which would help integrate into the receiving society); cooperation (state-level cooperation between receiving countries and country donors aimed at harmonization of external migration causes and related migration policies) (Solt, 1999). Besides that, additional elements in migration management were suggested as follows: stimulating qualified migration; encouraging business migration; attracting temporary and seasonal labourers; regulating migration of family members; the selective approach to refugees; preventing illegal migration; the social protection of migrants.

Within this framework agreement, all the EU members, including all Schengen group members, approved the so-called policy of "controlled migration" which was the system of measures related to border control and selective limitation of migration as well as control over international transport and migrants' deportation (Tsapenko, 1998, p. 38–40).

The next stage in the formation of all-European migration policy was marked by signing the Amsterdam Treaty in 1999. This document declared that the EU must develop a joint policy on asylum in particular and migration in general, keeping in mind the necessity for constant control at external borders in order to prevent illegal migration and fight against those engaged in it.

To follow this policy, the European Commission suggested the contingence mechanism for the migration policies of the country members. It covers the four fields: management of migration flows; receiving economic migrants; partnership with third parties; and integration of third countries' citizens into the receiving societies (Malynovska, 2006).

Unfavourable demographic situations and labour force deficits have led the European Commission to the thought which was voiced in 2000: the external inflow of labour force is vital for economic growth (Communication from the Commission to the Council and the European Parliament…, 2000). Then, in 2003 the directive was approved concerning the legal status of third countries' citizens which have stayed in the country members of the EU for at least five years. This directive guarantees migrants their key economic and social rights on an equal level with the EU citizens, and it also guarantees the right to free movement and free choice of a place to live within the EU territories for those persons which have the permit to stay issued by any of the EU member countries (Council directive…, 2004).

In 2008 the European Commission published the communication "Common Immigration Policy for Europe: principles, measures and instruments" along with the "Policy plan on asylum. An integrated approach to protection across the EU". Both programme documents were aimed to become part of the new five-year programme on freedom, security and law. The communication formulated the key principles of the future common migration policy. These principles were grouped in three directions: prosperity, solidarity and security. The principle of prosperity implied exact rules and equal rules of the game; compliance of the professional level of migrants to the labour force demand; importance of integration as a factor of successful migration.

The principle of solidarity covered the following: transparency, trust, cooperation between the member countries, overcoming specific migration challenges in separate member countries; cooperation with third countries on the problems related to migration. The principle of security included: visa policy being in compliance with the EU interest, easing the entry for responsible citizens and at the same time taking measures to increase security; comprehensive border management to maintain the unity of the Schengen space; taking radical measures against human trafficking, protection from human trade and slavery; efficient fight against illegal migration and illegal employment; efficient policy on migrants' repatriation (Communication from the Commission to the European Parliament, 2008).

The latter of these principles was applied through a wide range of actions: information campaign aimed at discouraging potential migration; severe border control; strict visa requirements; sanctions against migrants' transport carriers etc. Similarly to that, one of the instruments in migration policy became various visa regimes which served as counteraction against undesirable migration through the following requirements: grounding the travel purpose, providing financial, insurance and other documents, showing return tickets etc. Also, the system of work permits became much stricter. In contrast to the policy of preventing and fighting illegal migration, there are also regular amnesties carried out by the EU member countries aimed to legalize those foreigners who stayed in the country for a long time already and are able to support themselves financially. Such campaigns on illegal migrants' status regulation are carried out mostly in Southern Europe, however, quite frequently. According to the official data of the Ministry of Internal Affairs of Italy 294,744 applications on legalization were filed in 2015. At this, the Ukrainians are the leaders by the quantity of these applications, their share is 12.61% (Ukraiinski trudovi mihranty…, 2015).

Therefore, in the development of the EU migration regime we can distinguish four stages. The first stage was the constituting one and it lasted till the beginning of the 1980s. This was the period of common economic space formation and relative unification of the migration policy, formation of common grounds concerning free movement on the EU territory.

The second stage lasted from the early 1980s till the beginning of the 1990s. The key event of this period was the Schengen Agreement signing. At this stage the EU institutions' responsibilities and functions in the field of migration processes regulation were specified; the customs control on common borders was abolished; and the harmonization of migration legislation was initiated.

The third stage lasted from the Schengen Agreement signing till the end of the 1990s. During this period all the related legal norms and rules were specified, including: common standards and rules on family reunification; guaranteeing equality in rights for citizens and foreigners; simplification of naturalization procedures; promoting the participation of foreign citizens in political life; fighting discrimination on any ground etc.

At the fourth stage of its development the migration policy as such was shifted to the competence field of the European Union. This initiated wider cooperation between the member countries on the development of common policy concerning migration.

The current migration regime of the EU should not be treated as fully and finally established, it is still subject to further changes. As of today there is an ongoing debate concerning the model of common migration policy which has been provoked by the extremely numerous inflow of refuges from Northern Africa and the Middle

East. In this debate, on one side, there are voices demanding the guarantees of basic human rights for all migrants; on the other side, threats are voiced concerning the rising xenophobia in the receiving societies as well as risks related to certain conflicts with local national interests.

Today one of the key features in the migration policies in most of European countries is stimulation of highly qualified specialists' immigration. There are certain principles aimed at their attraction and encouragement of this type of migration. These include: the scoring systems (used in Switzerland, Great Britain, Czech Republic); the system of entrance quotas for the deficit categories of professions (Great Britain, Italy); special programmes and simplified procedures of employment for specialists in demand (Germany); programmes which motivate foreign students who got higher education in highly required fields to stay in the receiving country; simplified entry for researchers who have "scientific visas". In 2005 the European Council approved the directive that regulates the procedures of scientific exchange with third countries. Before that, in 2003 an all-European web portal on academic and scientific mobility was launched, supported by many related national portals and other sites of similar contents within the EU (Council directive..., 2005).

During the most recent decade Western European countries were much more active in using the labour force of seasonal foreign workers in various sectors, primarily in agriculture. Every year the Western countries of the EU recruit around 500 thousand agricultural labourers outside the EU. Back in 2005 Germany alone used the seasonal labour force of about 320 foreigners (Tsapenko, 2009, p. 65). Therefore, we can assume that attracting migrants became one of the ways to make the labour market more flexible and at the same time to reduce the problem of precarization of its own citizens, since a large share of temporary and seasonal work is transferred to migrants. However, at the same time precarization of the sending countries' citizens is ever increasing.

Today's migration regimes in the EU countries, on one hand, fully comply with the general humanistic principles and all framework agreements on the Eurounion level, but on the other hand, they also reflect the national interests of particular member countries and thus are aimed to protect the national labour markets, national social security systems and local sociocultural balance. The framework agreements acknowledge the right for free movement and the right for family reunification. However, a range of countries established specific requirements which somehow limit these rights, e.g., the limitation on the maximum age of children, on the level of income for the migrant inviting family members into a receiving country, on the length of migrant's stay in a receiving country etc. Thus, in the Netherlands the requirement on the minimum income level (which grants the right for family reunion) has been increased from 100% to 120% of the minimum wage in the country. Also the requirement on the length of migrant's previous stay (duration of stay in the country before the migrant is eligible for a family reunion application) became tighter. For example, in Switzerland, starting in 2004, a migrant is allowed a family reunion (with a spouse and children younger than 14 years old) only if he or she has already stayed in the country for at least five years. In Germany one of the requirements for family reunion is the migrant's language skills – he or she must speak German at a certain level (Yuskiv, 2009, p. 282). All these selective protection rules and requirements are usually explained by the necessity to protect national economy and society from the inflow of "fake refugees", which potentially might become the cause for social destabilization due to excessive numbers of social allowance users.

Concerning the opposite vector in the emigration flows from Ukraine the key direction is the Russian Federation. The Russia-Ukraine migration regime was formed gradually under the changing post-Soviet conditions. Its formation started with the President's Decree of 1993: "On attraction and use of foreign labour force in Russian Federation…" (Ukaz prezidenta…, 1993). It set the first legal requirement on migrants' employment – having a work permit from a local representative office of the Federal Migration Service; also, a new document was introduced called a "migration card". Later in 2001 the concept of demo-graphic development of the Russian Federation was approved which formulated the targets of the migration policy: regulation of migration flows aimed at creating the efficient mechanisms for overcoming the problems related to the natural reduction of the population in Russia, while increasing the efficiency of migra-tion flows' use by means of reaching the compliance between their volumes on one hand and socioeconomic interests of the Russian Federation on the other. Also, the same concept men-tioned the importance of migrants' integration in Russian society and the necessity for a tolerant attitude formation in the society (Kontseptsiya demograficheskogo razvitiya… 2001).

In 2015 a new concept was approved – "The Concept of state migration policy for the period till 2025". This was the first time Russian legislation mentioned the need to support the migration of qualified specialists and the necessity to establish the system to assess the actual need in the foreign labour force. Now amend-ments to migration legislation are being considered, aimed at legislation of those labour migrants who work for private individ-uals in the Russian Federation, namely through the mechanism of patent on foreign employment (Kontseptsiya gosudarstvennoi migratsionnoi politiki…, 2015).

Russian researcher V. Mukomel notes that despite the declared targets, today the migration policy of Russia has a range of weaknesses. In particular these include: concentration of attention solely on fighting the illegal migration, that is, considering migration as a purely negative phenomenon only; selectiveness of migration policy and its heavy dependence on the current political situation (for example, when relations with Baltic countries, Georgia or Ukraine got complicated, rules and general attitude to the migrants from these countries changed radically). In addition to that, Russian migration policy has very little support from the institutions and/or civil society; thus, all statements concerning migrants' integration and tolerant attitude to them remain declarative only (Mukomel, 2005, pp. 153–154).

Since 2014 the Federal Migration Service of the Russian Federation has new, very restrictive rules for Ukrainian migrants. At the same time, a preferential migration regime was introduced in relation to Ukrainian citizens residing in the Donetsk and Luhansk regions. This policy is very similar to that used in relation to the Caucasian region of South Osetia where Russia has been supporting anti-Georgian separatists.

For all other Ukrainians, Russia introduced the limited term of stay in its territory – up to 90 days per year. These changes provide additional advantages to migrants from the countries of the Eurasian Union (Belarus, Kazakhstan, Kyrgystan and Armenia) since Russian legislation treats labour migrants from these countries as equal to Russian residents when it comes to labour relations.

The Ukrainian answer to the changed situation was quite symmetrical. Today Russian citizens entering Ukraine have to use their international passports at the borders. Additionally, several documents are needed to verify the stay in Ukraine, including a notarized personal invitation.

Ukrainian migrants to Russian Federation have 90 days to define their status in the country. In case he or she does not want to receive the citizenship of Russia and/or is not asking for asylum as a refugee from the zone of military conflict, the length of stay in the country is limited to three months during half a year. Violation of this rule would lead to further rejection of entry to the country for the next 3–10 years. Therefore, the only choice for Ukrainian labour migrants to the Russian Federation is temporary (seasonal) work, and this logically leads to further precarization.

All these changes in the migration regime of the Russian Federation, which is one of the leading countries in Ukrainian external migration, have been caused by the worsening relations on the state level between Ukraine and Russia, and in particular, by bilateral political and economic sanctions. Additionally, if to follow the grounding by D. Massey, these changes are caused by the new demands of the general socioeconomic situation in the Russian Federation, and according to many expert assessments, the country is now at the edge of a serious economic downturn.

D. Massey (1987) also analyzed the case of the migration regime restriction between the USA and Mexico. He emphasized that the large-scale public and political campaign of this restriction was initiated not as much because of economic reasons, but mostly due to panic stimulated among the American population. This panic was one of the derivatives of the American protectionist policy favoured by both politicians and some of the key employers. From D. Massey's standing point, the aims of such migration policy is to create additional vacancies in the labour market, to smooth the social consequences of the economic crisis, to stabilize the political situation through satisfaction of trade unions' demands. Similarly, we can also interpret all the restrictions described above in the migration regime between the Russian Federation and Ukraine.

After the overview of the theoretical grounds of the migration policy models and development of migration policy in the European Union and CIS countries, let us now turn to the analysis of the current state of legal and social protection of Ukrainian migrants in destination countries.

Within the internal legal relation and international regulation of the migrant processes, legal and social protection of Ukrainian migrants can be viewed in the context of regional and global systems of control over illegal migration flows. Throughout the whole period of Ukraine's independence, its migration flows and migration policy have been asymmetrically mostly concentrated on the Eurasian direction. Today the political situation has changed in the diametrically opposite direction. On one hand, Ukraine has opted for a European vector of development, and on the other, meanwhile the Eurasian Economic Union has institutionalized as a structural unit. Therefore, the legislation on labour migration regulation and legal protection of migration on the post-Soviet territories is very much outdated and today it resembles more of an artefact of the most recent regional history[9].

---

[9] Multilateral and bilateral agreements on social protection between the CIS countries were mostly signed in early years after the Soviet split when legislation, other terms and conditions, types of social payments in all of these newly established countries were almost identical. However, over the course of time significant changes took place, in the pension systems especially. Namely, pension age was increased, as were years of pensionable service; a mandatory accumulation pension system was introduced. All these changes mean social guarantees related to pension are not as much affiliated to the country of permanent residence anymore and many of previous agreements between the CIS countries lose their sense.

In the early 1990s Ukraine signed several multilateral agreements within the CIS concerning pension provision, social protection for families with several children, compensations for industrial accidents or for professional diseases. Additionally, Ukraine also signed several bilateral agreements on social protection with Azerbaijan, Belarus, Georgia, Kazakhstan and Moldova. All of them were based on the principle of responsibility on the country of residence. The agreement of the CIS countries "On cooperation in the field of labour migration and social protection of migrant labourers" was signed in 1994 (Soglashenie o sotrudnichestve v oblasti..., 2005). In it, the parties agreed on the recognition of legalized documents about education, work experience and qualifications of migrant workers, on exclusion of double taxation of their wages, on the opportunities for transmittances etc. The same agreement also stated that social insurance and social protection of migrant workers are to be carried out according to the legislation in the country of employment.

These positions were reinforced in 2008 when within the same CIS framework a new document was approved – "Convention on the legal status of labour migrants and their family members in the member countries of the Commonwealth of Independent States". According to this new convention, all labour migrants, including seasonal and temporary ones, have rights equal with the citizens of the receiving counties, including the right for appropriate work conditions, the right for fair wages etc. Labour migrants are also eligible for a range of social rights (apart from pension provision), again, on equal terms with local residents. They also have the right for social protection (social insurance), including the mandatory insurance from industrial accidents and professional diseases, compensation for the related losses as well as the right for free-of-charge medical help in case of emergency (other medical services to be provided on regular financial grounds) (Problema sotsialnogo zakhystu..., 2013).

Concerning the European direction in migration outflows from Ukraine we should acknowledge that the issue of setting the migration regime with Ukraine was of interest for many politicians and experts in European countries since the early 1990s. This interest came from the perception of Ukraine as a risky area which potentially could become the source of illegal migration from the East.

Thus, in 1998 the Migration Management Program was initiated, aiming to counteract the unregulated transit migration. European countries provided assistance to Ukraine in the issues concerning registration of asylum seekers and transit migrants, and also while setting the Migrants Temporary Accommodation Centre in Pavlyshyno (Transcarpathia). Additionally, there were also special trainings for Ukrainian border officers and material and technical support was provided to cross-border stations (The cooperation process with Ukraine..., 1998).

Also in 1998, the European Union and Ukraine signed an agreement on partnership and cooperation. This agreement included the establishment of special working groups for customs interaction, transborder cooperation, fighting illegal migration etc.

For quite a long period of time the EU did not have an explicit concept of a migration regime with Ukraine, aside from the vision of Ukraine as a buffer state which could reduce part of the migration threats on the Eastern borders. Thus, for a long time Ukraine had neither an exact invitation for full-scale integration, nor an alternatively attractive offer (Fischer, 2008).

Significant changes came with the introduction of the Schengen visa zone. First of all, the Ukrainians were forced to apply for a visa each time they travelled to a territory of the EU. This became one of the major reasons Ukraine has had positive saldo of migration since 2004. Another reason for the different dynamics of external migration was quite noticeable economic growth, which hindered the socioeconomic push factors.

In 2004 the migration regime between Ukraine and the EU got new features in the context of the so-called "neighbourhood policy" which was aimed at creating "a circle of friends" on the borders with the EU. One of the first practical steps in the direction of this neighbourhood was establishing the European Union Border Assistance Mission (EUBAM) in the Odesa oblast not far from the border with the internationally unrecognized Transnistrian Republic in order to counteract contraband and illegal migration in the region. In the framework of neighbourhood policy during 2007–2010 Ukraine got the financial assistance in the amount of 494 million EUR which, inter alia, covered the creation of five centres for temporary accommodation of illegal migrants (Speer, 2008).

In 2008 Ukraine and the European Union signed the Readmission Agreement. This agreement concerned the deported citizens of Ukraine and also citizens of third countries who entered the EU from Ukraine's side.

Overall, we can say that during the long period of time between the 1990s and 2014 (the year when the Agreement on Association was signed) the European migration regime and migration policy had one leading line of motivation – the threats from uncontrolled and illegal migration from the East through the territory of Ukraine.

Throughout the analyzed period the European vector in the external migration from Ukraine was very much predetermined by the bilateral agreements of Ukraine with the receiving countries. For example, during 1993–1996 several agreements on employment were signed with Poland (and in 2005 a protocol was added to that concerning seasonal employment). Similar agreements were also signed with Czech and Slovak Republics, Lithuania and Latvia (Streimikiene et al., 2016). All of these agreements were very much identical in content and overall were more of a framework.

Agreements on employments signed in 2003 with Portugal and Libya were much more specific. They, inter alia, specified the employment mechanisms, the candidates' selection procedures and the key requirements to them, terms and conditions of labour contracts etc.

The agreement signed in 2009 with Spain mentions three categories of workers: constant, seasonal and interns. However, none of the Ukrainians was ever employed according to the conditions provided by all these agreements, primarily due to complex procedures which imply the participation of public authorities on both sides – Ukrainian and that of the receiving country (while both employers and workers usually try to avoid this).

According to a similar agreement signed with Czech Republic, the initial quota of Ukrainian employees was 25 thousand persons; later this number was increased to 60 thousand. However, this country in reality managed to employ only 16 thousand people. This demonstrates that all these agreements were more of declarative nature, not the automatic guarantee of wider employment opportunities.

On March, 16th, 2007, Ukraine also ratified the European Convention on the Legal Status of Migrant Workers (1977). This document obliges the countries which signed it to provide social protection for migrant workers and their families at the same level with its own citizens.

Ukraine signed bilateral agreements on social and pension provision with Bulgaria, Estonia, Spain, Latvia, Lithuania, Slovakia and

Czech Republic. A similar agreement with Portugal was signed in 2009 but only ratified in December 2011 (Problema sotsialnogo zakhystu ukrainskyh..., 2013).

According to Ukrainian experts, all the above-mentioned agreements were not able to regulate labour migration and/or guarantee migrants' rights protection. All of them have one similar major drawback – the complexity of practical application.

Till now, the level of social protection of Ukrainian migrants abroad is unsatisfactory. The largest problems are observed for those migrants who work without any contract signed and those who work seasonally. Besides, there are no agreements signed with the governments of Greece and Italy (and both countries are important destinations in Ukrainian labour emigration). There are also internal Ukrainian problems related to the implementation of these agreements; they concern mostly the deficiencies of administrative mechanisms, the lack of appropriate staff and underfinancing[10].

At the same time we can observe a gradual legislative process of Ukraine's adjustment to the requirements of the European Union in the context of a potential visa-free regime. Late in 2015 the Ukrainian parliament approved in the first reading the laws of the so-called "visa-free package": the Law of Ukraine "On the introduction of changes to the Criminal Procedural Code of Ukraine

---

[10] A lot of problems arise due to the absence of exact mechanisms for these agreements' implementation. The agreements define the bodies responsible for their implementation; however, in the structure of these bodies in Ukraine there are no structural units who could have been delegated such a responsibility. There is also a significant lack of people with necessary qualifications and knowledge of the needed languages. A range of very specific problems concerns the medical side of the issue: medical conclusions are hard to be mutually recognized by countries due to differences in medical indicators of health conditions, different terminology and methods used.

concerning separate issues in seizing property with the aim to remove the corruption risks at its application"; the Law of Ukraine "On introduction of changes to the Criminal Procedural Code of Ukraine concerning the compliance with the recommendations of the European Union on Ukraine's performance according to the plan of action on liberalization by the European Union of visa regime for Ukraine concerning the investigative jurisdiction of the pretrial investigation bodies"; The Law of Ukraine "On the introduction of changes to the Criminal and Civil Codes of Ukraine concerning the improvement of the institute of special confiscation with the aim to remove the corruption risks at its application", and finally, to the Law of Ukraine "On labour migration".

The latter has introduced a range of important innovations, namely: more state responsibility for migrants' reintegration in the societies upon their return to the country; it also emphasizes the right of labour migrants and their family members for mandatory state social insurance according to Ukrainian legislation. Labour migrants also got the right for family reunions in accordance with acting legislation. Civil unions of labour migrants which have been founded abroad have the right for the same, typical for civil unions, activity on Ukrainian territory as well. The state is to create better conditions for financial remittances transfer from labour migrants abroad to their Ukrainian relatives.

The same law also covers a significant part of migrants' labour rights. In particular, it stipulates that every labour migrant before leaving the country is supposed to get a labour contract which is provided by the party arranging this employment opportunity on the side of the sending country. This labour contract is presented in the state language of Ukraine and also in one (or more) languages used as official ones in a receiving country. The contract describes the liabilities of an employer, including the following, inter alia: work conditions (including a description of safety rules) and order of payment (mentioning the minimum guaranteed volume); exact deductions from the salary volume before tax; the duration of a working day; quantity and length of breaks during the working day; the general term of contract duration and the conditions under which it can be terminated; social and medical insurance included; potential compensation in case of production emergency; conditions when a labour migrant may be repatriated.

All of the innovations described here comply with the requirements of the European Union concerning external migration regulation. And secondly, these innovations have the potential to actually change the current situation of Ukrainian migrants for the better. However, the question still remains concerning the mechanisms of sanctions' implementation for the violation of this law by any of the parties involved.

The political process of the Association Agreement ratification is ongoing. Meanwhile, we can already trace certain changes in the migration policies of Ukraine's European neighbours. For example, already in 2014–2015 Poland had significantly increased the general quantity of multi-entry visas issued for the Ukrainians. In 40% of these cases the visas are for more than one year. This is considered to be an efficient mechanism to fight both bureaucracy and corruption related to visa processes. In the previous period the share of long-term Polish visas for the Ukrainians was slightly higher than 10% (Polsha znachitelno…, 2015). Speaking optimistically, those Ukrainians who got their several-year visas in 2014 or 2015 may have been applying for the last time, since a visa-free regime is expected by many soon.

The consequences of these changes in Polish visa policy were already noticeable in the first half of 2014, when over 400 thousand Ukrainians found jobs in Poland and entered the country.

This is twice over the same indicator in the previous year. Among these newly employed, around 70% found jobs in agriculture, the construction sector or in industrial production (Blaszczak, 2005). However, a vast majority of these migrants are only temporary and/or seasonal workers, and obviously, this form of employment only adds to the trends of precarization.

Since Ukraine overall today is experiencing a wide range of both political and socioeconomic problems, nearly all of them to this or that extent influence the processes of external migration, giving rise to a range of new threats which were registered within the EUMAGINE project.

Roughly, around half of the Ukrainian population has migration intentions, at least to some extent. The general dynamics of the fourth wave of Ukrainian migration was rather unstable: the decade of the 1990s demonstrated a rapid growth of emigration, while from the middle of the 2000s emigration tended to slow down, and even a positive migration saldo was recorded. A more or less optimistic situation lasted for almost a decade (Bilan, 2014b). The next phase of emigration growth coincided with the global economic crisis (which also contributed to the growing migration). The political crisis of 2013–2014 and the ongoing military conflict have contributed significantly to both migration processes and the migration intentions of the Ukrainian population.

For several decades of the country's independence the migration flows from Ukraine were very disorganized, without any guiding influence of the state or of large business. This was mostly due to political uncertainty and the absence of a long-term concept of migration policy. Now the conceptual issue of the country's general geopolitical choice has been solved; however, there is still a range of institutional and legal issues. For example, borders with the Russian Federation are still not delimited fully and officially.

International agreements of Ukraine on external migration by key directions in migration flows

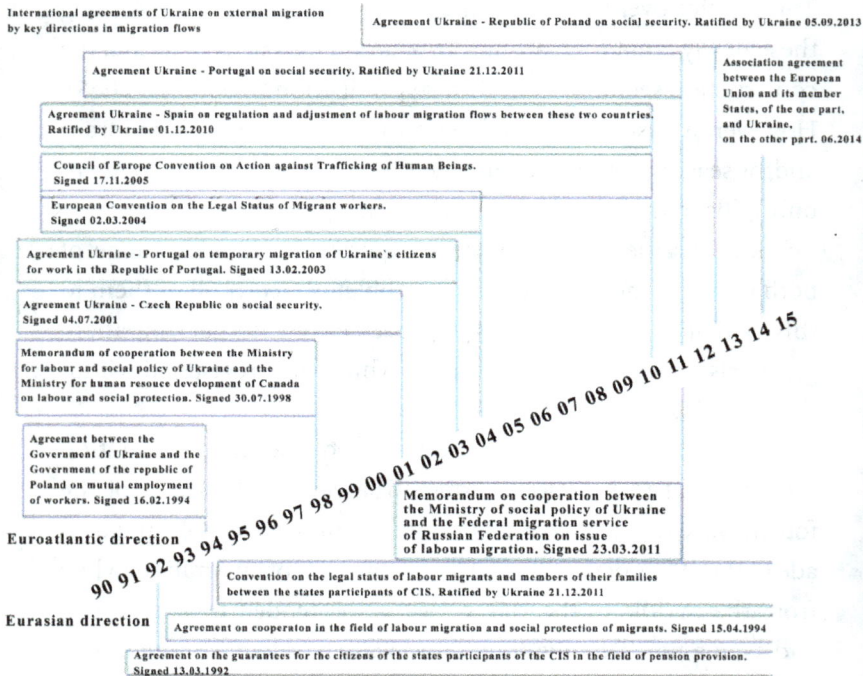

Agreement Ukraine - Republic of Poland on social security. Ratified by Ukraine 05.09.2013

Agreement Ukraine - Portugal on social security. Ratified by Ukraine 21.12.2011

Association agreement between the European Union and its member States, of the one part, and Ukraine, on the other part. 06.2014

Agreement Ukraine - Spain on regulation and adjustment of labour migration flows between these two countries. Ratified by Ukraine 01.12.2010

Council of Europe Convention on Action against Trafficking of Human Beings. Signed 17.11.2005

European Convention on the Legal Status of Migrant workers. Signed 02.03.2004

Agreement Ukraine - Portugal on temporary migration of Ukraine's citizens for work in the Republic of Portugal. Signed 13.02.2003

Agreement Ukraine - Czech Republic on social security. Signed 04.07.2001

Memorandum of cooperation between the Ministry for labour and social policy of Ukraine and the Ministry for human resouce development of Canada on labour and social protection. Signed 30.07.1998

Agreement between the Government of Ukraine and the Government of the republic of Poland on mutual employment of workers. Signed 16.02.1994

Euroatlantic direction

90 91 92 93 94 95 96 97 98 99 00 01 02 03 04 05 06 07 08 09 10 11 12 13 14 15

Memorandum on cooperation between the Ministry of social policy of Ukraine and the Federal migration service of Russian Federation on issue of labour migration. Signed 23.03.2011

Convention on the legal status of labour migrants and members of their families between the states participants of CIS. Ratified by Ukraine 21.12.2011

Eurasian direction

Agreement on cooperaton in the field of labour migration and social protection of migrants. Signed 15.04.1994

Agreement on the guarantees for the citizens of the states participants of the CIS in the field of pension provision. Signed 13.03.1992

Figure 12: International agreements of Ukraine concerning external migration by the key directions of migration flows.

* The political chapters of the EU–Ukraine Association Agreement were signed in March 2014. The remaining sections of the agreement were signed in June 2014. The agreement will enter into force once all EU countries, in addition to Ukraine, have ratified it.
Source: Data of Ukrainian Parliament (Verkhovna rada Ukrajiny). *zakon.rada.gov.ua*

With many countries, Ukraine still needs to sign the agreements on readmission. But the most sensitive issues in the context of Ukrainian external migration are the issues of social protection for Ukrainian migrants abroad and the problem of their reintegration into Ukrainian society upon return.

As we see, the activity of the Ukrainian government related to signing international agreements on regulation of various issues related to the life of Ukrainian migrants abroad throughout the period analyzed was in full compliance with the general logic of multivector vision which was announced as Ukraine's strategy at foreign arenas. At the same time, while in the Eurasian direction most of such agreements were signed within the CIS agenda, for the Euro-Atlantic direction of external migration and Ukraine's foreign policy, a more common practice was signing bilateral agreements with a range of receiving countries. This is a testament to the fact that throughout the whole period analyzed Ukraine had been gradually integrating with Eurasian structures, thus approaching the idea of a common legal field within the CIS, which became a pretty obvious idea straight before the framework agreement on the establishment of the Eurasian Union. This was the general external vector of Ukraine, up to the radical changes which took place after the political protests and change of powers from the end of 2013 to the beginning of 2014, when the country switched to the alternative, the opposite of the Eurasian scenario of integration.

Therefore, both researchers and politicians face the same issue: what must be the reaction of the state, of its political establishment, of business and civil society as the response to these new challenges? Since this problem is comparatively new, there is an obvious gap in the related research, both at the level of mass discourse of surveys etc. and at the level of expert evaluations. Thus, even smaller studies on this problem would be of interest in this context.

For example, during 2008–2009 a comparative expert evaluation of international labour migration problems by Ukrainian and Polish experts was carried out (Yuskiv, 2009, p. 360–361). Twenty Ukrainian and eleven Polish experts participated in their survey, discussing the problems related to international migration. In particular, there was a pool of questions concerning the experts' evaluation of the efficiency of state regulation of the international labour migration from Ukraine from the viewpoint of fast results and further development prospects. Also, a list of potential further measures was suggested for evaluation from the viewpoint of their effectiveness in the opinions of Ukrainian and Polish experts. This list included the following: the system of sanctions against illegal migration; counteracting illegal intermediary services in this field; administrative actions against illegal entry to the country and repatriation of migration; establishing specialized institutions with certain procedures on migration regulation; signing international agreements and other forms of supranational regulation; further improvement of national legislation on migration; limitations set on employment of foreign citizens; development and introduction of professional and sectoral priorities in foreign employment; indirect methods of migration regulation based on purely economic criteria, including investments, tax preferences and fines on both private individual and legal persons; information campaigns covering various issues related to migration processes.

To evaluate this list a nominal scale was applied, where: 1 – "would hardly lead to any positive result", 2 – "can be effective under certain conditions", and 3 – "would lead to the needed results". Evaluation of measures using this scale enabled the calculation of the measures' efficiency index. The value of this index would range between 0 and 1. If the value is closer to zero, that means that according to the experts' opinions, the given measure would not lead to the needed result. The value closer to 1 shows that most of the experts think this measure can be highly effective. Detailed results of Ukrainian and Polish expert evaluations are presented below in Figure 13.

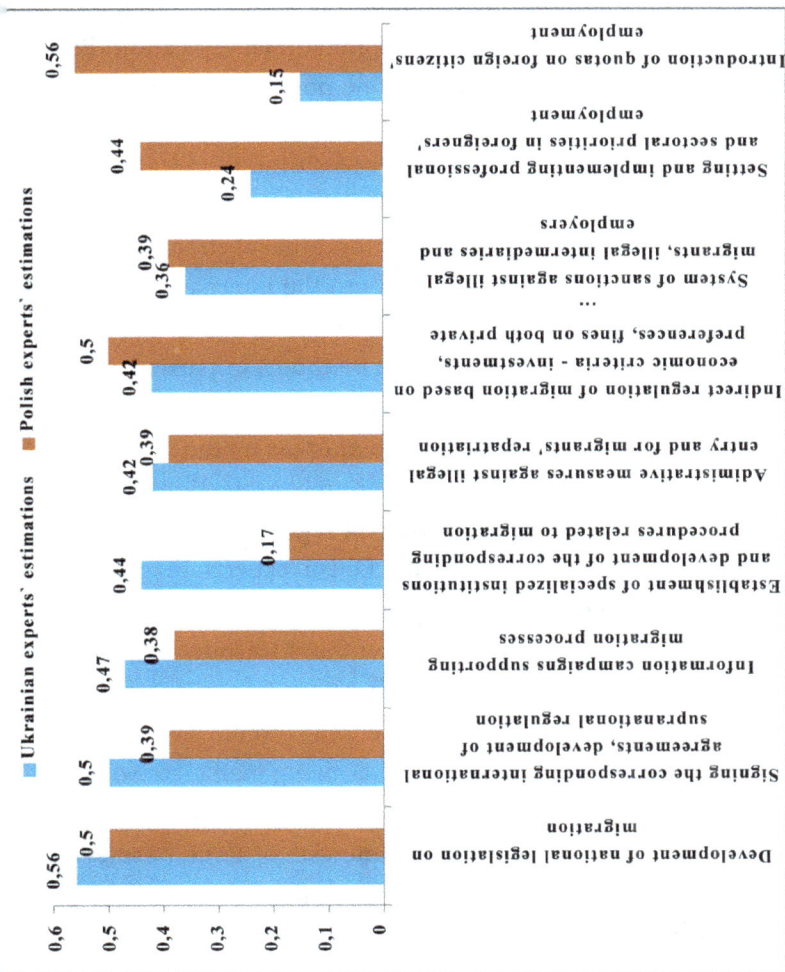

Figure 13: Measures regulating international labour migration in Ukraine, according to Ukrainian and Polish experts' evaluations. *Source:* Yuskiv, 2009.

In the intricate hierarchy of efficient regulation means for international labour migration, Ukrainian experts evaluated the following positions as number one: development of the national legislation on migration and signing the related international agreements, and development of supranational regulation. Polish experts' choice on the number one positions in this hierarchy was very different, namely: indirect regulation of migration using the economic criteria, and introduction of limitations on foreign employment. The differences in choice are significant and conceptual. Ukrainian experts opted for rather abstract solutions which shift much of responsibility onto the international community and foreign partners of Ukraine. Polish experts chose much more specific and measurable methods, in particular, the ones that are more limiting. However, at the same time, Polish experts evaluated quite a wide range of other methods as being efficient, from the above-mentioned purely protectionist methods in their own market up to indirect regulation. Two options were evaluated by Ukrainian and Polish experts in radically opposite ways. These are: setting professional and sectoral priorities in foreign citizens' employment and introducing quotas on foreign citizens' employment. There are several reasons for that. First of all, trade union movement in Ukraine has been and still is in crisis; by many it is viewed as being inefficient when it comes to protection of labourers' rights, since trade unions are often accused of representing the interests of large businesses rather than those of workers. Thus, protection of workers' interests at the level of professions and sectors is viewed by Ukrainian experts as inefficient.

Secondly, we can assume that at the time of this survey, Ukrainian experts tended to ignore the influence of labour market regulation in the context of international labour migration. Ukrainian experts overall tended to prefer legal (including the international law) and information means of regulation when it came to international labour migration. At the same time their Polish colleagues viewed these methods as inefficient.

Thus, the Ukrainian experts' assessment contradicts the vision of D. Massey, who emphasized that under crisis, experts would opt for restrictive measures.

Meanwhile, the current-day realia require the formation of the migration policy concept for Ukraine. The recently approved Law of Ukraine "On labour migration" covers mostly the issues related to social and legal protection of migrants as well as the issues of social reintegration upon return to Ukraine. The issues of state regulation of migration flows, the related challenges for the education system (mostly university education and professional training) have been left out of focus.

On one hand, the signed Association Agreement and also the agreement on a free economic zone have created the potential space for freer circulation of both economic and human resources. On the other hand, from the social viewpoint, external migration is becoming more dysfunctional: migration is currently escalating under great social pessimism and very low expectations about Ukraine's future, and it is often accompanied by the total loss of previous social connections, since migrants are concentrating their attention only on the receiving society, in which they are doomed to further precarization.

Therefore, the key task in the improvement of the institutional and legal regime of external migration from Ukraine lays in two dimensions: firstly, in granting all Ukrainian citizens the right to free movement, free employment choice as well as the corresponding legal and social protection in the most favourable receiving societies (according to our research, in the European direction these would be Germany, Italy, the UK and Poland); and secondly, in indirect discouragement of mass illegal labour emigration with emphasis on potential precarization.

Within the frameworks of the EUMAGINE project we have carried out research to reveal the social demand for a migration policy of certain contents. Namely, in the context of migration flows, regulation the respondents often mentioned low quality of life in Ukraine, and more specifically, a range of negative factors which served as the push factors for migration. At the level of mass discourse there is a widely spread perception of external migration as a dysfunctional phenomenon, not as a potentially positive one. Thus, concerning the institutional and legal aspects, external migration regulation is seen by the general public as "what the government must do in order to decrease the external migration from Ukraine" (that is, measure weakening and eliminating the push factors).

The key topics (or in other words, the key push factors) mentioned by the survey participants were: economic troubles, underdeveloped social infrastructure, political instability and corruption.

In this context, corruption is probably the most complicated issue of all. Obviously, the general corruption level in Ukraine is high; however, the level of corruption-related anticipation and panic is even higher, and thus, in mass discourse, media and political discourses its volumes are often exaggerated, while achievements related to fighting corruption are often ignored or downplayed – negative perception is widespread.

However, the same research also revealed another trend, which is less powerful so far, but can potentially form an alternative in mass discourse. This is the vision of external migration in a positive context. Mass expectations related to liberalization of the visa regime with European countries and to the legalization of many employment options for the Ukrainians within the EU have recently become widespread.

CHAPTER 3

Empirical Research on the Factors of External Labour Migration from Ukraine at the Current Stage

3.1 Overview of current research on the factors of external labour migration

The use of sociology in empirical research on external migration is important. In the absence of trustworthy tools measuring external migration, experts and media tend to use rather speculative estimations, especially when it comes to migration volumes. Overstatement and dramatization around migration in media usually takes place when the results of sociological research are presented without a detailed explanation of the tools, methods and indicators used.

How to cite this book chapter:
Bilan, Y 2017 *Migration of the Ukrainian Population: Economic, Institutional and Sociocultural Factors.* Pp. 141–224. London: Ubiquity Press. DOI: https://doi.org/10.5334/bbg.d. License: CC-BY 4.0

Studying external migration by means of demographic statistics does not allow considering numerous aspects of this phenomenon: precision in the volumes of migration; the intensity of migration mobility in various social and demographic groups; the influences of such factors as origin, education, social status and nationality; the dynamics of personal attitudes in the consciousness and behaviour of potential migrants; the contents of migration expectations and the level of these expectations coming true in time etc. As well noted by E. Jaźwińska, for a long period of time we were able to use only the state statistics data, various lists and registers. The advantage of this data, at least theoretically, is that they cover the whole population. The key disadvantage was, however, that they had very little information; at best, it was limited only to key demographic features, and these would tell us very little about the motives or aims of migrants, the way they made the decision to migrate etc. Besides, in the case of international migration the quality of official statistics is very low. Lack of and gaps in data are caused by differences in registration methods in different countries, and this does not allow us to compare the quantity of people leaving one country and arriving in another. Moreover, during the recent years illegal (unregistered) migration increased significantly, and in the absence of formal data it becomes even more interesting for researchers (Jaźwińska, 2000).

Today there is a wide variety of rather developed tools for statistically-oriented qualitative and quantitative research on migration. Every "family" of sociological methods has its strong and weak points. As mentioned by Balakireva et al. (2012), there are also certain limitations on using quantitative methods in mass surveys when it comes to migration. First of all, migrants have to return regularly home and/or have relatives who still live in the sending country. In this case both migrants and their relatives can be considered in research and further surveyed. Migrants that have nobody to return to in the sending country should be not considered. Secondly, migration should be numerous enough that the sample would provide enough material for solid conclusions.

While using quantitative methods in sociological research on migration there is always the issue of sample. Unspecified socio-logical research, being representative for Ukraine, with the prob-ability or quota sample of 1200 persons with the traditional set of social and demographic parameters, would have 32 persons who had experienced labour migration (if we assume that the total volume of labour migrants in the country is 1 million), or 64 persons (for 2 million of labour migrants), or 96 persons (for 3 million). Obviously, such a sample size does not allow for reli-able conclusions on the experience of labour migration or key features of labour migrants (including age, gender, duration of stay abroad etc.) (Balakireva et al., 2012).

In this regard E. Jaźwińska continues that studying migration using nationwide samples is nearly impossible since migrants represent only a minor share of the population. If we assume that their share is around 5–10%, then in order to obtain the migrants' sample of 1000 persons (or households), we need to survey about 10–20 thousand respondents (Jaźwińska, 2000, p. 19).

Thus, with the unspecified general sample, we get trustwor-thy sociological information on migrants only with truly large-scale research, and this requires a lot of resources, including time and labour. Clearly, crossover research would have a much smaller sample. However, the most a researcher can do with a small sample is a very careful statement of hypotheses, without overgeneralization.

In a similar manner, A. Gorny notes that the experience with migrant groups shows that applying only quantitative approach with surveys encounters many difficulties and as a consequence, there may be serious distortions in final data. One of the widespread problems which researchers are trying to solve while using quantitative methods is the lack of opportunity to create the needed sample of respondents. The major reason behind this is the lack of reliable statistical data on the actual volumes of migration, because a large share of it is illegal, and those who actually came to the country fully legally are usually hard to reach (Gorny, 2005).

A creative approach to sample formation was suggested by J. Fawcett and F. Arnold. They proposed finding potential migrants using the lists of people who apply for visas or work permits or who apply for citizenship status (such a sample will be partially random, partially purposive). For the formation of a sample of those who have actually migrated (or have a real opportunity to do so), they suggest using the lists of people who got visas (or work permits) or of those who have recently changed citizenship (Fawcet et al., 1987).

Qualitative research is used in cases of new subject fields, for example, new types of migration. Then researchers do exploratory research in order to study the very structure of the subject field. Qualitative methods are used when the application of quantitative methods is troublesome or impossible. They are also applicable to phenomena that are not widespread enough to be explored quantitatively. Also, qualitative methods are useful in sensitive issues like household relations, personal finance, family relations, illegal practices regarding employment, tax evasion, contraband etc. Besides that, migration research always works with the groups which are hard to reach, for example, high-status migrants, illegal migrants, people engaged in or related to organized crime etc.

Qualitative research does not concentrate on the volumes; it determines trends and patterns. These may include: behavioural strategies and the related decision-making; migration experiences; migration motives, values, perceptions and causal relation between factors. Flexibility of qualitative research allows us to explain differences and similarities in perception, even in changing cultural contexts.

Qualitative sociological research aims to find the true meaning of human attitude, to understand the social mechanics behind behavioural patterns and systems of values, to describe intentions and lifestyles. Qualitative research has its roots in anthropology and ethnography, which have formed the tradition that to study a certain culture, the researcher has to spend some time within it, inside it, observing its carriers and interacting with them in their everyday lives.

M.S. Knapp describes qualitative ethnographical research as a fully unbiased exploratory approach to a problem in question; intensive engagement, inclusion of a researcher in a situation; using multiple research tools with the emphasis on participant observation and the key role of interviewing informants; an attempt to understand the regularities in a studied phenomenon operating the same terms the participants of the studied social situation use; an interpretative approach with the key role of the context; the research the product of which, in a form of ethnographical descriptive text, provokes in the readers the sense of belonging (Knapp, 1979, p. 119).

Carrying out research using qualitative sociological methods raises questions concerning the selection of individual respondents and their groups, how to establish trust for more productive communication and how to process the obtained data afterwards.

The issue of a sample is also relevant for qualitative research. The major aim of a sample in a qualitative sociological research is to catch the variations in the aspects of social realia, to avoid repetitions and incompleteness, to prevent the focus shift. The most frequent choice in qualitative sociological studies is the snowball sampling. A theoretical (or typological) sample means that researcher chooses persons with certain features that are relevant for the subject field. These features, hypothetically, can differentiate the attitudes, values and practices (in our case these can be: absence or availability of migration experience; the level of migration mobility; availability or absence of migration opportunities; having relatives abroad; belonging to an ethnical minority group etc.).

The snowball sampling method can be especially useful in the research of specific types of external migration (for example, sports or academic migration). It is also a useful tool for studying social networks. The first person who introduces a researcher to a studied community is usually called the gate opener. Most often this would be a representative of an international organization or an NGO employee (including those providing support to migrants); this can also be a public officer from self-government or a community leader, a local celebrity. These people ease the first contact of the researchers with the so-called gate keepers – the key persons in a future study, the local experts who have the most knowledge about the local community life in detail. This first step is ethically important, since external migration is a highly sensitive issue and setting trust is vital.

In many cases doing a regular survey would kill all hopes of getting trustworthy data, especially when it comes to shadow or illegal practices of migrants. For example, back in 1995 the Centre for Migration Research surveyed 792 former citizens of the Soviet

Union. For this, 20 interviewers were working on two border points, trying to survey every tenth traveller crossing the border from the side of once-Soviet territory. For obvious reasons, being on the border, with the customs officers around, the respondents were not particularly ready to tell about their real intentions concerning employment (which might be illegal) or how exactly they got their visas. This method was borrowed from the British Passenger Survey but clearly did not work well in this specific case (Okolski, 1997).

There are specific requirements to both gate openers and gate keepers, especially when it comes to polyethnical societies or societies divided in other ways which usually have significant socioeconomic differentiation. The universal advice would be to start the research with several people who potentially could become gate openers, then expand to several more gate keepers who ideally will represent various stratas in the local society.

A good example of such a sample formation is provided by Jonczy (2003) who studied the external labour migration from Opole, Poland. Since none of the statistical databases had information on the needed population group, Jonczy turned to key informants in the selected 12 territorial units of Opole, and those introduced him to the households the members of which were working abroad. In such a way he managed to conduct interviews in 45% of the households which were mentioned by the key informants. Thus, the author reached quite a high representativeness level.

Although in quantitative research the sampled population is usually around 1000 respondents, in quantitave research the sample can be 1 informant only. In less extreme cases, as for example, in Volodko's study (2007), the sample consisted of 14 semistructured interviews with the ladies who had experienced working in Poland. Social facts stated verbally by the respondents may be enough for further narrative analysis. That's why the life story of one informant only in a certain social context can be enough (Sandelowski, 1991). One of the most important studies for sociology overall and migration research in particular also did not have a large population sample (Thomas et al., 1918).

The location choice within national borders is also important for the empirical research on external migration. In some cases, especially when it comes to explicit seasonal variations in the intensity of migration processes, both location and time factor are important for field research. Thus, the researcher must have advance knowledge about both location and good timing.

The next step is the selection of informants. A popular approach is expert choice, as experts are the carriers of the most widespead and generally accepted knowledge, attitudes and experience. Contacts with experts provide information on both the studied phenomenon and also on the community around it.

As noted by E. Jaźwińska, P. Kaczmarczyk and J. Napierała, there is a way to solve the dilemma between quantitative and qualitative methods by combining them as suggested by D. Massey. This approach was called ethnosurvey by D. Massey (Massey et al., 1987).

This was implemented during one of the most magistral studies of the recent decades in the field of migration (Massey et al., 1987), and it happened to become the methodological reference point for many followers. The Mexican Migration Project (MMP) study of the migration between Mexico and the USA has the following key elements: 1) a set of both qualitative and quantitative methods to collect data; 2) comparatively symmetrical samples in various locations; 3) combining data at different level of analysis (starting with separate life stories up to the level of macroanalysis); 4) the interdisciplinary nature of the research.

Another reputable project on migration was MAFE – Migration Between Africa and Europe (Beauchemin et al., 2009). This project included biography studies (the so-called close-ups) in three sending and six receiving countries (Senegal, Ghana and the Democratic Republic of Congo; and Belgium, France, Italy, Holland, Spain and the UK accordingly). The MAFE database had the following parameters: 1) it was multifocused (various aspects of the respondents' lives were studied – work, family relations, mobility, legal status etc.); 2) the data were compared by the cross-level principle (meso- and macrodata were compared with microlevel data, on specific respondents); 3) this was a longitudinal research (the retrospective analysis for reconstruction of migration trajectories); 4) the research was transnational (the gathered data concerns both sending and receiving countries).

Similar variants of combining quantitative and qualitative methods are also present in Polish research. For example, in the early 2000s the research group under the leadership of K. Iglicka carried out a project titled "Migration and its influence on the labour market in Poland". The study was based on the use of quantitative methods with further thorough statistical analysis of the obtained results and in-depth interviews with hundreds of migrants which had returned to Poland from Great Britain, USA and Germany (Iglicka, 2003).

Overall, a perfect sociological research has to combine various methods, and their diversity and combination at various stages of hypotheses' formulation and their further verification raises the quality of subsequent sociological knowledge. Combining qualitative and quantitative methods in the research aims to: 1) discover both quantitative and qualitative dimensions of the studied phenomena; 2) reveal and explain the complex interrelation between structures and individuals who finally have to choose whether to migrate or not (Findlay et al., 1999). Combining tools, methods and approaches allows us to validate the research results and significantly improves the methodological foundations of the research. This creates the conditions for performing truly fundamental research which will enrich scientific knowledge rather than provide basic knowledge on fragmented realia.

Another curious aspect is the cross-national dimension of such research. Internationality is vital for sociological knowledge, since the whole cycle of migration concerns both sending and receiving societies, and only cross-national research is able to reveal the universal, most widespread features of the migration phenomenon. Moreover, even within the national limits it would be more preferable to compare several socioeconomic contexts, both promoting and preventing external migration (in the case of a sending society) or various degrees of a society's attractiveness and social comfort for emigrants (in the case of a receiving society).

Therefore, a reference sociological research on external migration must be based on a smart combination of quantitative and qualitative sociological methods in its collection and processing of information for further cross-national comparative case studies in a diversified social context (preferable also multi-sited). As many researchers note, such a research design is extremely important for overcoming the so-called methodological nationalism (Wimmer et al., 2002). As D. S. Massey and J. Durand (probably the most influential contemporary scholars in the field of external migration) wrote in their joint study: "qualitative and quantitative procedures complement one another, and when properly combined, one's weaknesses become the other's strengths, yielding a body of data with greater reliability and more internal validity than would be possible to achieve using either method alone" (Durand et al., 2004, p. 332).

Along with combining methods in data collection, the quality of sociological information can also be increased by combining the methods of its subsequent analysis. There are two opposite poles in the wide range of possible methods for qualitative sociological analysis of data. One of these poles is absolute interpretation, which can easily and often does devolve into speculations; it is also characterized by the rejection of *a priori* statements and theory is thus constructed in the process of data analysis as such. This approach is most explicitly represented by the so-called Grounded theory (Barney et al., 2006). The opposite pole is the total quantification of data, solely computer analysis of the raw data obtained. This can be done, for example, by means of NVivo, AtlasT or other software. Classification and sorting out the data obtained by means of qualitative methods, first of all, releases the researchers from accusations in speculation, and secondly, it directs scientific search on truly well-grounded conclusions.

Obviously, combinations of research methods can be very diverse since the sociological methodological toolkit is quite rich. A. Singleton proposes using the above-mentioned methods in combination with official demography statistics and analysis of political decision-making, since the latter, actualized through the actions of the state and other influential factors, may create new opportunities for the migration process to develop. Singleton is rather critical regarding official statistics; however, she does not fully reject their use. International migration is a cross-national phenomenon, but at the same time international migration statistics are the product of national governments, related ministries and other offices. Researchers need to remember that official instruments for migration calculations are limited in many aspects – conceptually, linguistically etc.; besides, they are always carried out within certain national legal frameworks (Singleton, 1999, p. 156).

The topic of external migration appeared in the mass consciousness of Ukrainian society with the fall of the Iron Curtain at the end of the 1980s when, on one hand, crossing the national borders became easier, and on the other, the socioeconomic crisis started, reaching its peak in the early 1990s. Further dynamics of socioeconomic development of Ukraine was also characterized by the crisis features, especially after the start of the global financial and economic crisis in 2008, and later, due to the military conflict with Russia in the Donbass region (2014–present).

While the first crisis of the 1990s had rather obvious internal causes, the following two crises were mainly caused by external factors of both economic and geopolitical nature. Let us consider the influence of socioeconomic development dynamics in Ukraine on the mass discourse of Ukraine's population as applied to external migration.

First of all, we need to note that formation of the mass discourse on external migration was happening under the influence of significant decrease in quality of life at the beginning of the 1990s. As I. Prybytkova wrote, this decade of reforms and uncontrolled market transformations was accompanied by quantitative and qualitative changes in the labour market and economic environment as such: suddenly there were fewer opportunities for the application of one's labour potential since now getting state-funded education did not automatically guarantee the availability of a job. As was traditional for the Soviet Union, economic connections were ruined, and overall, labour demand decreased, many enterprises that were still operating had serious delays with wage payments. Full-time jobs were radically cut, part-time and temporary jobs were much more available than before, informal employment became widespread (Prybytkova, 2009). All these features of labour relations' instability led to ever-increasing threats of poverty due to sudden loss of jobs and rather chaotic redistribution of employment forms between those enterprises that managed to survive under such conditions. All of the above made external migration quite a topical issue for many.

As a result, one of the largest European migration flows was formed, and this gave several researchers enough grounds to call Ukraine "European Mexico" (Duvell, 2006). Unlike its closest neighbours (Poland, Hungary, Romania and Slovakia), which also had quite intensive migration during the same period, Ukraine was not successful in developing its national economic and labour market, and that only aggravated the consequences of the world financial crisis for the country.

Slow dynamics and lack of radical innovations in the socioeconomic development of Ukraine can be partially explained by the specific features of both the national political class and the mass consciousness in Ukraine. In particular, one of the barriers on the way to system reforms, in our opinion, is the deeply rooted paternalism of the Ukrainian population, traditionally high demands to the state in terms of social protection, work guarantees and labour rights' protection. Paradoxically, this sort of paternalism is combined with citizens distancing themselves from state authorities and with significant distrust of public institutions. Ukrainian researcher V. Susak is of a similar opinion and wrote the following: "counterinnovative conservatism... is dominating over... the desire for innovative development, and this is the sign of post-Communist transformations in Ukraine being incomplete" (Susak, 2009). This very specific distortion in the mass consciousness of the Ukranian population forms citizens' disengagement from civil and political life due to their distrust, their inability to believe in potential constructive changes. We can assume that migration intentions are partially preconditioned by these attitudes within the mass discourse.

Despite such trends and after the years of massive migration outflows from Ukraine, 2005 became the turning point in migration development since that was the year of the first-recorded positive saldo in migration (mostly due to the inflows from the CIS countries), and thus, Ukraine turned from being a migration donor into a migration recipient (Balakireva et al., 2012).

During the first years after gaining independence Ukrainian sociology was in a crisis condition, mostly due to a generally weak economic situation and scientific financing by the leftover principle; besides, Ukrainian sociology was hardly integrated in any regional or global research. Therefore, the key problem in studying the external labour migration from Ukraine was the absence of common methodological approaches to measuring and assessing migration processes. Also, there was no unified database for calculations and further analysis. Thus, all data on the volumes of labour migration from Ukraine, both statistical and demographic, including the data presented and analyzed in this book, is not completely trustworthy, but in many cases it comes from the only source of information available to us.

Further, we would like to overview the available corpus of sociological studies dedicated to the selected issues of mass discourse dynamics in Ukraine concerning external migration. One of the first attempts of the sociological research on mass discourse concerning external migration from Ukraine after the country got its independence was the joint work of S. Pyrozhkov, O. Malinovska and N. Marchenko titled "External migration in Ukraine: causes, consequences, strategies" and published back in 1997 (Pyrozhkov et al., 1997). This research was carried out in the National Institute for Strategic Studies in cooperation with the Social Monitoring

Centre during the autumn and winter of 1994–1995, with support from the Department of Population of the European Economic Commission, United Nations. The key topics of this study were: causes and consequences of migration; strategies and models of labour migration; influence of historic and cultural traditions on migration; economic and social influences on migration; and family situation influences. For the analysis, both qualitative (migrants' life stories, interviews with experts) and quantitative (surveys of migrants' families using the standardized survey form) methods were used. The authors came to the following conclusions: early in the 1990s migration was primarily short-term; the dominating forms of external migration were trade and labour migrations; and sociodemographic features of migrants were described (these were mostly young and middle-aged people with higher education and developed qualifications). The study also revealed that incomes from such migration were later spent mostly on consumption, not as investments.

Another contribution to the initial sociological research of external migration from Ukraine was made by the above-mentioned V. Susak. The study "Ukrainian host workers and immigrants in Portugal (1997–2002)" was published in 2003 (Susak, 2003). It was dedicated to studying the reasons behind Portugal's popularity as a receiving destination for Ukrainian migrants and these migrants' social and demographic features. The research used the data of the PEMINT project "The political economy of migration in an integrating Europe" (http://pemint.ces.uc.pt). The study was using mostly quantitative methods to reveal that Portugal managed to attract Ukrainian migrants mainly thanks to the construction boom which started in 1997 due to the EU preferences provided. Thus, the vast majority of Ukrainian migrants in Portugal were (and still are, actually) men from Western Ukraine.

As already noted in the previous chapters, for the analysis of migration phenomenon, parallel bilateral research would be useful, in both sending and receiving societies. Sadly, in Ukrainian sociology this is a very rare case. One of these rare – and hence extremely valuable – examples is the project "Social portrait of the recent Ukrainian labour migration" which was carried out in January 2002 by the Western Ukrainian centre "Female perspective". In their study, 441 persons were surveyed, all working in Italy (or upon return from this country) (Sotsialne oblychchya, 2003).

That same year another large-scale study on labour migration saw its results published. The study "Life journey of Ukrainian population" was carried out in 2001 by the State Committee for Statistics and National Academy of Sciences of Ukraine (Zovnishni trudovi…, 2002). This study covered eight regions (oblasts) in Western Ukraine and also Donbass.

The first attempt to describe the dynamics of external migration from Ukraine was made in 2003 within the framework of the research "External labour migrations from Ukraine: socioeconomic aspect" (Pyrozhkov et al., 2003). The empirical basis for this research was made up of the interview materials with 150 migrant families in Kyiv, 100 such families in Chernivtsi and 100 families in the village of Prylbychy (Lviv oblast). Very similar research had been carried out in the same location back in 1997, using roughly similar methodology; thus we can consider this study longitudinal. The evolution of external migration features was described: the duration of stay abroad became longer, while educational and qualificational features of migrants changed – in 2003 the migrants were mostly people with vocational education, not a higher one as previously. Moreover, the research noted the diversification of destinations: Russia and Poland were still popular; however, increased outflows to Italy, Portugal and Spain were noteworthy.

In 2005 a research group headed by I. Markov published a collective book titled *Ukrainian Labour Migration in the Context of Change in Today's World* to summarize the then-available corpus of sociological studies on external migration. Also in 2005, N. Parkhomenko and A. Starodub published the study *Ukrainian Labour Migration to the European Union in the Mirror of Sociology: Information-analytical publication*. This work managed to use the principles of parallel research of migrants in two societies – sending and receiving ones. Empirical data in Ukraine was gathered in eight oblasts, while Polish materials were gathered in Mazowieckie voivodship (Ukrainska trudova migratsiya…, 2005). The author came to the conclusion that the key reason and the leading pull factor for Ukrainian-Polish migration was potential for higher income.

One of a few comparative studies on migration processes in various regions of Ukraine was the joint research by A. Kizilov, V. Nikolaievskyi and Ya. Petrova under the title "Peculiarities of migration processes in Ukrainian transborder regions (according to the results of sociological research in Kharkiv and Lviv oblasts)" (Kizilov et al., 2006). This study was carried out within the framework of the international project "Models of migration in new European border regions" (INTAS). The research was based on the quantitative methods and was rather limited in terms of representativeness, since only 400 respondents from two regions of Ukraine participated. Still, the study managed to distinguish three key models in migration behaviour: labour migration, education migration and relocation with residential purposes. Migration intentions in Lviv oblast were significantly higher than those in Kharkiv oblast. For obvious reasons, the migration directions in this study were completely opposite: Russia for Khrakiv oblast, and the member countries of the EU for Lviv oblast.

In 2009 one of the most systemic and multi-aspect studies on external migration factors was published by I. Prybytkova. The key aim of this study was formulated as the synthesis of the available studies in order to describe fully the preconditions for external labour migration. This author used quite large volumes of data, from 1992 through 2006, including, inter alia: a) materials of the annual monitoring by the Institute of Sociology, National Academy of Sciences of Ukraine; b) data of the State Committee for Statistics; c) the data of the International Centre for Migration Policy Development. The author's results were quite curious, namely: most Ukrainian citizens identify themselves as being "the poor" and have the feeling that their quality of life is decreasing, despite the objective improvement of certain related indicators. For example, in the middle of the 2000s the general situation in the labour market was quite satisfactory, speaking statistically; still, about 43% of the adult population in Ukraine were convinced that finding a job was problematic. Prybytkova also revealed the dependence between migration experience and migration plans (and attitudes). The people who already had migration experience had higher and more frequent intentions to emigrate with residential purposes. The key innovative feature of this study was the systemic view on the range of factors in their interrelation – quality of life, welfare level, general situation in the labour market and migration experience.

The first large-scale sampling investigation of labour migration issues was carried out in June 2008 within the framework of the project "Studying labour migration in Ukraine" by the State Committee for Statistics of Ukraine and the Ukrainian Centre for Social Reforms. The project was financially and technically supported by the Fund of Arseniy Yatsenyuk "OpenUkraine", the representative office of the International Organization for Migration in Ukraine, the International Bank for Reconstruction and Development in Ukraine (Zovnishnya trudova mihratsiya, 2009). This study was based on the sampled population of households, covering 48.1 thousand people. The repeated research was carried out in 2012, then covering already 45.5 thousand people. The study managed to reveal the volumes of external migration from Ukraine at the estimated level of 1.5 million throughout 2005–2008, and then 1.2 million more during 2010–2012. Till now, the most trustworthy source of information on external migration (including the one with labour purposes) remains the results of two household surveys carried out by the State Committee for Statistics in 2008 and in 2012.

According to the Committee's data from the period of 2007 through the first half of 2008, the volume of migration was 1.3 million people. We need to note here that statistical research of this type are extremely labour-consuming and also expensive; thus, it is nearly impossible to carry them out more often than once in several years.

Another attempt to assess the volume of external migration was done by the Ukrainian Institute for Sociological Research and the Social Monitoring Centre. In December 2008 and May 2013 they carried out the monitoring surveys, "Your opinion", the samples of which were 2097 and 2009 persons accordingly (and this is representative enough in relation to the adult population of Ukraine). In 2008 2.8% of the respondents answered that they had labour migration experience during 2007–2008, and this means that in the corresponding year about 1.1 million people in the country overall had this experience. The second survey (May 2013) showed that already 3.6% of the respondents had the experience of working abroad (that is, 1.3 million in the country overall).

A comprehensive study on a variety of aspects of Ukrainian external migration was carried out in 2009 by the Institute of Ethnology, National Academy of Sciences (Markov et al., 2009). This study used in-depth semistructured interviews and also focus group discussions with migration, experts' survey in the receiving countries, monitoring of legislation trends and changes in these countries, and monitoring of Ukrainian media space. Considering a wide range of the used methods and their smart combination, we can state that this research study was probably the most multidimensional one and the most methodologically thorough.

In 2010–2013 the international project "Theorising the Evolution of European Migration Systems" came to Ukraine. Its key aim was to determine the motives behind migration decisions. The leading organizer of the project was the International Migration Institute (Oxford, UK). Within this project 45 detailed interviews were done with Ukrainian migrants in four European countries (the UK, Holland, Norway and Portugal), and also, 420 structured interviews were done in Kyiv (city) and Lviv oblast. The latter part of the study aimed to describe the public opinion on external migration and to reveal how widespread migration intentions are.

About that time the first generalizing studies on external migration from Ukraine showed up. For example, in 2010 one more collective study was published under the title *Labour Migration as an Instrument of Internationalization: The Collection of Materials of the Comprehensive Research on Labour Migration and Labour Markets* (ed. Kis, 2010). This collective book summed up the results of regional studies on external migration from Ukraine to such countries as Spain, Italy, Moldova and the Russian Federation as well as on the consequences of migration in the context of individual life stories, family stories, career success stories etc. Consequences for the receiving societies were also described.

At the same time, separate studies concentrated more on the local cases. In 2010 a group of researchers headed by K. Levchenko published a collective book under the title *Ukrainian Greece: Causes, Problems, Prospects*. The book analyzed the influence of the world financial and economic crisis on Ukrainian emigration to Greece and migration intentions of the Ukrainians as such (Ukrainskaya Gretsiya, 2010). This work used large volumes of empirical data: expert interviews with Ukrainian and Greek public authorities' representatives, with NGO officers and experts on the issues of external migration, as well as interviews with migrants themselves (in Greece and in Ukraine, upon return); sociological survey results were also used. The authors got quite interesting results. As it turned out, during 2009–2010, mostly females of middle age and older, with higher or vocational education, primarily married and with children moved from Ukraine to Greece. The developing financial crisis had its negative influence on migrants' expectations and their levels of income; however, mass return back to Ukraine was still not observed. Many migrants in this regard stated that the Ukrainian state does not encourage this return and in case of actual return their reintegration into Ukrainian society is very complicated. The important useful feature of this study is that it contains recommendations on the institutional improvement of external migration regulation and in the related legislation.

Another interesting study was published in 2011. In the book titled *Labour Migration: Social Consequences and the Ways of Reacting*, O. Malinovska grounded her own interpretation of the dysfunctional influence of external migration in its contemporary volumes and manifestations (Malinovska, 2011). She stated that intensity of migration processes is directly correlated with real estate prices, the phenomenon of social orphanage and the poor state of the social care for the elderly in Ukraine. In her opinion, optimal migration policy must be managed so that to "keep people in Ukraine by means of creating decent living conditions, through development of internal labour migration as an alternative to external one, through protection of Ukrainian labour migrants' rights abroad and development of stimuli for reverse migration" (repatriation).

Among all European destinations in Ukrainian labour migration, the most thoroughly studied ones are Poland and Greece. In particular, in 2011 V. Volodko published the thesis study under the title "The influence of labour migration on the family roles of Ukrainian women (with work experience in Poland and Greece)" (Volodko, 2011). This study is dedicated to the sociological analysis of the family roles' structure, family life practices of female migrants, comparing that among premigration, migration and postmigration time periods. The study was based on the qualitative sociological methods (semistructured interviews) and reached the following conclusions: Labour migration to Poland and Greece does not have any radical influence on the structure of family roles. The most significant changes occur during the migration period. However, during the postmigration period, all practices attributed through migration experience cease to exist gradually, including the features related to the EU emancipation.

In 2011 Lviv-based researcher O. Rovenchak published her thesis on the conceptualization of contemporary international migration as a sociocultural phenomenon of the globalization epoch. In it, inter alia, she presented the results of her comparative research on female labour migration from Ukraine to Poland and Greece. This research was carried out during 2008–2010. The author did 120 semistructured interviews with female migrants in Poland, Greece and back in Ukraine (Rovenchak, 2011). The results of this research confirmed the growing importance of noneconomic factors as the causes for migration. The key models of female Ukrainians' adaptation in Greece were based on diaspora groups and voluntary segregation, while in Poland the assimilation trend is more obvious. A collective book by O. Ivankova-Stetsiuk, H. Seleshchuk and V. Susak (Ivankova-Stetsiuk et al., 2011) had a similar research focus.

Therefore, we can generalize the following key features of the sociological corpus of work on external migration from Ukraine. First of all, the dynamics of the studies is noteworthy: until the early 2000s the issues of sociocultural nature, identity transformations and migrants' adaptation to a different cultural environment were totally out of the scope of research. Secondly, a large share of empirically oriented research on external migration from Ukraine does not go over the national boundaries; that is, they miss the foreign component – the actual migrants staying in receiving countries are seldom covered by such research. And thirdly, nearly all of the studies can be divided into two types – they are either too local or all-Ukrainian. Thus, while the former do not allow generalization of the results on the national scale, the latter do not reveal the regional features of external migration and the key geographical differences.

3.2 Theoretical-methodological fundamentals and general framework of the EUMAGINE project[11]

The EUMAGINE project is quite different from the previously mentioned studies by its object field: this is a large-scale cross-national project which managed to cover four countries (Ukraine, Turkey, Senegal and Morocco) and, therefore, it also covered several migration flows, most of which are directed toward the receiving countries within the European Union. The project methodology is very comprehensive; the research object is concentrated not only on the socio-demographic structure of migration, but also includes a wide range of sociocultural issues (namely, the stable correlation between migrants' imaginations and imagined demography, their ideas about democracy, human rights and institutional efficiency in the potential receiving countries etc.).

The project's methodology synthesizes the neoinstitutional grounds and social constructivism. The institutional focus of the study is predetermined by the contemporary international regime of state obligations related to human rights protection and democratic support. Today the international influence of human rights and democracy worldwide is undeniable and thus, it always becomes the object of many studies with an obvious institutional focus.

---

[11] The research study "EUMAGINE: Imagining Europe from the outside" was carried out by the consortium of universities and research centers: University of Antwerp (Belgium), Oxford University (UK), Peace Research Institute Oslo (Norway), University of Koç (Turkey), Mohammed V University (Morocco), Center for Sociological Research (Ukraine) and Cheikh AntaDiop University (Senegal). The research was carried out during the time period from February 2010 till January 2013 in four countries. In each country 2000 respondents participated in the questionnaire survey. Project #: SSH-2009-4.2.2.

The project analyzes the functional roles of various types of discourses (media, political, popular etc.) in the emergence of: 1) perceptions of human rights and democracy in Europe; 2) migration intentions; and 3) final migration decisions in regional, national and international contexts. This particular interest in the individual perceptions and decision-making is in line with several other international studies on migration, including the previously mentioned studies by Massey et al. (1998). It was Stark (1984) who first introduced the importance of individual-level migration decision-making. According to Carling (2002), intentions to migrate can be analyzed at macro- as well as microlevels. On the macrolevel, this author refers to the question of why a large number of people wish to emigrate and attributes this to the emigration environment. This emigration environment is made of social, cultural, political and economic contexts on the one hand, as well as the nature of migration as a socially and culturally constructed project on the other.

The latter refers to the discursively constructed meanings of migration. In this, the second component of the project's methodology is manifested – social constructivism. The microlevel approach to intentions puts forward the question: who wants to migrate and who wants to stay? There are various individual-level factors influencing migration-related intentions, such as gender, age, migration experience and social strata affiliation. The EUMAGINE project aims to combine these two approaches to explore how macrolevel (media discourse and political discourse) and mesolevel (popular discourse) impact individual-level perceptions, imaginations and later, actual intentions.

The project's key hypothesis is that macro- and mesolevel discourses in the emigration environment would influence intentions directly through the perception of human rights and democracy, and this influence can be positive and/or negative. The conceptual model of the project demonstrates that perceptions of human rights and democracy, migration and geographical imaginations play a crucial role in shaping migration intentions. The core assumption is that human rights and democracy perceptions, intentions and decisions are structured by various discourses, i.e. they are preconditioned culturally and socially.

Perceptions have become very important in the context of contemporary international migration, in which an ever-increasing number of people are exposed to migration ideas as such because of overwhelming mass communication and wider transportation possibilities and also due to the growing role and widespread activity of migration-facilitating institutions, such as human traffickers, international recruitment offices, marriage bureaus etc. (Carling, 2002).

The project also assumes that the perceptions of human rights and democracy may impact the so-called "culture of migration"; that is, migration is getting deeply rooted into behavioural repertoire (Massey, 1998). This "culture of migration" – frequently present in popular discourse, media, cultural artefacts and especially in social networks – somehow enthrals potential migrants' perceptions and affects their further behaviour (Collyer, 2006; Pang, 2007).

Till now, comprehensive empirical research on migrants' perception of human rights and democracy, and further migration-related intentions at the premigration phase remains too limited (de Haas, 2007). Various recent studies on international migration point out the importance of discourses and imaginations concerning potential destination countries in generating migration-related intentions and decisions. Discourses and imaginations concerning democracy and human rights focus mostly on the individual level (since these are often related to asylum-seeking situations and other humanitarian issues) or a more general level (human rights under the conditions of free-market economy; social welfare characterized by the rule of law; democracy limiting the government influence). The role of perceptions of democracy and human rights and their possible connection to migration motives remains very much understudied (Boneva et al., 2001).

As already mentioned above, the project has studied various types of discourse. Popular discourse here is understood as socially and culturally determined narratives and practices about migration, migrants and destinations. Discourse as such within the framework of this research project includes representations, practices and performances through which meanings are produced and legitimized (Gregory, 2000, p. 180–181). Also, the project focuses on the way the political/governmental discourse on human rights, democracy and migration impacts the perceptions of human rights and democracy, and also how it impacts the geographical imaginations.

Malmborg and Strath argue that "Europe is an imaginary discursive construction, emerging out of nation state debates within the imaginary frame of a European identity" (Malmborg et al., 2002). This holds equally true for many other possible destination regions since a vast majority of potential migrants have never actually visited the destination point before the deciding to migrate and thus, they usually have very limited knowledge about their future destination countries (Efionayi-Mader et al., 2001). Media discourses and discourses of returning migrants, friends and family abroad are also important sources for perceptions and imaginations about democracy and human rights (Koser et al., 2004). This limited, (second-hand) information, often responding to local actual social and pragmatic needs, appeals to potential migrants of certain destinations. In this context, the project specifically explored individual perceptions in the source countries concerning human rights and democracy in order to analyze the link between these perceptions and migration decision-making.

Three major parts can be singled out in the conceptual framework of the impact of macro- and mesolevel discourses on the development of human rights and democracy perceptions, migration intentions and migration decision-making: 1) the impact of various types of discourses on perceptions; 2) the further impact of perceptions on migration intentions; 3) the relation between perceptions, intentions and migration decision-making. Therefore, the first part deals with perceptions, the second explains the motivation and the third studies the related behaviour.

It is also important to add here that in this research gender is treated as the core factor in shaping perceptions of human rights and democracy and migration-related imaginations, intentions and decisions.

Thus, the conceptual framework of this research, putting it simply, basically means that: the attempts to migrate to Europe are preceded by the development of certain finalized perceptions on human rights and democracy development in Europe and in a home country, and the related decision to migrate. Intentions in this context may vary from very broad wishes to go to Europe or elsewhere to more specific preferences in terms of destinations and migration modes (e.g., family reunification, creating a family, temporary/seasonal work, asylum or illegal entry for various purposes). Migration-related perceptions and intentions develop within specific geopolitical, economic and cultural settings which are often referred to as emigration environment (Carling, 2002). The project described is based on a specific analytical framework which has predetermined the project design. This analytical framework assumes that migration behaviour is being influenced by the factors at three levels: macro, meso and micro. At the macrolevel, political and socio-economic contexts, the acting migration regimes in the countries of origin and receiving countries and also the influence of mass media – namely, its discourse concerning both countries, sending and receiving ones, and also migration as such – are important. The mesolevel factors influencing the migration behaviour include local and transnational communities and social networks as well as cultural phenomenon, e.g. local subcultures. And finally, at the microlevel the most significant influences on migration behaviour exercise the individual features, such as age, gender, social status, education achievements etc. Besides that, migration intentions and migration behaviour can be partially influenced by an individual's experience of previously successful (or not) external migration.

Numerous ethnographic studies have already shown how migration intentions are linked to socially and culturally constructed perceptions. These include the ideas and meanings attached to migration process, subjective images of one's own current environment, thoughts about potential destinations. The EUMAGINE project seeks to understand how perceptions of human rights and democracy are formed and then translate into intentions and, further, into the decisions to migrate. These processes are influenced by the factors at three levels.

The *macrolevel* includes the factors common to all potential migrants, such as national policies on emigration/immigration, general economic and political situation in a country, mass media, situation with human rights and the maturity of the democracy.

The *mesolevel* covers the factors in between an individual and the society (Goss et al., 1995). Local and transnational networks through which people gather the needed information and exchange ideas are most important here.

Finally, the *microlevel* concerns specifically individual features. Perceptions are shaped not only by human rights conditions in a country, but also by individual-level factors, such as gender or political views (Carlson et al., 2007). The resulting intentions to migrate are clearly influenced by gender, age, education level, current labour market situation, political sentiments etc. Each migration act has its impact on the context in which subsequent migration decisions are made (Massey, 1998). Therefore, the project treats all related perceptions, intentions and decisions as dynamic processes, open to changes in location and time. Individual features as well as meso- and macrolevel factors affect the degree to which people with intentions to migrate are actually able to go. There are substantial barriers (for example, but not limited to, European restrictive immigration policies) and literally millions of people have dreams to go to Europe that will never be fulfilled.

The project also aims for a dynamic non-Eurocentric analysis of the impact of human rights and democracy perceptions on migration intentions and decisions in important source countries, including Ukraine. The project particularly focuses on the contribution of such perceptions on migration intentions and decisions in emigration and transit regions outside the European Union. Four related topics are addressed: 1) the relation between perceptions among people living in the selected source countries concerning human rights and democracy situation in Europe and in their own countries and their migration intentions; 2) the influence of human rights and democracy-related perceptions on migration as compared to the effects from other determinant factors; 3) the extent to which migration is perceived as a life project; and finally, 4) how potential migrants compare Europe with other major destination regions such as the USA, Russia, Canada or Australia when it comes again to their perception of human rights and democracy.

The fundamental background for this project has been formed by the systemic analysis of the existing literature on the issue and other quantitative and qualitative data, and also the collection of new materials by means of both quantitative and qualitative methods in the selected regions of the source countries.

The project has an innovative methodological design. The post-structuralist era in international migration and human rights research is in need for a multidisciplinary, multilevel theoretical framework within which migration is seen as a social and cultural construct. The research design enables full-scale comparison of the perceptions of human rights and democracy, migration-related intentions and decisions between the countries on the one hand, and also the comparison of the processes under study within a single country on the other hand. Within countries the following is in focus: triangulation of data material; comparisons between different types of data, different regions, and different profiles of potential migrants. Between countries the following is emphasized: transcending the country level for cross-country comparison.

For theoretical and methodological reasons, the project ana-lyzes the perceptions of human rights and democracy by poten-tial migrants, i.e. migrants, but also of the large number of people who have not (perhaps yet) moved. Thus, the research got its con-trol group – the non-migrants.

In order to study the variety of contextual influences on the per-ceptions of human rights, democracy and subsequent migration intentions and decisions, the project has opted for the case study approach. The project is based on the assumption that by comparing and contrasting a diversity of local contexts, it is possible to generalize how these perceptions are formed and how they influence migration intentions and, then, migration decisions. Therefore, the starting point will be to reach an in-depth understanding of perceptions, intentions and motivations in the selected areas of migration sources.

For this, four countries have been chosen as important as areas of origin: Morocco, Senegal, Turkey and Ukraine. All four countries are the sources of substantial migrant inflows in Europe. They also are attractive areas for migrants from more distant countries (remember that back in 2005 the external migration saldo in Ukraine became positive, and this happened primarily due to migration from other CIS countries). Migration flows to Europe from and through these four case study countries include regular migration (including that for family reunion purposes), asylum or employment, as well as irregular migration.

In order to reflect the diversity within each country, four types of locations have been selected. These 16 "cases-within-cases" were carefully selected, using the information provided by the project partners based in Morocco, Senegal, Turkey and Ukraine. To guarantee the diversity of perceptions, intentions and motivations in each country, four research locations have been chosen using the following selection criteria: 1) an area characterized by high emigration rates; 2) the second comparable socioeconomic area with low emigration rate; 3) a comparable area with a significant immigration history; and 4) a location with a specific human rights situation.

The target population of the study is the general population in the 18–40 years old age range, that is, those who are most likely to consider emigration as an option. Besides other relevant individual-level variables such as age, gender, socioeconomic, political and legal status within the target population, the project compared the perceptions on human rights and democracy, and then migration intentions and decisions of three primary categories of individuals: voluntary non-migrants, involuntary non-migrants and migrants (Carling, 2002).

Theo (2003) states that "imagination may be interpreted in general terms and forms a basis for understanding the world and making decisions". The methodology of this project has enabled the in-depth study of local processes and people's subjective perceptions, their systematic comparisons and further quantitative generalizations.

There have been three major methodological components in the study: 1) ethnographic fieldwork; 2) a large-scale survey; and 3) qualitative interviews with the selected respondents directed by an interview guide. The research uses three-method triangulation by means of combining the quantitative method with two qualitative methodologies, namely, in-depth interviews and observations in the communities. Taking into account the choice of research methods, the major challenge in this research was to draw together quantitative and qualitative research parts.

The project is conceptually innovative. Until recently, the link between democracy, human rights and migration has been hardly discussed. Moreover, the very notions of "perceptions", "migratory imaginations" and "geographical imaginations" remain rather unexplored and hardly used in the external migration research. Various authors have already pointed at the power of perceptions and imaginations in inducing decisions to change the place of residence. However, how exactly this concept relates to the other concepts in migration research such as the culture of migration, intentions, migration decision-making etc. so far remains out of the scope of migration research.

The project will be relevant for the following target audiences: 1) academic and university researchers; 2) policy developers; 3) NGOs working in the related social fields; and 4) human rights activists. This and similar projects are especially relevant for NGOs and other civil society organizations since they can indeed play a crucial role in the related information campaigns, since information distributed by public authorities and other representatives of power is often distrusted by potential and actual migrants (Koser et al., 2004). The project may also be interesting and useful for the staff of embassies and consulate offices engaged in social protection activities in key destination countries of labour migration.

3.3 Quantitative research of the factors in external labour migration of Ukraine's population in their cross-country and internal dimensions

Here we would like to describe the methodology, the programme and the key features in the design, procedures and tools applied for research in EUMAGINE. The authors of the project were trying to take into account the previous experiences in external migration research in Ukraine, namely, to dispose of probably the most widespread disadvantage of such studies – excessive ethnocentrism.

The international project "EUMAGINE: Imagining Europe from the outside" was carried out by the consortium of universities and research centres from February 2010 till January 2013 in four countries. The cross-national dimension of this project is quite impressive – Ukraine, Turkey, Morocco and Senegal.

All four countries are the starting points in the quite numerous migration outflows to the EU.

The EUMAGINE project had quite an ambitious aim – to apply a rather non-Eurocentric approach to assessment of a wide range of socioeconomic, cultural and political contexts of migration as well as the microlevel variables of the related mass discourse and intentions of migration to the EU countries.

Obviously, when the research goes beyond national borders, it creates additional requirements for research teams and puts forward additional methodological problems, widely known as the dilemma of maximum quality: research framework, methods and tools are maximally adjusted to the local context under study; however, further comparison of separate cases is rather problematic. On the other hand, there is the consistent quality approach, under which the research design, methods and tools remain unchanged; however, there are risks that the local specificity of the context would be lost, left out of research scope.

Within the project in question this dilemma was solved in the following way: the quantitative side of the project presupposed the use of the common for the entire toolkit, without any adaptations, but local specificity was still taken into consideration because the qualitative methods and tools were also applied (the semistructured interviews with experts and representatives of power).

The quantitative part of the research was represented by the survey covering 500 people at each of the 16 territories (that is, 8000 respondents overall). The random selection method was used to get the sample of respondents aged between 18 and 39. Below we present the analysis of the quantitative component of the research for which SPSS was used. In the following subchapter we will present the analysis of the qualitative components (NVivo software package applied).

In Ukraine four territories were chosen for the research. Just like in three other countries, the criteria of the "theoretical sample" have been considered during the selection: Solomyanskyi district of Kyiv (the territory with a high positive saldo of migration within the country); Zbarazkyi district of Ternopil oblast (the territory with high indicators of external migration); Znamyanskyi district of Kirovogradska oblast (the territory with a low indicator of external migration) and Novovodolazskyi district of Kharkiv oblast (the territory with a high indicator of external migration and a rather specific situation with human rights).

The quantitative side of the project covered the issues related to the household's composition, external migration experience, availability of relatives abroad, migration intentions (rather abstract or more specific and exact), the desired directions for migration, the evaluation of the situation in the home country and in European countries (as the leading choice between the desired directions for external migration).

While studying the perception of the situation in receiving countries, the notion of "geographical imaginations" was applied. This concept means the subjective perception by a person of space, specific locations, people residing there and political and economic opportunities related to these specific places in question. Such perceptions/imaginations are formed partially chaotically, in the regular course of everyday life, and partially intentionally – under the influence of specific political and cultural discourses. They can also be "inherited", since such imaginations are part of national identity formation. Regardless of the level of objectiveness in such geographical imaginations, in time they tend to actualize since they may have very explicit, materialized consequences, just as any other cultural symbolic construct.

While studying the migration intentions the following screening question was used: "Ideally, if you had an opportunity to go abroad to live and work there for the next five years – would you go or stay in your country?" The answers to this question demonstrated that in all the studied territories the share of females with migration intentions ranged from 25% to 76%, while for males this variation was from 43% to 90%. Thus, in all the studied territories the share of respondents with migration intentions was higher among men than among women (a drastic difference in this regard was also observed in Turkey). We can assume that such distribution was influenced by the traditional gender perceptions of the role of man (the breadwinner, ready for hardships and risks for the sake of his family) and that of woman (the preserver of the hearth).

Further, we determined the preferences in migration destinations among the respondents who had confirmed their migration intentions. In three other countries, aside from Ukraine, the most preferred destination was always the EU, while for the Ukrainians the most desired destinations were Germany, the USA, Russia and Italy (that is, generally speaking, the preferred destination is not exactly European, but "Western"). The actual statistical leader in Ukrainian emigration is the Russian Federation; however, in the "wish list" of countries for migration, this country is ranked only the fourth. Obviously, one of the key reasons for that is a much easier migration regime between Ukraine and Russia. However, it is worth noting here that this data was gathered before the annexation of Crimea and further geopolitical and military conflict in the border region between the two countries. Most probably, at the time of publication, the results in terms of both actual statistics and respondents' answers would be very much different.

Table 4 presents more details on the respondents' answers regarding migration intentions.

As we can see in Table 4, the Western Ukrainian region (represented here by Zbarazkyi district) and the centre of the country (Solomyanskyi district of the capital city) are more Europe-oriented, while the Mid-Eastern and South-Eastern regions of Ukraine have very mixed preferences, partially European, partially Eurasian. In Novovodolazskyi district, which borders Russia, the first choice is Eurasian; however, the second choice is still Europe-oriented. While the respondents in Znamyanskyi district (which is quite in the middle of the country, far from national borders) the first choice is European, while the second choice is Eurasian.

Since, when studying the geographical imaginations and migration intentions in their regional dimension, we have to pay some attention to the problem of sociocultural differences present in Ukrainian society, we need to introduce additional methodological and theoretical instruments. One such instrument is the assumption that specificity of mass consciousness of the population in certain regions of Ukraine is predetermined by peculiarities of these regions' historic development: here the so-called "lonque durée" are manifested, truly significant and resistance to changes in social properties. The social space of today's Ukraine has been formed as a result of historic confrontation of various state-level, religious and cultural formations from the West to the East, and this long-term confrontation has formed a sort of historic zonality on the territory of Ukraine. This zonality is first of all manifested while comparing those Ukrainian regions which used to be included into different countries. As well noted by Belarusian researcher S. Kandrychyn (2008), the explanatory power here has the very notion of a historic border. These historic

Table 4: Migration intentions of the respondents and the preferred destinations for emigration.

Country / oblast (regional unit)	% of the respondents with migration intentions		% of the respondents wishing to migrate to Europe under the conditions all needed documents are available		% of the respondents who had international passport and who took specific steps to emigrate		The most desired migration destination (first choice)	The most desired migration destination (second choice)
	F	M	F	M	F	M		
UKRAINE								
Zbarazkyi	50	58	56	71	21	39	USA	Italy
Znamyanskyi	35	44	33	48	11	11	Germany	Russia
Solomyanskyi	43	53	43	55	35	34	Germany	USA
Novovodolazskyi	44	49	46	52	8	12	Russia	Germany

Source: "EUMAGINE: Imagining Europe from the outside".

borders have special significance in the case when political barriers and sociocultural differences overlap. In this sense, the largest gap between societies would be between those which are attributed to different civilizational areas. This idea was well explained by S. Huntington, and in its own time got many followers as well as criticism. Applying this to Ukraine, this idea is interpreted as – according to the above-mentioned author – Ukraine belongs to the so-called "torn societies", that is, those societies in the territories in which there are borders between different cultural and civilizational areas. In our case, this important border is determined by two historic borders: the border of 1772, which existed before the Rzecz Pospolita split and further inclusion of Right-Bank Ukraine to Russian empire, and then, the border of 1939, the one which was valid right before World War II (after the war this border was removed and Western territories of Ukraine were joined to the USSR). Ukraine's example of social space differentiation is probably among the most known ones; however, it is definitely not the only case when the historic factor has so much value in today's civil life.

Below we present the map from the widely known Huntington's work, in which Ukraine, along with some other European countries, is presented as the territory that contains the border between two civilizations – the Western and the Orthodox (Huntington, 1993).

The discussion on whether Huntington was wrong or right is still ongoing. This active discussion concerns both general methodological grounds of his theory (see, for example, the work by E. Said, "Class of ignorance" (2001), in which Huntington is viewed as the representative of orientalism), and also more specific criticism of his empirical results of cross-national comparisons and conclusions on civilizational differences (see, for

Figure 14: Civilizational divide and torn countries in Europe, according to S. Huntington.
Source: Huntington, 1993.

example, the joint work by R. Ingleheart and P. Norris, "The true clash of civilizations" (2003)). To some extent, this discussion also concerns the adequacy of this theory in its application to Ukraine specifically. For example, Ya. Hrytsak emphasized the dynamic nature of sociocultural identities and on the significant changes in historical limitations, as mentioned in Huntington's work. Ya. Hrytsak considers his vision to be too sketchy and too primitive in its dichotomy presentation of sociocultural realia (which are far more complex than banal dichotomy) (Hrytsak, 1995). Speaking rather metaphorically, this author states there are not two Ukraines, but twenty-two.

On the opposite side, S. Kandrychyn supports Huntington's vision and empirical results concerning the differentiated social space of Ukraine, and in particular, concerning different dimensions of social pathologies in historically different regions of the country. Huntington's view is seen as also relevant by Ukrainian sociologists O. Kutsenko and A. Horbachuk (2014) who supplements the ideas suggested by Huntington with their own theoretical postcolonial studies.

The choice of four regions for the research within the EUMAGINE project enabled covering the above-described zonality of Ukrainian social space and thus, one more time reinforced the statement about the importance of regional community affiliation as a factor which socially differentiates the Ukrainians. Below we present the map of Ukraine on which one can see, firstly, the political borders of 1772 and 1939 which played their significant differentiating role in the formation of Ukrainian mass consciousness, according to Huntington's concept, and secondly, the location of all four communities in which the EUMAGINE surveys were carried out in Ukraine.

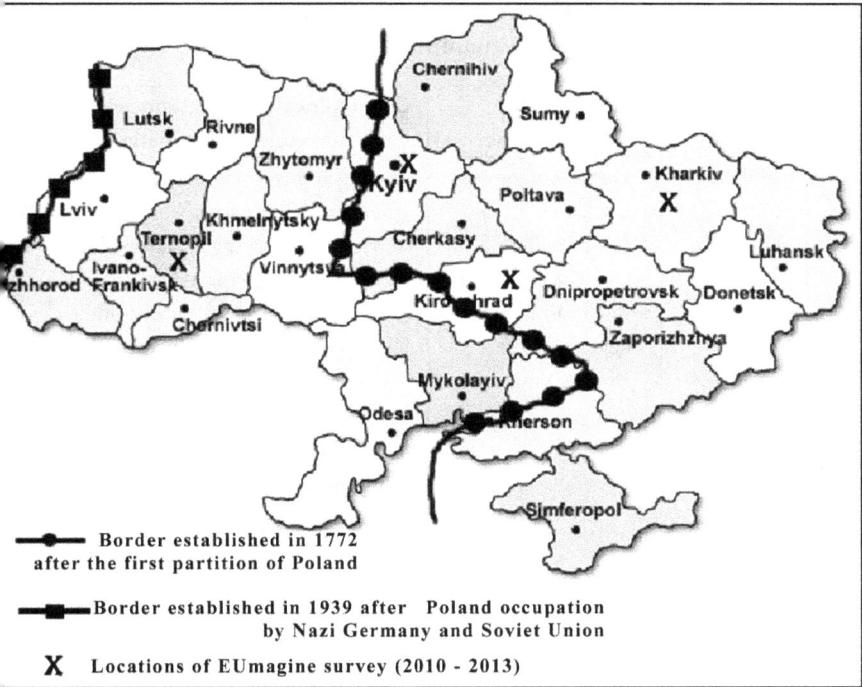

Figure 15: Historical borders and locations of the field stage of EUMAGINE survey on the territory of contemporary Ukraine. *Source*: Author's own figure.

As one can see, the choice of locations for Ukrainian surveys on external migration issues gave us an opportunity to verify the availability of a certain sociocultural gradient, which has been many times detected by other authors in relation to such subject fields as political and geopolitical orientations, historic memory etc.

The topical toolkit of our quantitative research was divided into the following groups and subgroups as seen in Table 5.

Table 5: The covered aspects of the quantitative research on mass discourse related to external migration from Ukraine.

Wider aspects	Migration projections	Geographical imaginations related to the receiving destinations
Family and gender issues	– Life of women in Ukraine – Life of men in Ukraine – In Ukraine women have equal life chances with men	– Living and working in Europe is a good experience for a woman – Living and working in Europe is a good experience for a man – People who leave for Europe often lose connections with their family back in Ukraine – Life of women in Europe – Life of men in Europe – In Europe women have equal life chances with men
Discrimi-nation, criminality, corruption	– There is a lot of cor-ruption in Ukraine – In Ukraine it is not safe to walk in the streets during the night time	– There is a lot of corruption in Europe – In Europe it is not safe to walk in the streets during the night time – In Europe people from Ukraine are treated badly
Financial and professional success	– Finding job in Ukraine is easy – In Ukraine one can reach real success by hard work	– Finding job in Europe is easy – Most of the Ukrainians working in Europe become rich – Most of the Ukrainians working in Europe get valuable professional knowledge – In Europe people can reach success by hard work
Institutional efficiency	– Schools in Ukraine – Healthcare system in Ukraine – Government sup-port for the poor in Ukraine	– Schools in Europe – Healthcare in Europe – Government support for the poor in Europe

Wider aspects	Migration projections	Geographical imaginations related to the receiving destinations
Democracy, freedom of speech, cultural diversity	– Politicians in Ukraine work for the sake of the people – In Ukraine people can publicly speak up on whatever they want – The government of Ukraine respects various languages which Ukrainian citizens speak	– Politicians in Europe work for the sake of the people – In Europe people can publicly speak up on whatever they want – European governments respects all languages which their citizens speak

Source: "EUMAGINE: Imagining Europe from the outside"

Concerning the first aspect of the survey (family and gender issues), over 40% of the respondents agreed that women in Ukraine have equal life chances with men. Interestingly, in all the regions men confirmed this statement much more frequently than women. Almost half (45%) of the respondents noted that women's life in Ukraine is "neither bad, nor good", while 36% opted for "bad" or "very bad". "Good" options were chosen only by 17.4% of the respondents. Negative answers on women's lives in Ukraine are much more frequent in the East of the country: in Kharkiv oblast they totalled 62%, while in the capital their share was 44%.

Twenty-eight percent of the respondents agreed with the statement that people leaving for Europe lose family connections back at home (no significant difference between genders on this issue). This answer in Ukraine got the lowest confirmation within the project overall (in Turkey 39% of the respondents confirmed this loss of family connections, in Senegal, 42%, and 49% in Morocco). This may be explained by the relative welfare of the families of Ukrainian migrants, as compared to other studied countries which suffer from large-scale migration outflows. Interestingly, this problem, even though nearly denied by our respondents, is very often mentioned by mass media.

Indicators of discrimination, criminality and corruption got the following results. Thirty-four percent agreed with the assumption that migrants from Ukraine are treated badly in Europe, while 30% disagreed. In the cross-national comparison the following curious observation was recorded: in other three countries the share of those who disagreed with this statement was always larger. For example, in Turkey 44.8% of the respondents disagreed with the statement that their compatriots are being discriminated in Europe, while 36% agreed. In Morocco this ratio was 52.7% to 21%. In Senegal, 41.4% to 35%. Only in Ukraine did more respondents think that their compatriots are discriminated against in Europe. This result can be partially explained by regional differences in the attitude toward discrimination as such. As our more detailed analysis shows, the largest share of confirming discrimination answers was in Kharkiv oblast – 45.2% of the respondents (while 28.6% disagreed). Most of those who agreed with this statement in Kharkiv oblast were women with no migration intentions. And this indirectly confirms that in the mass discourse on migration there is the topic of exploitation of Ukrainian women in European countries.

The lowest confirmation for bad treatment of the Ukrainians in Europe was recorded in Zbarazkyi district, Ternopil oblast – 28.7% (while 30.7% objected to this statement). It is worth adding here that in Zbarazkyi district only 8.8% of the respondents got visas for European travels during the last five years at the time of the research, while in Novovodolazskyi district (the most convinced in discrimination of the Ukrainians in the EU) only 1.4% of the respondents got European visas during the same five years.

Therefore, we can observe that the most convinced of a bad attitude from Europeans toward the Ukrainians are the respondents in the regions that have the least experience with European travels as such. This is probably one of the most obvious examples of imagined geography. We can also conclude that one of the key features of mass Ukrainian discourse on external migration is the negative stereotyping of this phenomenon, in particular, in the aspect of national discrimination. We can assume that this imagined discrimination is partially the fruit of mass media influence, since this stereotype finds its place mostly in the heads of those who were never abroad themselves. A significant role is played by the mass media's choice in topics, which is often predetermined by their rush for dramatic front-page materials like the deaths and sufferings of Ukrainian migrants abroad, as was already described in the previous chapter.

Additionally, we can also consider the hypothesis on the influence from neighbouring Russian mass media, which often has clearly anti-European rhetoric. N. Bitten also noted in this regard that in the today's Russian media discourse "European stands for alien, dangerous, deviant" (Bitten, 2015).

Concerning the issue of security – the Ukrainians rated security in European countries higher than at home (similarly to other three countries' respondents, actually). Thirty-eight percent of the Ukrainians agreed it would be dangerous to walk in the streets during the night time in Ukraine (while 22.8% stated it would be dangerous to do so in Europe).

Similar results were obtained for corruption: 80.7% agreed on widespread corruption in Ukraine, while only 13.1% of the respondents thought that it is widespread in Europe.

When it comes to financial and professional success, Ukrainian respondents are very critical in relation to their own society. Only 8.3% agreed that it would be easy to find job in Ukraine. And only 22.8% agreed that hard work in Ukraine leads to real success. The results for the same questions but regarding Europe got the following results: 34.1% of Ukrainian respondents think that finding job in Europe is easy, while 66.1% are convinced that in Europe hard work can lead to success.

Thirty-five percent of the Ukrainians think that they can become rich thanks to European jobs, and 65% of them are sure that while working in Europe the Ukrainians get valuable professional knowledge.

Obviously, in the mass discourse of Ukrainian society the image of Europe is rather complex, if not confused: it combines negative stereotyping of Ukrainian society with rather positive stereotyping of European target societies for potential migration.

The answers related to institutional efficiency make the mass discourse's larger picture more complete. The survey had several questions to reveal the key features of the imagined Europe. When it comes to efficiency of education and healthcare systems, putting it simply, we can state that the vast majority of the respondents, in all places, perceive these systems as operating poorly in Ukraine and operating well in Europe.

Here we also record the correlation between such assessment and the desire to emigrate. Therefore, we can note that mass discourse on institutional inefficiency in Ukraine and institutional efficiency in Europe as a potential receiving destination determines migration intentions to a very large extent.

We also recorded a bidirectional correlation between the negative evaluations of schools in Ukraine and the desire to emigrate. Even higher correlation values are recorded for the healthcare sector: 78.2% of the respondents in Zbarazkyi, 77.3% of the respondents in Novovodolazkyi district, 58.8% of the respondents in Znamenskyi district and 64.5% of the respondents in Solomyanskyi district of Kyiv think that the healthcare system in Ukraine is "bad" or "very bad". The assessments of the European healthcare are almost exactly the reverse: positive answers were given by 74% of the respondents in Znamenskyi district, while in Zbarazkyi district they reached the level of 90%. Therefore, we can again record the phenomenon of positive stereotyping of European countries (simply because it is rather hard to imagine that these 90% of the respondents in Zbarazkyi district have real knowledge of the actual healthcare situation in Europe).

Another dimension of institutional efficiency covered by the survey was governmental support for the poor. The vast majority of the respondents think that in Ukraine this support is "bad" or "very bad" (82.3% together). Only 3% of them find this support to be "good" or "very good". And again, a mirror-like situation is observed: at the same time over 70% of Ukrainian respondents think that in Europe governmental support for the poor is "good" or "very good".

The next group of questions concerned the imaginations related to democracy, freedom of speech and diversity. In this group the answers were divided in the following way. The statement "Politicians in Ukraine do what is best for people" got critically low support, while over 70% of the respondents partially or fully disagreed with this statement. Twenty percent provided no answer at all. High level of distrust, huge distance between political elite and population were manifesting themselves long before the events of late 2013 through early 2014. This was the process of power delegimitization formation, and this deligitimization and it had quite significant regional differences. In Western Ukraine (which later in 2013–2014 was most involved in protests) over 90% of the respondents had very critical attitudes to politicians. As with the previous answer, there is a correlation between this political criticism and migration intentions of the respondents.

Overall, quantitative estimations demonstrate that in mass consciousness, institutional efficiency in Ukraine is assessed very poorly and negatively.

It is important to note, however, that in Kharkiv and Kirovograd oblasts the share of those who did not have any answer at all is quite large (the "no answer" option was used here four times more frequently than in Kyiv or Ternopil oblast; in Znamenskyi district is was actually over 40%). This signifies serious uncertainty and disorientation in Eastern Ukraine overall, and later on this was transformed into a rather "floating" mass consciousness phenomenon.

At the same time, according to the already revealed positive stereotyping of European countries, the activity of European politicians was also assessed positively: over 48% of Ukrainian respondents agreed with the statement "Politicians in Europe work for the sake of people".

Cross-regional analysis of the answers concerning freedom of speech and democracy demonstrated that the largest share of those who believe in Ukrainian freedom of speech live in Western and Central regions of the country, while on the East and South East this indicator is lower.

The most optimistic view on the freedom of speech in Europe (over 60%) is recorded among the respondents in Zbarazkyi and

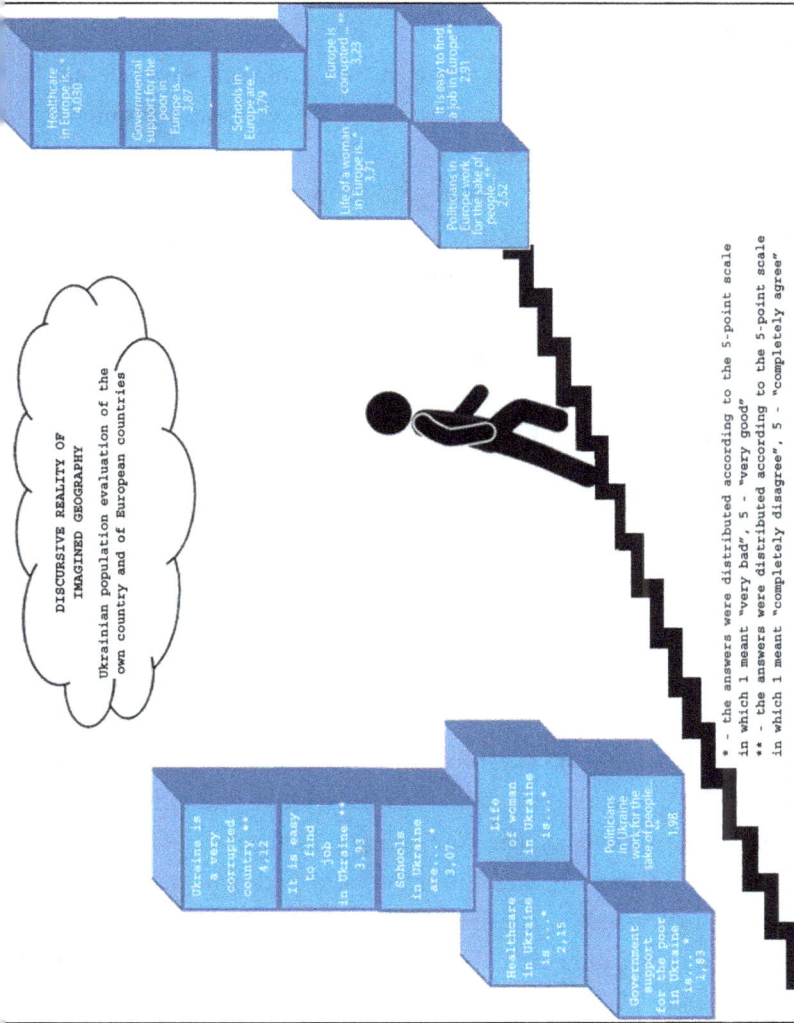

Figure 16: Discursive reality of imagined geography (assessment of own country and European countries by Ukrainian population). *Source:* "EUMAGINE: Imagining Europe from the outside"

Solomyanskyi districts (that is, Western Ukraine and the capital of the country). The least sure group in this regard is represented by men residing in Znamenskyi district (South-East of Ukraine) – also over 60%.

Therefore, we can summarize that in Ukrainian respondents' perceptions of their own country and of the countries for potential migration there is clearly negative stereotyping of their own country and positive stereotyping of European countries.

When it comes to positive stereotypes about Europe, the regional factor is very important, since residents of Western and Central Ukraine tend to imagine European countries in a much more positive way as compared to other regions which are much more distanced from the EU.

Statistically significant correlation is observed between the geographical imaginations of Ukrainian citizens about institutional efficiency of domestic and European institutions.

3.4 Qualitative study of the factors in external labour migration of population from four macroregions of Ukraine

The qualitative field research in the EUMAGINE project consists of two equally important aspects: observation and interviews. While some aspects of the research topics may be sufficiently covered by interviews with informants, others will have to be observed by the researcher in the field.

An interview guide and scenario for the observation and the interviews are elaborated, partly on the basis of the quantitative data collected during the first half of 2010. However, the proposal (suggested at the kick-off meeting in Antwerp) to locate the persons to be interviewed for the qualitative data collection among those persons that have participated in the survey (quantitative data collection) was not withheld for two reasons. First, choosing informants from among the survey respondents may be considered a breach of confidentiality by some, and secondly, the purpose of the qualitative data collection is not to further explore individual factors of migration motives. While informants may include persons who have responded to the survey, the information in the two data collection formats will not be linked.

Within the EUMAGINE project 80 in-depth interviews were performed – 20 in each district with specific migration situations. These interviews were semistructured, and the selection of individuals for them was carried out according to the principle of maximum coverage by the following criteria: gender (the sample had to be balanced by gender); current status in the labour market (both unemployed and those working in various sectors); migration experience (the informants were both with migration history and without it); migration intentions (informants having such intentions and informants without such intentions). Regarding the age, the category of those between 18 and 39 years old was chosen since this is the most economically and migratory active population.

This subchapter uses the sequences borrowed from one of the most well-known and most innovative studies on external migration from Ukraine (from the position of qualitative methods) – this is the research study by A. Rishko-Porcescu titled "Transformation of social space in a big city in time and societal dimensions" (2015). Sequences from this work were applied to the topical elements of this subchapter, dedicated to migrants' perception of discrimination in receiving societies (namely, in Poland).

We do hope that our data contributes to filling in the general research canvas on Ukrainian perceptions of Europe as "the country of El Dorado". The qualitative approach used for this helps achieve maximum precision and detail of the data obtained, according the strategy of comparative research known as "maximum quality approach" (while as already noted in the previous subchapter, quantitative research in this cross-national study was carried out according to the maximum consistency approach).

The qualitative part of our research, as with the previous quantitative one, recorded differences in migration perceptions between the residents of various regions (which are not only geographically different, but also socioculturally). These differences most of all concern the experience of cross-border movements (including the illegal ones), the experience of working abroad and the related imaginations about such work as well as the imaginations of the most-desired directions for external migration. However, the image of the "imagined Europe" among our informants from different sociocultural regions of Ukraine turned out to be rather comprehensive.

One of the introductory questions in these interviews concerned the migration intentions in a hypothetical, ideal situation, when "somebody provides the necessary documents for life and work in Europe", and the answers showed that overall the Ukrainians are ready for such travels, however, under certain conditions:

"If there were such conditions: here you have your documents, money, we have already made arrangements for you – you would have there a job, which suits you well, you can do it" (42206, Zbarazh research area).

It was also recorded that Ukrainian informants are rather tolerant of illegal migration when it is related to Ukrainians leaving the country; however, they consider this to be a negative phenomenon when it comes to illegal immigrants coming to Ukraine. The most important excuse for the practices of illegal emigration they see in the pragmatic reason to work abroad, while the ways of doing so is seen as the matter of secondary importance:

"There are different ways of going abroad: legal and illegal. It depends on the possibility – what kind of possibility you have. If it is possible to go legally, you can get all the documents for work and travelling there, you go legally...

I.: And what are the reasons to emigrate illegally?

R.: Life forces… (smiling).

I.: Do you accept this kind of emigration or don't?

R.: I can understand it. If there is a need to go abroad, to earn money, but there is no opportunity to leave, people emigrate illegally. The most important thing is that a person is solving his/her problems, does something for it" (41244, Zbarazh).

Several informants additionally clarified that border crossing is usually legal, however, further migrant's steps on getting job, performing it and staying in a country against visa-specified conditions and terms are often illegal:

"The border crossing was legal, and then – you never know" (41124, Zbarazh).

"Oh well, people were leaving with the hope that they would later be legalized and would work officially" (41124, Zbarazh).

A typical pathway of border-crossing and further employment in the most prosperous (in their imaginations) European countries was legal entry to Poland, and then – not quite legal migration within the Schengen zone:

"The most important thing is entering Poland. This is the first aim of everyone, then you will see how it goes" (41245, Zbarazh).

The most informationally substantial (in terms of their own memories and thoughts about their own experience) were the answers to the questions on illegal migration of the informants from Western Ukraine. The general perception is obviously distorted and thus requires more detailed further research. We can only assume that the repertoire of described behaviour has been forming for decades and has been impacted by the migration experiences of various sociocultural regions of Ukraine during the second and the third waves of migration. It is important to emphasize here that in the history of Ukrainian migration only the first wave was completely legal, and that was hundred years ago.

An important notion which explains these or that migration intentions is the so-called "geographical imaginations". These imaginations, first of all, reveal the potential and the most-desired countries for migration. So, what are those countries associated with Europe in the minds of Ukrainian informants?

Answering the question: "Which countries do you think of if you hear the word 'Europe'?", the majority of the informants answered it is Germany. This country was described as the most developed country in Europe by 42110, 42203, 43104 and 44208.

It was also viewed as being economically and politically powerful and also as providing security (legal, financial, social) for all – its citizens, migrants and future generations. This country is seen as the one with stable conditions which enable planning for the future and development of life projects for themselves and their children. Germany's economic power and state of development is a geographical imagination that fulfils one of the primary migration intentions – economic stability and security (41114, 41242, 42107, 42104), and "a salary one can live on" (42105) while "nothing will change in our country" (44109).

"Germany. It is the most powerful country of the whole European Union" (43123); "the government cares about them" (41121), "the biggest one… leader of Europe in fact, the biggest economically developed country" (41122). "This is evident and everybody knows who watches at least television. Germany and France are in the first place, holding the entire European Union" (41238).

At the same time, the informants refer to Germany as not only an economic power but also as the source of social welfare, imagining that this "state will not leave you alone, will not let you starve" – while this is one of the major disappointments the informants had experienced during the early years of Ukraine's independence. For instance: "Most of all, I am impressed with Germany (economically it is a very powerful country)" (41117), "but there are also all sorts of social programs that I liked (when I was) in Germany" (Ibid). Also, "there are totally different priorities for employment there ... you will be valued highly ... I think people are better protected there (socioeconomically and by the police)" (42107).

Aside from Germany being probably the most imagined country of Europe, there are also mentions of France:

"Of course, when I think of Europe, I first of all, don't know why, think about France, about Paris, as about the country to which I would really want to go. I think that the quality of life there is really high" (41116, Zbarazh).

In several cases the informants mentioned the countries in which they personally had been to or they have friends who had travelled there and had been working there. For example: "I once was abroad myself, in Czech Republic, so I more or less have an idea what is Europe... and now I imagine it to be like that" (41112, Zbarazh); or, "first associations are Italy, Spain, Portugal, this is where our people go for work" (41238, Zbarazh).

Now let us turn to more clarifying information obtained from the in-depth interviews by the following topical groups of issues: 1) problems of the external migrants' families; 2) gender models and gender inequality in Ukraine and in European countries;

3) discrimination against Ukrainian migrants in the receiving countries; 4) corruption in Ukraine and in European countries; 5) assessment of life quality, social protection and opportunities for financial and professional success – in Ukraine and in European countries; 6) human rights' protection, freedom of speech and democracy in Ukraine and in European countries; and 7) institutional efficiency and politicians' role in Ukraine and in European countries.

Problems in the families of external migrants

The fourth wave of external migration from Ukraine was the most gender-balanced, as compared to the previous three waves. Previously, external migration from Ukraine was mostly a "man's job", and only in very rare case females emigrated (mostly that was the case when the whole family was relocating at once).

Besides that, the current, fourth wave of external migration from Ukraine is the first one in which a large share of migrants is formed by single females, the largest share of which belongs to divorced and widowed women (Virc, 2012, p. 127).

Thus, for obvious reasons, during the fourth wave such issues as gender models and roles, transnational families, social orphanage and lack of home care became extremely urgent. Under "care" here we mean all possible forms of both professional and informal care and support for all who need it.

In the mass discourse on external migration negativism is especially powerful, first of all and most of all in the context of family issues. Comparing sociodemographic, economic and sociological data, as well as the related features of media discourse on external migration we can assume that this negativism was formed already at early stages of the fourth migration wave from Ukraine, and in time we can observe its weakening. However, it is still too early to talk about new, positive discourse related to external migration from Ukraine.

External migration of one spouse is often perceived as a threat to a couple's existence as such: "there are many cases when one is leaving, and the family stay, and then the family falls apart..." (41118, Zbarazh)[12]. In the cases when a husband or a wife is leaving, the threats are different essentially but have the same strength of impact: "When a woman leaves, then the man does not know what to do, and there are a lot of men, not all of them, who lose oneself in drinking, or find another family. And when a man leaves, very often he will find another woman there. Because we all understand, when still young people live separately, the families often get separated" (41116, Zbarazh); "parents must be with their children. And we have such cases, when children are being brought up here, while parents, their *mother* sets her personal life in a different country, and in time children literary forget their *mother*, forget this word. This is very bad" (41116, Zbarazh); "Recently more women leave for abroad. Maybe, it is easier for them to find work there. But I think this is a negative moment. A negative moment in relation to their families which they leave behind. If a man leaves, this could be okay, but if a woman leaves, this is almost 100% guarantee that the family will split up" (41245, Zbarazh).

Within the gender dimension in migration imaginations of Ukrainian informants, there is a certain moral panic in relation to the very phenomenon of external migration, and this panic is both a symptom of family problems and their cause. One of the

---

[12] In this and several other topical groups, the most informative and substantial were the answers from the informants in Western region (due to obviously much more experience related to external migration).

informants described the connection between external migration and family troubles in the following way:

"I.: And is this a problem only for the Ukrainians that someone goes abroad, while other stays here?

R.: Yes, this is a big problem. It broke a lot of families.

I.: Are there any examples among your friends, colleagues?

R.: Yes, there are" (41126, Zbarazh).

Here is another example describing the negative influence of external migration:

"I.: Do you think that migration somehow splits up families, that it destroys families because a woman or a man leaves the country and then their relationships deteriorate?

R.: It happens, certainly it happens, even often. Especially in young families, when they get married, a child is born, a man goes, for example, abroad. Here is this girl sitting with her child and has to look after it, then begins the kindergarten, school, and her husband is abroad and there is no family reunion, there is no intimacy between them because they become in years, almost strangers, and only their child ties them together. So if a man or a woman does not come back for a long time young couples in most cases divorce. Even though they have a child, they still divorce" (41240, Zbarazh).

Thus, the key family threat in the mass discourse on external migration is seen in long-term migration. E. Libanova agrees with this and also adds that "long-term labour migration often causes separation. And the divorce can be initiated by both the emigrant and also by the one left at home" (Libanova, 2011, p. 25)[13]. Note

---

[13] Here we need to add that this problem in external migration was partially solved by the latest communication and transport possibilities which were not available during the early years of the fourth migration wave. Today communications and information exchange in the Internet provides better chances for at least virtual presence of family members, for their direct participation in economic and other decisions of the family.

that short-term labour migration is not considered to be a threat for family life:

"For example, a lot of people want to go to Poland. It is good there because it is not far away. You work there for three months, three at home, for example. And here you are again, the same. As if you don't go away from the family for a long time and you have a job" (41121, Zbarazh).

Traditional gender models, roles and values in the context of external migration demonstrated another interesting turn: for some people external migration became a means of actual divorce. On one hand, they wanted to get separated, but on the other, they are afraid to do this officially due to family pressure and/or traditional family values in the local community. As A. F. Vianello mentioned in this regard: "Female migration is often the cause for divorce, but sometimes the decision to leave is a strategy developed to distance oneself from the spouse; in other cases the divorce is caused by the fact that the man found another partner while the wife was absent. And finally, families get separated because the woman has found another partner in a receiving country" (Vianello, 2012). This phenomenon of the so-called "migration divorce" in Ukrainian mass discourse has another name – the Italian syndrome.

Another important family problem for external migrants is upbringing children left in Ukraine: "I think that in the country a new generation is being formed, of senseless children, who want to achieve nothing in their life, they only want to rest, since they are used to money they have. They do not feel the lack of financial means … To some extent, this is degradation, because they do not develop, they only rest" (41245, Zbarazh).

In this regard mass discourse is in line with the research/ expert one. Among the key threats to children's upbringing in the situation of labour emigration the researchers mention the following: the threat of stigmatization – in child's consciousness there soon arises the narrative of being a victim – and the threat of social disorientation – these children are not able to fairly evaluate their life situation, to set relations or to have emotional connections with other people due to lack to communication and emotional support in their early age (Ivankova-Stetsiuk et al., 2012, p. 18).

Nearly one-fifth of all Ukrainian families are multigenerational (Ukraiinske suspilstvo..., 2012). This form of family living is especially spread in rural communities, and at the same time it is one of the sources of migration outflow from Ukraine. These multigenerational families usually live under the conditions of the so-called subsistence economy. That is, they are highly dependent on natural production (they consume what they grow and breed), they also have informal exchanges with other households (including labour resource exchanges and agricultural equipment exchanges). In such families and such situations transborder migration attracts the middle generation (and to a lesser extent, the younger generation). In this regard it is worth noting the "specialization" of functions which has been establishing itself for years: the elder generation is mostly responsible for economic and financial issues, while the middle generation is responsible for the upbringing of children. This function is now being left on the spouse who stays in Ukraine. In this context the role of elder generation changes somehow; now this generation has to ease the negative consequences from this new gap in the family, in both economic and sociopsychological senses. The only resource the members of this elder generation have in abundance is time. Due to this functions' redistribution inside the family, the representatives of the elder generation have no chance but to find themselves in the situation of forced "active aging".

Migration decisions are initiated by migrants independently; however, the final decision-making is usually done upon approval from other family members. Among the reasons for going abroad the respondents most often mentioned the financial interests of the families. Representatives of the younger generation also mentioned other, less materialistic motives, like self-fulfilment or getting new experience. Long-term migration is seen by many as a much bigger problem than short-term stay. The most problematic variant is seen when a long-term migration act is done by a mother and a wife.

Therefore, we can conclude that transborder migration not always ruins families, but it can increase the interdependence of its members. This, in its turn, does not damage families, but helps establish better connections between generations inside a family due to the situation in which many responsibilities inside a family are exchanged and delegated to each other.

Overall, we can conclude that the influence from transborder migration on the functioning of multigenerational families is rather contradictory, while for nuclear families this is indeed a much bigger problem.

Gender models and gender inequality in Ukraine and in European countries

Describing traditional distribution of responsibilities and competences, the majority of our informants relate to comparatively egalitarian models:

"Well, I would not say that somebody is leading at ours. As agreed by parties, I would put it like this. We find agreement. The wife told me 'I want this', and I say 'Maybe we don't need this', then we find agreement, and we will do first one thing, and later – another" (41112, Zbarazh).

In their answers concerning the life chances of men and women in Europe and in Ukraine our informants were rather unanimous; nearly all acknowledged higher life chances of females in Europe:

"I think women have more opportunities to work there [in Europe]. If one will consider a factory, there are women and men, all working there. Here, we just have such jobs when men get more. With pleasure one will hire a man for a job rather than a woman; they think that a woman cannot work that way. And here, as people say, only in some shops, in bars, so women go only there. And it is all around. Women are at any firm" (41112, Zbarazh).

"I.: Please, tell us from your own experience, is there any difference between men and women in your town? I mean, are there any priorities for employment or, suppose, during local government elections, are men or women preferred, or to the same extent?

R.: The fact is that I've never seen any woman run for the position in our local government" (42105, Znamyanskyi).

Informants see the cause for such a situation the in the great conservatism of Ukrainian society, under which traditional values and lifestyle significantly limit women in their choices, force them concentrate on family responsibilities, on children's upbringing, but not on career growth, education or development of new skills.

"I.: Well, if we exclude the authority sector and leave the sectors of business, education and services. It is possible for women to reach self-fulfilment in Europe?

R.: Of course it is. Why not?

I.: On the same level with men?

R.: I think yes. I think that in Europe it is possible. Here also if someone would like to – he/she can. Obviously, in our case, woman is more in the family, with kids, due to mode of life ... and because of all of these women simply cannot reach something greater. Woman has to take care about everything. The work plus all the rest – home and everything for home" (41114, Zbarazh).

A large share of the informants of both genders justifies the existing gender barriers in the labour market and difference in pay: "Taking into account the physical features of a man, he can bear more. Of course, for a man it is easier to find a job. Because, first of all, he can work under much worse conditions than a woman. Besides, he can endure more than a woman ... And you know, our men work for 12 hours, or even for 18 hours a day. You just give them work, and most importantly is that the woman at home does not scold for money" (41245, Zbarazh).

We have to note here that traditional perceptions of the gender model of employment, conventional attitude toward professional and career growth are more inherent to the Western region of Ukraine. In other sociocultural areas, urban territories especially, the attitude toward traditional gender models is less explicit, and the issues of work specificity and the required qualification in the labour market are of primary importance:

"I.: It is not important – man, woman – if there is a vacancy, then people are equal...

R: If there is a vacancy and if this person has some education, some work experience or something like this, then it will be set-tled" (VN850005, Znamyanskyi).

"I.: Okay, and what do you think, who have more chance to get employed – men or women?

R.: There is no difference, here, because it depends on the sector.

I.: What do you mean under 'depends on the sector'?

R.: Yes, in some cases it will be harder for men to get employed; in other cases, for women. For example, accountants – they can be both men and women, but for some reason I have never met a male accountant" (43143104, Solomyanskyi).

Describing disproportions in the labour market and differences in career prospects for the people of both genders and various ages, the informants from all territories, except for Western Ukraine, were concentrated not as much on the traditional distribution of functions between men and women, but more on the specific interests of specific employers which may be not willing to employ specific groups:

"Nobody wants to employ a single girl of a marriageable age who in a year or two will be on the maternity leave, that's right. And nobody would hire you if you are five years from pension age" (VN850006, Znamyanskyi).

"Many employers are afraid to hire women, because before 20 a woman is too light-minded, and after 25 she will want to have children and will be on maternity leave, plus this is a gap in work, plus this means additional expenses for the employer, and if there are no children so far, she will definitely will leave to have them in the nearest three or four years. While every employer want the employee to work for at least 5 years" (43143135, Solomyanskyi).

Another aspect of gender imbalance indicated by several informants was the imbalance in authorities' representatativeness: "Concerning local self-government bodies, I have never seen a woman running ... Only men are running for such positions" (VN850010, Znamyanskyi).

Informants' opinions concerning the role of external migration in the lives of women and in the lives of man correspond to the traditional perceptions of gender models and the related behaviour. Woman must stay at home as the hearth-keeper and the mother, while man is allowed to go for external migration and in some cases must do it as the breadwinner:

"Well, men are still breadwinners in their families. They provide and they must support their family ... Perhaps most men consider themselves to be breadwinners and if a man doesn't have a decent salary then he has to search for other variants which would fit better in supporting the family" (42103, Znamyanskyi).

Following the logic of V. Volodko, we can assume that Ukrainian men, like Ukrainian women, are themselves the carriers of rather traditional perceptions of gender roles. In those cases when women return to Ukraine from migration, there is a short period of her rather innovative behaviour, when a woman has more financial influence on the household, and thus, there is more equal distribution of home labour. But very soon the gender behaviour returns to the traditional patterns which are more socially approved in Ukrainian society (Volodko, 2009).

This vision is additionally confirmed by the qualitative data obtained in our project. Ukrainian women are family-oriented and rather conservative when it comes to choosing a place of living. Above 40% of them prefer staying in a home area, even if it is possible to consider options of moving to another part of Ukraine or going abroad.

In the group of answers concerning the discrimination of Ukrainian migrants in the receiving countries we revealed that in most cases the informants have not observed any discrimination in the treatment of the Ukrainians in European countries. But at the same time we can note the phenomenon of self-stereotyping of the Ukrainians. In several answers the informants were complaining that Ukrainians are "not civilized", "not law-abiding" and "not polite" while being abroad, and in this way they explained and justified the negative attitude toward the Ukrainians:

"Well, there were different cases, but generally the attitude was good depending on how one behaves" (42112, Zbarazh).

"Well, you know how they call it, 'crowd overrunning the city'. Well, because our people probably spoil their cities, because Ukrainians are not that civilized, and because … we are different people … there are those that can steal, and it is a minus for our country" (42121, Zbarazh).

A. Rishko-Porcescu also gathered some evidence describing the mass discourse of Ukrainian migrants in Poland concerning the feelings and experiences related to discrimination. While describing their social environment in Poland, the migrants usually use the categories of nationalities, meaning, they are using some sort of "national optics" in their vision of the world around them. As Rishko-Porcescu revealed, Ukrainian migrants frequently prefer to reside with people of the same nationality. Very often they note that they keep close contact only with other Ukrainians, while with the Pols they have only business/work-related contact. Seldom exceptions are those Ukrainian migrants who have family connections with the Pols.

At the same time there is another social criteria in Ukrainian migrants' descriptions of their experiences with discrimination in the receiving societies. Evidence of this discrimination is divided into nearly equal halves, depending on life success achieved in emigration. The migrants that are more successful and thus, more integrated into the receiving, society stress that there is no discriminatory treatment from Polish side: "Throughout all my stay here, I never and from nobody heard anything negative in relation to myself" (male, 26 years old, two years of permanent stay, highly qualified worker) (Rishko-Porcescu, 2015, p. 153).

Less successful Ukrainian migrants mentioned there is both discrimination and some sort of social distance between Ukrainians and Pols. "I did not have conflicts with the Pols, but I always felt I am alien here. Despite all the demonstrative tolerance and culture, they always show that you are Ukrainian. I feel this everywhere, especially in administrative institutions. I think this is some sort of historical stereotype, because we are poorer. But Ukrainians are more open to Pols. Maybe because we are in an alien country, and they are in their own country" (female, 30 years old, 12 years of permanent stay, temporary unemployed). "The negative thing here straight from the very beginning is the situation when you are alien by 100%. You don't know anything, there is no sense in speaking Ukrainian here, people maybe will understand you, but they will not respond. I was shocked. And I was very ashamed to show that I am a foreigner, moreover, than I am from Ukraine" (female, 24 years old, eight months of permanent stay, on the maternity leave) (Rishko-Porcescu, 2015, p. 155). "Now I have all documents, and I am absolutely legal here, nobody is saying anything to me. But I had problems in the past. I even had to change my last name" (female, 35 years old, 15 years of permanent stay, works as a sewer) (Rishko-Porcescu, 2015, p. 156).

It is interesting to note that distancing and distrust, and even negative (self)-stereotyping are being formed in the minds of Ukrainian migrants in relation to other Ukrainians in very similar life situations. "Recently I was sitting on a bus stop, and two Ukrainians were sitting and talking about their work, about how to switch on some equipment and other details. I could get acquainted with them, but we are here like ants. I would get acquainted, then they will want my job, and I don't need this. This is self-defence" (female, 48 years old, four years of permanent stay in Poland, a nurse) (Rishko-Porcescu, 2015, p. 144). "I don't have Ukrainian circle at all, maybe there was no such opportunity to find people, or maybe I did not want that so much, it is always very complicated with them, they also want something from you..." (female, 35 years old, 15 years of permanent stay in Poland, a seamstress) (Rishko-Porcescu, 2015, p. 136).

Thus, we can observe that parallel to the formation of migrants' communities and social networks there is another trend – isolation from other Ukrainian migrants. The socioeconomic and sociocultural factors which lead to this isolation most definitely require additional research. So far we can only assume that this phenomenon, according to the neoinstitutional theory, can be called "downward levelling pressure". And as noted in this regard by A. Portes and J. Sensenbrenner: "successful individuals are beset by fellow group members relying on the strength of collective norms, and highly solitary communities restrict the scope of personal action as the cost of privileged access to economic resources. The last form discussed in this section conspires directly against efforts toward individual mobility by exerting levelling pressures to keep members of downtrodden groups in the same situation as their peers. The mechanism at work is the fear that a solidarity born out of common adversity would be undermined by the departure of the more successful members. Each success story saps the morale of a group, if that morale is built precisely on the limited possibilities for ascent under an oppressive social order" (Portes et al., 1993, p. 1342).

To the best of our knowledge, this mechanism has never been studied in relation to the communities of Ukrainian migrants. While we have found enough evidence to state that this phenomenon is extremely real for the Ukrainian migrants' community. Ukrainian migrants who are highly qualified and have decently paid jobs (and often, also a completely legal status) are not really willing to be in any sort of relationship with other Ukrainian migrants who have much less favourable life circumstances. Thus, some migrants are reluctant to reveal their national identity in order to avoid unexpected contacts with other Ukrainians. This is also confirmed by A. Portes and J. Sensenbrenner: "Perhaps, the most destructive consequence of this negative manifestation of social capital is the wedge that it drives between successful members of the minority and those left behind" (Portes et al., 1993, p. 1343).

On the other hand, Ukrainian migrants who are unskilled labourers do not feel any discomfort or threat from their relations with other Ukrainian migrants since for them this communication is providing additional resources, but not consuming them (this includes emotional and psychological support, exchange of useful information, finding ways to deliver remittances to Ukraine, getting recommendations for potential employers etc.). "Women who do the cleaning are trying to stick together, we are a band. That's right. This is only because we need support and information. When I get back to Ukraine, the woman from next door in my village will go to Poland to fill in my place. And this is constant, we are trying not to lose employers" (female, 34 years old, three years of commuting migration, cleaning) (Rishko-Porcescu, 2015, p. 139).

Corruption in Ukraine and in European countries.

The informants' answers concerning corruption in Ukraine and in Europe are fully concordant with the results of our qualitative survey. We revealed that mass discourse in Ukraine agrees on the widespread corruption in Ukraine. As noted by one of the informants: "I do not know any single sphere which would be not infected with corruption" (43135). The informants stated that corruption is "everywhere in Ukraine" and they also provided more specific examples; namely, they mentioned:

- education, including both schools and universities, and especially corruption at the stage of university entry and corruption related to various exams and grades (41240; 41242)
- labour market and corruption related to job search and employment, corruption related to well-paid and high-profile jobs (41242; 41125; 41127)
- healthcare system and, more specifically, bribing doctors during the medical services' provision (42104, 41240, 42105, 43131, 41242)
- corruption at the level of central and local authorities (41117; 41122; 41124)
- law enforcement units and courts (43112; 44121)

Concerning the latter, our informants, in particular, told the interviewers that law enforcement units in Ukraine take bribes and violate human rights so frequently that it can be considered their everyday practice. Many informants are of the opinion that there is a huge gap between law enforcement in Ukraine and their counterparts in European countries:

"work for the people's benefit, but not for the benefit of some distinguished rich population groups ... in Europe police tries to fight criminality somehow, they try to catch some specific criminals, and in our case criminals can pay off to be left in peace ... our police can catch some criminal and then just let him go" (44121).

Along with the self-stereotyping we can observe the stereotyping of imagined Europe. For example, concerning corruption, the vast majority of the informants believe in the "zero level, as compared to Ukraine" corruption in Europe, not specifying which European countries they actually mean here. According to these stereotypes, imagined Europe does not have corruption-related problems as such: "If to compare with our actual situation here, corruption in Europe is equal to zero. In Ukraine today it is blossoming so much, that there are no limits to it" (41116, Zbarazh).

The next group of questions was related to the quality of life, social protection and opportunities for financial and professional success – in Ukraine and in European countries.

Concerning all these issues the majority of informants are very critical and sceptical describing life in their places of residence:

"Mainly ... life isn't easy here, it is very difficult" (44121, Novovodolazskyi). "In my opinion, we have very poor quality of life, because there is lack of everything. The town is small ... here healthcare is very poor, one might even say that there is nowhere to study and to work. There is lack of everything, and we want something better" (42109, Znamyanskyi).

The objective indicators of socioeconomic situation, among all four studied territories, were the lowest in Zbarazkyi district, and some of the informants' answers fully correspond to the state of affairs:

"Quality of life ... quality of life, of course, we have no quality of life; because salaries are low ... for example, my salary is enough only to pay for gas, for electricity, but it is not enough for the phone already" (41121, Zbarazkyi).

While the largest group of informants confirmed that the quality of life is really low, the second-largest group is formed of those informants who had no certain answer or who provided rather contradictory statements:

"The quality of life is average, I won't call it high, because people have low salaries. Taking into account that we live in a village, many people have gardens, they work there all year round, so they don't have to spend money on food" (42204, Znamyanskyi).

Evaluating social support by the governments in Ukraine and in Europe (and comparing them), the informants tended to state that in Ukraine this sort of support is at a miserable level and can only help them to survive physically, while in Europe state financial support for the poor is high enough, if not to say generous:

"There, maybe, people are socially protected better. Because the level of life is higher – and accordingly, social protection level is also higher. And at ours it is so low, because life level is miserable, that's it" (41114, Zbarazkyi).

An interesting phenomenon is revealed here (and it is worth more in-depth research): a large share of the informants see all European countries in a very generalized way, imagining them all to be almost socialistic and exaggerating the role of the state in the process of overcoming poverty problems: "there people are more protected by the state. The state helps its people to have at least something and helps in everything" (41118, Zbarazkyi); "As far as I know, there pensioners are much better taken care of, more than in our state ... Their rights are protected, they have preferences, they get good pensions" (43143104, Solomyanskyi); "Europe means happy, smiling, travelling pensioners, citizens are protected by the state ... retiring on pension in the European Union is a dream, a person worked for the state, and then this state, when the person is already free and can rest, will take care of him…" (43143135, Solomyanskyi).

There are also more realistic assessments, but those are also very positive in terms of quality of life in Europe as compared to the one in Ukraine. Moreover, many informants repeated nearly the same statement – that Europe is the benchmark of the socially fair system: "I am not saying that in Europe one can be not working and still having a beautiful life. Of course, I have such associations that one needs to work there, and really hard. Maybe even really a lot, and overtime. But for your work you can also get decent salary which corresponds to your hard work, so that you can rest, you can feed yourself accordingly etc." (41116, Zbarazkyi).

Comparison of employment opportunities in Ukraine and in Europe revealed that the informants mostly think that it is hard to find job both in Ukraine and in Europe. However, significant differences are noted:

"In Europe ... they can find a deserving job with the diploma they get. And with our diplomas, I do not know, maybe except from a few schools, but I am not sure about it as well, that it is not possible to find a good job" (42108, Znamyanskyi).

"Well, I think they should have such governmental programs that help a person to find a job if he/she wants, of course. I think anyway, the government in Europe takes care about people much more" (41240, Zbaraz).

There was also a question on the opportunity to "go up" or "achieve the state of welfare" by hard work, and Ukrainian informants mostly stated that they do not believe in such an opportunity. This common answer has correlates with the objective economic situation in Ukraine, since in the country overall it is typical to work (even to work in several places) and still be poor. Many actively working people, despite all their efforts, are not financially able to purchase durable goods, let alone a car or real estate:

"We work from 9 to 6 without lunch and still receive the minimum rate – it is not enough ... Quality of life, of course, we have no quality of life" (41121).

Thus, if a person manages to find a job, that does not automatically mean that he or she will be able to provide for the family: "...you can find a job. It's possible, but again, the salary is low, everything is about money. I see people working really hard, hellish hard, I would say, and people work just for 800, 1000–1200 gryvnias and this is not enough" (42104). "They want too much for too low price. They won't raise the salaries, but we are supposed to meet their crazy demands" (43102). The informants often reiterated the same descriptions of the situations in which it is impossible to make a living on one salary: "the prices are rising, you can only survive, you can't live" (41122).

At the same time the informants' imaginations of Europe are much more optimistic. One of the most important statements in this regard is that in the imagined Europe, rewards for your work allow you to improve your quality of life gradually:

"If a person has a good job here, and he works there efficiently, can he hope for the improvement of life, of family welfare, some kind of progress?" (44121).

"One can count on gradual improvement of life level" (44125).

Such imaginations of Ukrainian informants go really far; we even came across the following statements:

"I: So, what makes people go abroad? What are their reasons?

R: Some people want to get rich. They strive for enrichment and better living" (43111).

As with many other topics and issues, in the discussions on life quality in Europe we reveal the stereotyped perception of Europe – in the imagined Europe there are no differences between separate countries. There are a few exceptions though;

several people mentioned the difference between "old" and "new" EU members:

"If not to speak about Bulgaria, Romania and other recently added countries, in general, in the older members of the European Union the level of life is so high that we can only dream about it … Bulgaria and Romania even though de jure are in the European Union, but de facto they are still very far from the same level of life" (43143135, Solomyanskyi).

Apart from the financial dimension, in the eyes of many Ukrainians Europe is the place where one can get valuable experience and improve one's qualifications. Such imaginations add to the image of Europe as the place of not only financial enrichment, but also the place of certain cultural values and worldviews:

"Well, I agree with that. I think everything they do there might be useful in future life. What I know for sure that if a man goes to work on construction he can later use it in his own life. I have the example that my friend's father went to work in Russia on construction and when he came from there he built a cottage house himself. He got experience, skills and now he knows how to build, how to do other things. Now he has almost finished a two-storied house" (41244, Zbarazh).

"I encourage people not only to study in Europe but, in general, learn something new, be tolerant to the people who, for example, have come from other countries and learn a lot of interesting things about them" (44101, Novovodolazskyi).

In the informants' attitude to the topic of human rights protection, freedom of speech and democracy in Ukraine and in European countries we recorded the following peculiarities. The majority of informants agreed on the high level of freedom of speech in Ukraine. However, significant regional differences can be observed in this regard concerning the freedom of speech of the informants themselves, especially when it comes to the issue of corruption. People on the West of the country were more eager to speak about it (Zbarazkyi district – 153 mentions), while informants on the East are rather reluctant to communicate on this issue (Novovodolazkyi district – 48 mentions). One of the very rare mentions of the problems with human rights in Novovodolazkyi district was voiced like this:

"Well … there was a situation in our place … one boy was beaten by the police and then they said that he had fallen from stairs and had hit himself. And in another place a few men supposedly jumped out of the windows. So yes … you do feel frightened and scared for your life" (44121).

It is important to note here, though, that the general situation with freedom of speech, human rights and democracy in Ukraine became much more sensitive in the years following this gathering of empirical material. As recorded by the UN representatives and numerous international NGOs, the political conflict of 2013–2014 has led to serious radicalization of the society, popularity of many extremist groups and numerous human rights violations, primarily in the territories which are not under state control today, namely, violations of the Crimean Tatars' rights in Crimea and significant pressure on the Ukrainian-speaking population on the Donbass (areas controlled by separatist groups).

The group of questions concerning institutional efficiency and political performance in Ukraine and in European countries covered the following sectors: education, healthcare and political institutions' functioning. More specifically, Ukrainian informants tended to explain low quality of education in Ukraine by low wages of teachers, by lack of motivation of the latter to do their job well:

"School education is horrible, it is just a fake. Because of the lack of financing teachers are not so eager to teach kids properly – they teach just for the kids to get their school leaving certificates" (44128, Novovodolazskyi).

Regarding the general situation with school education, the informants also noted a huge gap between education in cities and in villages, stating that the former is much better:

"What is a village school? Even if we compare a village and a district school, the latter is at an upper stage. Kharkiv and a village – it is just like heaven and earth" (44211, Novovodolazskyi).

They imagine school education in Europe to be of good quality, whether they themselves were in Europe or not:

"...education obtained in Europe is more valued than education obtained in Ukraine in many educational institutions of Ukraine since most of these educational institutions have not reached the international level yet" (41130, Zbaraz).

"I don't know for sure whether education in Europe is better than ours and to what extent, but I consider it to be good. They don't come here to study. On the contrary, our students go there" (42103, Znamyanskyi).

Several informants mentioned that the advantage of the European education system, as opposed to the Ukrainian one, is that it is better oriented toward the labour market; getting education is directly related to one's further work:

"People, getting a particular education, know for sure what will be required from them. So they try to get employed according to the education they got. And at ours, we graduate from an institute or a university, have a specific specialty, but very few actually go work according to this specialty" (43143104, Solomyanskyi).

At the same time there are also informants who compare education in Ukraine and in Europe by means of comparing the skills and talents of Ukrainian and European students, and they mostly assess skills and talents of Ukrainian children rather highly:

"You know, I always knew and I know now that our education is at a very high level. Especially it was so when I was in school. You can ask students of European schools some questions, from the same secondary schools as we have here, they do not know many things than our children know. I think the education we have here is at the good level, it is okay, and our children can compete with European children, because our kids are really smart" (41238, Zbaraz).

We can record quite a similar way of thinking regarding the state of healthcare in Ukraine and in Europe: "I know that medical services should be of high quality in Europe because there are social programs there. They also have social insurance, and it pays for advanced medical equipment etc." (44116, Novovodolazskyi).

There is also a popular thought that rich Ukrainians prefer European medical services. This is presented as additional proof that European healthcare is of high quality:

"All our businessmen, the so-called 'new Ukrainians' are treated there and they are satisfied. Apparently, their healthcare is much better than ours. Though we have good experts, we lack support from the government and lack equipment first of all" (42207, Znamyanskyi).

There are also mentions of the personal experiences or experiences of friends who travelled in Europe. The medical insurance of European countries got positive assessments:

"My cousin lives and works in Germany ... so he has told me that healthcare is on a higher level, dentists' service is cheaper there ... he has his medical insurance included into his work contract" (44118, Novovodolazskyi).

"The key advantage of healthcare abroad is, of course, insurances. They provide 100% guarantee of high-quality medical services provision for population. Because in the opposite case the doctor will be legally punished. So he is making sure he is providing real help, of good quality, and he is trying to cure to the maximum. Because he will be later responsible for this, even his license can be revoked if anything…" (41245, Zbarazkyi).

Concerning the comparison of Ukrainian and European politicians, our qualitative data confirms the results we got in the quantitative part of our research. It is important to take into account the general political and social situation in the country at the time of these interviews. The situation then and mass discourse specifically was characterized by significant frustration, political apathy and citizens distancing themselves from political events; the protest potential was very low. Radicalization of the society obviously happened later, and being provoked by a range of events, it ended up in the mass protests of late 2013 through early 2014.

Frustration and absolute disappointment can be illustrated, for example, by the following statement: "our government cannot even repair the roads, so all the rest is out of question as such" (42105).

Here we can also observe self-stigmatization and extremely low expectations of politicians:

"Our government is wrong, and our people too … Everything is wrong here. For the most part it is all about the government. Look, people are trying to get their attention, standing near the Verkhovna Rada, but they get no response at all. They care about their own business in this Rada. They don't care about anything else" (43114).

The informants were also very sceptical answering the question whether Ukrainian politicians are doing anything good for the society. This large distance, if not gap, between Ukrainian general population and public authorities was previously noted by numerous other researchers.

"To be honest, there is a small percentage, maybe five percent of probability that the situation will change. This can happen if the government of the country, as they say, changes its direction and improves social protection. That is, pensions will be increased, adequate medical care will be provided. If the whole financial situation is improved, there is a small percentage of probability that people will get the feeling of success in life then. It is not even zero level now, you cannot even feel like a human being" (44106, Novovodolazskyi).

Negative assessments of institutional efficiency in Ukraine (and high level of corruption in particular) is also observed in the informants' comments on the prospects of starting one's own business in Ukraine as compared to doing the same in Europe:

"Today in our country, starting a business is a very unpredictable thing; you are not able to guess what will be next … if some magnat wishes, they will tear you into pieces, and it does not matter how well or how right you were in your business. Plus corruption of the judiciary system … Today even teenagers already understand that here nobody will guarantee you anything … and if fiscal authorities do not let your business dream come true in – then naturally, we will choose the path of least resistance, we will try to leave" (43143135, Solomyanskyi).

There was also a question concerning the potential abolition of visa regime by European countries, and in this regard the informants were very straightforward – the migration outflow from Ukraine will grow significantly and quickly:

"I.: And if, for example, they introduce the visa-free regime?

R.: Then – that's it!

I.: People will all go – or maybe…?

R.: Massively. All would be gone, including me" (41245, Zbarazkyi).

Therefore, let us conclude this subchapter. The conclusions are rather gloomy, since they point to a range of interrelated and serious socioeconomic, institutional and sociocultural problems:

- Social infrastructure (education and healthcare) is greatly below the expectations of the Ukrainian people, whereas perceived good education and medical service in Europe are the incentives for the Ukrainians to migrate.
- A large majority of the Ukrainians do not trust their political representatives whilst the performance of European politicians is assessed highly by them.
- Corruption is seen by over 70% as a huge problem for the country's further development and prosperity; in contrast, corruption in the EU is imagined to be generally low.
- A majority of the Ukrainians consider their chances to achieve success by working hard in Ukraine much lower than the chances for the same in Europe.
- Gender equality and freedom of speech are believed to be higher in the EU than in Ukraine.
- People in Ukraine do not seem to be well informed about actual conditions in Europe.

Imaginations about Europe are rather idealized. We got an impression that in the minds of the Ukrainians, imagined Europe is some sort of discursive structure, some sort of foretype of "good society", in which everything is "tuned" to the optimal level: state guarantees on social protection, perfect work of all institutions and an enormous open field for self-realization. As the results of the qualitative part of the research show, there is a strong correlation between such idealized imaginations about Europe and the migration intentions. This discursive structure becomes one of the pull factors. Elements of mass discourse which add to more realistic or negative imaginations of Europe are not widespread and not so pronounced.

In this study we recorded the state of mass consciousness of Ukrainian population as being rather frustrated, pessimistic and even fatal. We can assume that after the political events of autumn 2013 through winter 2014 and further military developments, such sentiments in Ukrainian society are only increasing, and in the background of rather unpopular and complicated reforms, and considering the potential visa regime abolition with the EU, all of the above would lead to significant increase in the migration outflow from Ukraine, which might be comparable in volume with that of the middle through the second half of the 1990s.

CHAPTER 4

System Analysis of External Labour Migration of Ukrainian Population at the Fourth Stage

4.1 Theoretical and methodological fundamentals of system analysis of external migration processes

External migration is a complicated phenomenon which is predetermined by a wide range of socioeconomic and culture-oriented factors. In today's world the issue of external migration becomes especially real due to intensification of multi-sided interactions which nearly always disregard state borders and become global. Also, due to a range of potential new opportunities and threats which arise between the sending countries and the receiving countries. Along with this there are also new opportunities to

How to cite this book chapter:
Bilan, Y 2017 *Migration of the Ukrainian Population: Economic, Institutional and Sociocultural Factors.* Pp. 225–245. London: Ubiquity Press. DOI: https://doi.org/10.5334/bbg.e. License: CC-BY 4.0

study this phenomenon since we can observe some sort of standardization of the indicators relevant to external migration and of the procedures for accounting them. Statistical data also grows in size; thus today there is much more available statistical, demographic and sociological information on our subject matter.

At the same time we can also observe the growing interest from the side of political and managerial circles to the possibilities of science-based measuring and forecasting of migration flows. In particular, from the administrative viewpoint, there is an ever-growing demand for detecting and measuring the migration-related risks and also for the mechanisms regulating migration flows, mechanisms which may help integrate and adapt migration communities. The multidirectionality of these tasks straight from the very beginning renders it impossible to provide clear and simple answers within a single discipline; still, problems related to external migration traditionally and even today are covered mostly by economic research discourse.

This is additionally proved by the intensive development of the neoclassical theory of external migration which operates not only traditional economic categories of demand and proposition at the labour market, dual economies which combine capitalist segment and economic of subsistence, and also micro- and macroeconomic push and pull factors, categories and patterns which cover institutional and sociocultural factors: key features of migration regimes, migration intentions, geographic imaginations about the potential countries for migration etc.

The obvious mainstream of the contemporary research on external migration is based on the acknowledgment of the narrowness of single-discipline approaches and thus, the necessity for interdisciplinary integration to be able to take into account the wide range of factors that determine the phenomenon of migration.

The complexity and multi-aspect nature of external migration lead us to the necessity for applying interdisciplinary analytical schemes as well as a range of other methods which would catch the very essence of this phenomenon in all of its dynamics and complexity. The fundamental work in this regard was created by Polish sociologist P. Sztompka in his study "Sociology: Analysis of Society" (Sztompka, 2002). According to this work, social practices are being formed by two groups of factors – institutional and discursive ones. These two dimensions, which are in the research focus of sociological science, are necessary to consider external migration from the angle of the micro- and macroeconomic dimensions of these former factors' formation.

Each group of these factors is comparatively autonomous and represents (operating the terminology of A. Schutz) "the finite province of meaning" – which is a specific, comparatively separate field of human experience determined by a logic of its own (Schutz, 1962). Thus, the economic field is primarily described using the model of homo economicus which considers rational buyer, employer, employee, investor, creditor etc., while the institutional field follows political and organizational logic. The sociocultural field is determined mostly by intangible factors which are hard to detect and measure; these are values, norms, hierarchies of identities, loyalties and behaviour. At the same time all these rather autonomous fields are combined by means of an intricate two-sided interrelation, and in this regard external migration is just another complex social phenomenon. For example, certain institutional changes can cause rapid economic growth or, on the other hand, can lead to economic troubles at the national level. These troubles, in turn, would change the priorities in the value system and thus, the life strategies of the general population would also gradually change. On the other hand, the institutional features of any society (its political and administrative organization, first of all) as well as the functioning of any economy are determined by the priorities and values of its political elite – and the population too, by the role of labour ethics and the power of its influence on the society, by the most common social practices etc.

In today's research the attention of researchers working with human rights and democracy issues in general is primarily focused on the institutional side of the problem. The following aspects of democracy and human rights in the EU, their most common discourse and attitudes toward them in source countries may influence migration processes: free elections (including passive and active political rights necessary for that, like freedom of opinion, the right to vote, the right to be elected, the degree of freedom of political association); parliamentary democracy; rule of law (limited government, division of powers within the state system, independent and impartial courts and legal procedures); individual rights and freedoms; social, economic and cultural rights and freedoms (including free market area and the state of social welfare); and recognition of multiculturalism by public authorities and by the society at large.

We also suggest to take into account various types of discourses that can influence migration plans and the corresponding behaviour. It is important to focus on macro- and mesolevels of these discourses within the emigration environment since they influence through the so-called "migration imaginations" and "geographical imaginations", and this sort of influence may be positive and/or negative. In the EUMAGINE project the conceptual model hypothesizes that perceptions of human rights and democracy manifested through migration and geographical imaginations probably play the most crucial role in shaping

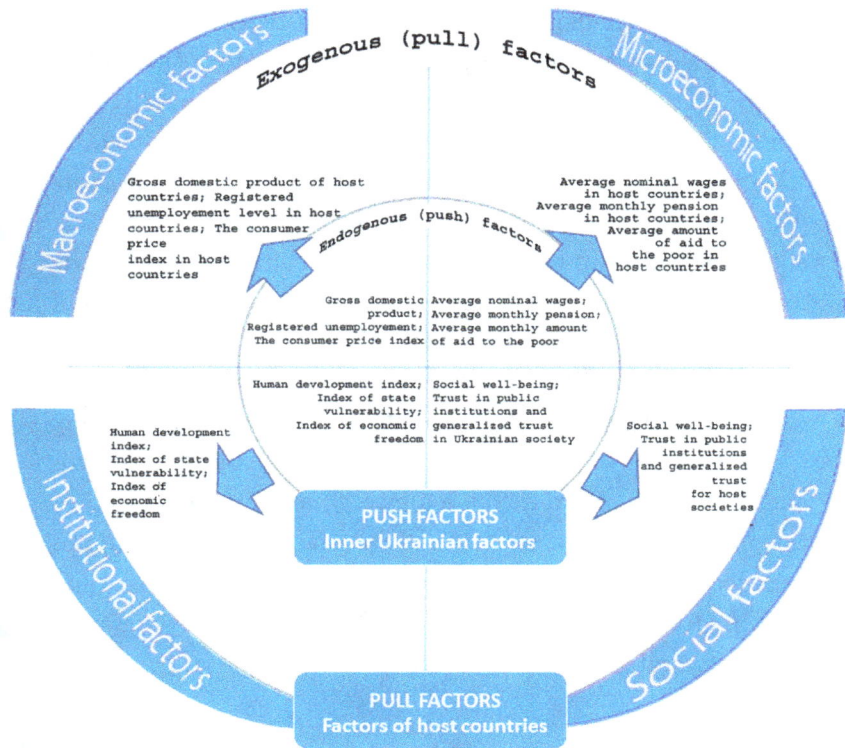

Figure 17: Theoretical modelling of the factors determining external migration from Ukraine. *Source*: Author's own figure.

migration intentions. A core assumption of the project is that perceptions of human rights and democracy, intentions and decisions are structured by various discourses; that is, they are culturally and socially embedded.

Therefore, modelling the interrelation of a wide range of factors determining external migration include taking into account the relative autonomy of these "finite domains" in their interrelation too. In analytical terms the model here can be presented as a system of push and pull factors which become real in comparative autonomous fields – microeconomic, macroeconomic, institutional and socio-cultural. Below we present the graphical interpretation of this vision, which will be further applied in modelling the external migration from Ukraine during the fourth wave (see the next subchapter).

Within the system of factors determining external migration, just as it is done traditionally, it would be reasonable to differentiate between two types of factors – push and pull factors. The former ones mostly determine why people leave their country of origin, what exactly does not satisfy a potential migrant in his or her own country. While the latter factors determine the vector of migration and the specific country chosen by a migrant according to his or her knowledge and imaginations. Besides that, in accordance to the theoretical methodological framework of neoinstitutionalism chosen here we divide all these factors into four groups (macroeconomic, microeconomic, institutional and social), and their mutual interaction is actually determining the migration intentions and migration behaviour.

4.2 Statistical model of economic, institutional and sociocultural factors of the external labour migration from Ukraine

External migration today attracts the attention of the many – general public, media and writers, politicians and researchers. Today's Ukrainian society is experiencing the fourth wave of emigration which partially has common features with the previous three waves but in some aspects it is also unprecedented. First of all, the scale of the phenomenon is impressive as such. During the first wave of emigration from Ukraine (1880–1914) about 1.5 million people left the country; during the second wave (1914–1939) around 200–300 thousand more people left Ukraine; during the third wave (1939 through the end of 1950s) over 300 thousand people moved abroad. As of 2015 (and we do not have data on 2016 so far), the fourth wave of emigration from Ukraine, according to some estimations, already involved over 7 million Ukrainian citizens.

This number may be somewhat misleading since it creates an impression of a truly catastrophic depopulation of Ukraine. It is important to remember here that the absolute majority of these migrants return to the country, sooner or later, sometimes for good, sometimes to engage in external migration later again. The impressive number of several millions of Ukrainians in this context should be treated as an indicator of a truly contemporary, highly dynamic society with its open migration regime and "rubbing out" of national borders. Remigration, circular migration, multiple citizenship, transnational families – all of these are the signs of the twenty-first century society.

As is well noted in this regard by E. Libanova, "it would be impossible to determine the real volume of migration transfers in Ukraine today. The differences are so big, they are twice as large as the average indicator. Thus, it is feasible to concentrate not on the absolute numbers as such, but on the structure and trends which are much more realistic" (Libanova, 2011, p. 15).

However, the impossibility of exact numerical calculations does not mean we cannot analyze the factors which force Ukrainians leave their country. This study is the attempt to combine the specifics of economic theory, statistics and sociology in studying the external migration factors for Ukraine on the basis of a wider spectrum of macroeconomic, microeconomic and sociological data and applying the statistical procedures of correlation, factor and regression analysis.

In the research field (primarily the economic one) similar studies are not numerous but we still can mention the availability of a certain corpus of works in this direction. Thus, Ukrainian researcher O. Pasichnyk used factor analysis to study the migration process as having several stages: the stage of potential migration, the stage of the immediate migration act, and the stage of migration process consequences (Pasichnyk, 2012).

V. Borshchevska applied correlation and regression analysis of an econometric model and came to the conclusion that external migration from Ukraine was primarily caused by low monthly average salary, as compared to other countries, and in time this emigration becomes more and more determined by the economic development factors (Borshchevska, 2012).

K. Shekhovtseva also applied correlation and regression analysis in her study to conclude that two factors influence, most of all: the number of Ukrainian emigrants: unemployment rate for the age group of 15–70 years old and the state of social protection measures (Shekhovtseva, 2013). Yu. Kurunova used regression modelling and created an econometric model for the influence on external migration of a range of economic factors (GDP per capita, income per capita, average monthly salary, indebtedness in salaries, consumer prices index, cost of bank credits in foreign currency, level of unemployment, the number of vacancies, the rate of employment via the state employment agency etc.) (Kurunova, 2012). All these studies contribute to the systemic re-evaluation of the external migration phenomenon and help develop the necessary tools for monitoring and forecasting the dynamics of emigration.

At the same time there are several gaps in the related research field and we are trying here to fill in these gaps. These are, namely: 1) little attention to institutional and social factors due to over-concentrated attention on macro- and microeconomic factors of emigration only; 2) analysis of the external migration factor for the whole period of the fourth wave, starting from the early 1990s till now, without distinguishing it specific phases. Only such an uninterrupted study could reveal the dynamics of factors forcing the Ukrainians to go abroad during all the years of the country's independence.

This work is based on the theoretical model which covers microeconomic, macroeconomic, institutional and sociocultural factors of the external migration of the Ukrainian population. The socioeconomic factors which determine external migration during the fourth wave need to be considered within the general socioeconomic context of Ukraine's development since the early years of its independence through now. In this regard, we suggest dividing the whole time period under study into two halves which are differentiated by the socioeconomic context of migration decisions and by the motivation of external migrants.

The first half – from the early 1990s until the start of the new millennium – was a period of severe socioeconomic crisis, radical decrease of life quality, money depreciation and critical indicators of GNP. During this first period, external migration from Ukraine was determined primarily by the economic factors: many enterprises stopped operating, delays with salary payments lasted for many months, the unemployment rate in the country was growing month by month. The key motivation of external migrants then was "escaping from misery"; going abroad was not the enrichment strategy, this was a strategy of survival.

The beginning of the second half of the fourth wave was in 2003. This year was the first one to record the growth in gross product. Here the process of gradual improvement began, and therefore, during this period Ukrainian migrants were driven by completely different motives: the desire to increase the family welfare rate, the need to settle issues with real estate, the necessity to finance education for children etc.

The whole analyzed period (more specifically, from the first quarter of 1992 through the second quarter of 2013) is divided into halves according to the dynamics of Ukrainian society's development. Tentatively, we can call the first half the period of deep socioeconomic crisis, while the second half is the period of stabilization and relative welfare. We assume that during these two periods the systems of external migration factors for the Ukrainians have changed: during the first half of the fourth wave (deep socioeconomic crisis) the most important were the factors of macro- and microeconomic nature, while for the second half (the period of relative stability and at least minimal welfare) the influence of sociocultural and institutional factors grew significantly. The dynamics of migration saldo throughout the whole fourth wave actually confirms this periodization of ours.

According to the selected theoretical model for further statistical modelling we have chosen the group of factors which are presented in Table 6.

The comparative analysis performed, of the average values of all factors throughout the whole period, indicates the statistically significant ($p < 0.05$) differences for the following factors: macroeconomic variables (budget deficit, GDP per capita, employment level, poverty index); microeconomic variables (the average monthly pension, the average monthly salary); institutional variables (the following indices constructed by World bank experts: Voice and Accountability index, Political Stability and Absence of Violence/Terrorism index, Regulatory Quality index, Rule of Law index, Control over Corruption index); and sociocultural variables (anomic demoralization index, anxiety index, social well-being index, the average point in the answers to "To which degree are you satisfied with your work?").

We performed the regression analysis for the dependence between migration saldo in Ukraine and each of four groups of

Table 6: Indicators and sources of data used in the modelling of Ukrainian external migration factors.

Indicators chosen	Data source
Macroeconomic variables: Budget deficit GDP per capita Employment rate Poverty index	Statistical data from public institutions of Ukraine and from international organizations: State Statistics Service of Ukraine; World Bank; UN Economic Commission for Europe
Microeconomic variables: Food products and soft drinks in the general structure of Ukrainian households' spending Average monthly size of pension Average monthly salary	
Institutional variables: Voice and Accountability index Political Stability and Absence of Violence/ Terrorism index Government Effectiveness index Regulatory Quality index Rule of Law index Control over Corruption index.	The World Bank's Government Indicators which combine statistical data with expert evaluations
Sociocultural variables: Anomic demoralization index Population anxiety index Social well-being index Average point of the answers to the question "To what extent are you satisfied with your work?" Yes-answers to the questions: "Do you plan to go abroad for temporary work in the nearest year?" % of the Ukrainians who answered "I am completely happy" on the question about happiness Average rate in the answers concerning the level of satisfaction with life	"Sociological monitoring"; "World Values Survey"
Dependent variable: Ukrainian migration saldo	Department for Immigration and Citizenship of Ukraine

Source: Author`s own data.

factors in the period from 1992 till 2002, and the influence on migration saldo turned out to be significant for one factor only – the average point of satisfaction with work ($p < 0.1$). However, in the period from 2003 till 2013 the influence of such factors as the Voice and Accountability index ($p < 0.1$), Government Effectiveness index and Control over Corruption index ($p < 0.05$) were also significant.

Further, we have performed the exploratory factor analysis to determine which factors influence migration saldo. This was carried out for each period separately by means of the key components method and setting the maximum at two forming factors. The choice of two factors only is confirmed by the scree test.

The matrix of factor loads for the period 1992–2002 (Table 7) shows that two factors explain 68.77% of the whole variation in the variable "migration seldom for Ukraine", and this is quite a high indicator of the explanatory power of the model. At this, the first factor is more correlated with the rest of the variables than the second one.

Factor 1 is closely correlated with the following indicators: Poverty index, Voice and Accountability index, Government Effectiveness index, Control over Corruption index, Social well-being index, and the average point on satisfaction with work answers.

Factor 2 is determined by the following indicators: budget deficit, unemployment rate, the share of food and soft drinks in household spending, and the average monthly pension.

To perform the multiple regression equation further, we select the most meaningful variables among the independent ones. According to our factor analysis these would be: budget deficit, unemployment level, poverty index, the share of food products and soft drinks in the general structure of household spending, the average monthly pension, Voice and Accountability index,

Table 7: Matrix of factor loads (1992–2002).

	Factor 1	Factor 2
Budget deficit	−0.074248	0.910809
Unemployment rate in Ukraine	0.370515	0.859785
Poverty index in Ukraine	−0.791954	0.326490
The share of food products and soft drinks in the total structure of household spending	−0.102500	0.978898
The average monthly pension	0.230740	−0.922528
Voice and Accountability index	−0.801065	0.211504
Government Effectiveness index	0.940492	−0.004137
Control over Corruption index	0.915296	0.130315
Social well-being index	0.891796	0.049519
The average point in the answers to the question "To which extent are you satisfied with your work?"	0.748246	−0.112219
Expl. Var	6.675087	5.016660
Prp. Totl	0.392652	0.3

Source: Author`s own data.

Government Effectiveness index, Control over Corruption index, Social well-being index, and finally, the average point in the answers concerning satisfaction with work.

The calculated correlation ratio is R = 0.76008663, and this means that there is a strong correlation between the selected indicators and the migration saldo, the determination coefficient $R^2 = 0.57773169$ shows that 57.77% of change in migration saldo is explained by the selected above factors. Our conclusions concerning the right choice of factors and correlation and also the adequacy of the model built (and of the obtained regression equation) is also confirmed by Fished-Snedecor distribution criterion ($p < 0.03179$).

Table 8: Regression model parameters (1992–2002).

	Beta	Std. Err.	B	Std. Err.	t(8)	p-level
Intercept			−1698.37	617.5295	−2.75027	0.025048
The average point in the answers to the question "To which extent are you satisfied with your work?"	0.581672	0.230623	554.17	219.7182	2.52218	0.035688
Budget deficit	0.542556	0.230623	16.25	6.9081	2.35257	0.046495

Source: Author`s own data.

It is noteworthy here that, in the regression equation (Table 8) only two factors are statistically significant ($p < 0.05$) – the average point in the answers related to work satisfaction and the budget deficit (in % of GDP).

The regression equation for the influence of selected indicators on migration saldo takes the following form:

(Migration saldo in Ukraine) = 0.581672 * (Average point in the answers to the question "To which extent are you satisfied with your work?") + 0,542556 * (budget deficit in % to GDP).

For the period 2003–2013 two factors (see Table 9) explain 73,82% of the whole dispersion (variation) of the dependent variable (migration saldo). The first factor is more correlated than the second one.

For the second half of the fourth wave in Ukrainian migration (2003–2013) Factor 1 is mostly correlated with the following independent variables: GDP per capita, Poverty index, the share of food and soft drinks in general household spending,

Table 9: Matrix of factor loadings (2003–2013).

	Factor 1	Factor 2
Budget deficit	−0.354665	−0.773621
GDP per capita	−0.915259	−0.347657
Unemployment rate in Ukraine	0.506409	−0.825809
Poverty index in Ukraine	0.960251	−0.078178
Food products and soft drinks share in the total structure of Ukrainian household spending	0.974427	0.005811
Average monthly pension	−0.867769	−0.472459
Average monthly salary	−0.983261	0.085343
Voice and Accountability index	−0.881809	0.218262
Political Stability and Absence of Violence/Terrorism index	−0.765230	0.468480
Government Effectiveness index	0.816837	0.508004
Regulatory Quality index	0.179896	0.436508
Rule of Law index	−0.537559	0.405754
Control over Corruption index	0.151452	0.917018
Anomic demoralization index	−0.066490	−0.005862
Social anxiety index	0.905230	0.119766
Social well-being index	−0.913262	0.312473
The average point in the answers to the question "To which extent are you satisfied with your work?"	−0.337341	0.349087
Expl. Var	8.957714	3.593120
Prp. Totl	0.526924	0.211360

Source: Author`s own data.

the average pension, the average salary, Voice and Accountability index, Political Stability and Absence of Violence/Terrorism index, Government Effectiveness index, Social anxiety index and Social well-being index.

Factor 2 is determined by the following factors: budget deficit, unemployment level and Control over Corruption index.

We should note here that for this period no correlation at all is observed for the following factors: Regulatory Quality index, Rule of Law index, Anomic demoralization index and the average point in the answers concerning satisfaction with work.

For further calculations of the multiple equation regression we select the most significant independent factors. According to the factor analysis above, there would be: budget deficit, GDP per capita, unemployment rate, Poverty index, the share of food products and soft drinks in the total household spending, the average monthly pension, the average monthly salary, Voice and Accountability index, Political Stability and Absence of Violence/ Terrorism index, Government Effectiveness index, Control over Corruption index, Social anxiety index and Social well-being index.

The correlation coefficient $R = 0.99994560$ confirms strong correlation between the selected factors and migration saldo, while the determination coefficient $R^2 = 0.99989119$ shows that 99.98% of changes in migration saldo can be explained by these selected factors. The conclusion on the right correlation and the adequacy of the built model (regression equation obtained) is confirmed by the results of Fisher-Snecedor distribution criteria ($p < 0.01956$).

In the regression equation statistically significant ($p < 0.05$) are the following parameters: Poverty index, GDP per capita, average monthly pension and Voice and Accountability index. Only for two factors (Government Effectiveness index and Social well-being index) $p > 0.05$ is insignificant but $p < 0.1$.

Thus, the regression equation would be as follows:

(Migration saldo in Ukraine) = -0.64972 * (Poverty index) + 0.21584 * (Government Effectiveness index) + 1.46783 * (GDP

Table 10: Regression model parameters (2003–2013).

	Beta	Std. Err. of Beta	B	Std. Err. of B	T	p-level
Intercept			−626.530	56.11770	−11.1646	0.056870
Poverty index in Ukraine	−0.64972	0.042703	−19.463	1.27919	−15.2149	0.041782
Government Effectiveness index	0.21584	0.033434	32.487	5.03230	6.4556	0.097837
GDP per capita	1.46783	0.081764	8.833	0.49204	17.9521	0.035426
Average monthly pension	−1.09797	0.083399	−0.047	0.00360	−13.1653	0.048263
Voice and Accountability index	0.42528	0.033201	22.557	1.76096	12.8094	0.049599
Social well-being index	−0.37216	0.038234	−6.007	0.61709	−9.7339	0.065174

Source: Author's own data.

per capita) -1.09797 * (average monthly pension) + +0.42528 * (Voice and Accountability index) -0.37216 * (Social well-being index).

We need to mention here additionally that all these factors determine Factor 1.

The regression equation for the newly formed factors' influence on migration saldo (Table 11) would be as follows:

(Migration saldo in Ukraine) = -0.874957 * (Factor 1) + 0.147494* (Factor 2), and Factor 1 is the only statistically significant factor (p<0.05). The calculated correlation coefficient R = 0.78730470 means there is a significant correlation between the selected factors and migration saldo, while the determination coefficient

Table 11: Parameters in the regression model of the newly formed factors (2003–2013).

	Beta	Std. Err. of Beta	B	Std. Err. of B	t	p-level
Intercept			6.0375	2.843875	2.12298	0.087175
Factor 1	−0,874957	0.206250	−12.8973	3.040230	−4.24222	0.008152
Factor 2	0,147494	0.206250	2.1741	3.040230	0.71512	0.506527

Source: Author`s own data.

$R^2 = 0.78730470$ shows that 78.73% of change in migration saldo is explained by these newly formed factors.

Therefore, we can conclude that the system of factors that determine the scale of external migration from Ukraine throughout the whole fourth wave has been changing. These changes are obviously caused by the related socioeconomic, sociocultural and institutional changes which took place in Ukraine during the period analyzed. These two periods in the post-Soviet development of Ukraine (the period of deep crisis – 1991–2002, and the period of stabilization and relative welfare – 2003–2013) concerning the migration behaviour factors presumably had the following specific features discovered by means of regression analysis. We have created two models to describe the impact of external migration factors for the two periods described above. For the first half of the fourth wave the regression equation shows only two significant factors – the average point in the answers to the question "To which extent are you satisfied with your work" and the budget deficit. During the same period of time the key factors of external migration were related to the specific features of the labour market and labour activity as such; this was also the period of long-term delays in salary payments and overall, the period of the lowest level of life quality. A significant correlation with budget deficit, in our opinion, reveals the sensitivity of the population to the problems related to public financing of the social protection system, infrastructure development and social services for population.

For the second half of the fourth wave the key factors determining external migration were the poverty rate and the institutional factors related to efficient governing, the ability to influence political decisions in the country and corruption fighting. It is obvious that during this period of time social demand becomes more complex, more diversified, and so does people's vision of life quality level. This shift can be described as the move from purely materialistic demands (and accordingly, factors of external migration) to mixed ones (materialistic and also post-materialistic) (R. Inglehart et al., 2005).

The data presented by other authors are relevant to our results. For example, O. Hodovanska noted: "Research materials provide us with the evidence to state that the aims of labour migrants during the mid 1990s–early 2000s include excessive savings, up to the most vital items, so that to satisfy the family needs back in Ukraine, while at the current stage most of the earned money are used for satisfaction of the own life necessities, including intangible ones, which is partially related to getting to know the country of work better, its culture and traditions" (Hodovanska, 2010).

The same trend, in the context of more systemic value and sociocultural transformations was emphasized by Zaremba (2014): "view on the migrant as a physical labour force is transformed under the concept of postmaterialism … today's Ukrainian labour migrant is more often the carrier of highly specific professional skills, also having certain set of values and life priorities, strategies and standpoints which are being formed within the general orientation on 'searching for the better' (life, conditions, opportunities)".

Described here, by means of system modelling, dynamics of external migration factors at the fourth wave in its publicistic discourse is described as being in transition to the fifth wave. For example, Shafranosh (2016) put it like this: "the fifth wave of Ukrainian emigration will be different from the previous ones in its important detail – the portrait of Ukrainian emigrant, since today's Ukrainian is looking for not only higher income and security for him/herself and his/her family, but also wishes to integrate into the international community, but not to be simply a cheap labour".

Overall, today the term "fifth wave" in relation to external migration is already used by several authors to describe the dynamics of external migration factors; however, it requires its deeper conceptualization, and as of now, we can forecast that in the next couple of years this term will quickly get conventional. There are also several important factors influencing the volume of external migration but not considered in this model. Taking them into account would be necessary and appropriate in further research on external migration factors in Ukraine. These are, first of all, the features of migration regimes in the countries that became the key recipients of migration inflows from Ukraine. Adding these indicators of migration regimes to the model of external migration factors would require creating the system of related indicators. As of today all scientific attempts to measure and quantify the features of migration regimes have been rather sketchy: usually only two types of migration regimes are mentioned – the one requiring a visa and visa-free. A more detailed system of migration regime indicators in the future should include the following issues: the rate of visa rejections, visa costs, opportunities for further legal employment once a visa is obtained etc.

The forecast on further transformations within the system of migration behaviour factors in Ukraine must proceed from the current trends among which there are two major ones: the first one is related to the crisis phenomena in Ukraine, radical poverty and high unemployment rate, depreciation of hryvnya, inflation growth and problems related to the military conflict on the Donbass; while the second one is directly connected to the expected liberalization of the migration regime with the EU countries in parallel to complicating migration regime with the Russian Federation. Both trends suggest that in the near future external migration from Ukraine will only increase.

Conclusions

External migration in today's world occurs in unprecedented volumes, and new forms of it are emerging all the time. Growing mobility of population, new transport, communication and other technological opportunities, liberalization of migration regimes and emergence of supranational regional structures have all caused the current situation in which opportunities to go abroad at nearly any age got the largest ever possible share of population, and this becomes the reality for nearly all countries of the world. And Ukraine is no exception to these processes.

The country has a rich history of external migration which is rather well studied. Two of the four waves in external migration

How to cite this book chapter:
Bilan, Y 2017 *Migration of the Ukrainian Population: Economic, Institutional and Sociocultural Factors.* Pp. 247–257. London: Ubiquity Press. DOI: https://doi.org/10.5334/bbg.f. License: CC-BY 4.0

from Ukraine (the first and the fourth) were voluntary, while the two remaining waves (the second and the third) were forced ones. Historical reconstruction of the key specific features of Ukrainian emigration is experiencing a range of problems, among which lack of available data is probably the most serious one. At the same time, the current stage in Ukrainian emigration is open for research, and an extremely wide range of sources, methods and tools for data collection and further analysis is available. However, we should note there is a certain methodological gap in this field since theoretical and methodological achievements of various related disciplines are not yet integrated into the system of joint research on external migration processes.

Speaking chronologically, the fourth wave of external migration from Ukraine started with the fall of the Iron Curtain. According to many researchers, it is still ongoing. However, its qualitative features have been changing all the time, and thus, external migration today is very much different from the migration of the early 1990s. The socioeconomic factors determining the dynamics of external migration from Ukraine are to be considered in the general context of socioeconomic dynamics of Ukrainian society development. Within the fourth wave of Ukrainian emigration we see at least two periods which are rather different from each other in terms of institutional regulation of external migration and also in terms of the socioeconomic context of migration decision-making, migrants' initial motivations and socioeconomic consequences from migration processes.

The first period lasted from the beginning of the 1990s until the early 2000s. It was developing on the back of severe economic and political crises, both having consequences easily comparable with the Great Depression in the USA. Aside from economic crisis, this time period was also characterized by a dramatic decrease of the welfare level in the country and nearly absolute depreciation of all people's savings. At the very beginning of the first period of the fourth emigration wave, the migration flow consisted mostly of the representatives of ethnic minorities which had strong institutional support for their migration decisions and support on the side of informal social networks in the receiving societies. Highly qualified professionals followed them, and their leave was a typical example of the brain drain, that is, the loss of valuable human capital by the country of origin.

In the middle of the 1990s emigration attributed new economic and social features: this was the time of mass migration of people with blue-collar qualifications, rather vulnerable in both economic and social senses. Most of them were employed illegally in the receiving countries. The specific features of this period were:

- Materialistic motivation to emigrate, orientation primarily on the opportunities to earn money and solve the financial problems of the families back at home
- Absence or low intensity of communication between the migrants and their families left in Ukraine
- Circular migration was hardly possible due to illegal employment (and thus, the related risk of being deported) and also due to problems with getting a visa again later
- Absence of social and legal protection caused by illegal employment; human trafficking was a common practice which led to further victimization of Ukrainian emigrants. Additional problems with the law were caused by minor illegal activities practiced by the migrants, frequent visa regime violations etc.

- Remittances from Ukrainian labour migrants mostly became part of a totally inefficient "economy of subsistence" within the migrants' households in Ukraine (that is, they have been only consumed, disinvested, spent by the families on current spending by the principle "to get by not to get ahead")
- Labour emigration is socially perceived as a key problem, accompanied with alarmism and moral panicking in media; in mass perception external migration is envisioned as a negative phenomenon, comparable with country's depopulation and/or severe economic crisis

These rather negative features of the first period in the fourth wave of emigration caused the widespread use of the notion "zarobitchanyn" in relation to labour migrants which has an absolutely negative connotation and thus adds to a rather distorted imagine of labour emigration from Ukraine.

The second period of the fourth wave of Ukrainian migration started in the 2000s, with the start of an economic revival and the first indicators of economic growth in the country. The specific features of this period in external migration are the following:

- Change in motivation for migration, shift to the mixed materialistic-postmaterialistic motivation which was mostly explicitly revealed among younger migrants who demonstrated such new motives for migration as the desire for self-actualization, wishes to get new knowledge, skills and impressions, strive for better education etc.
- More attention to non-financial aspects of life in the receiving societies, namely, the level of institutions' efficiency, higher quality of education, better developed healthcare and legal support etc.

- Intensified communication between migrants and their families back in Ukraine, and consequently, less destructive influence on the families previously caused by constant absence of some family members which is not compensated by their virtual presence
- Circular migration became more frequent and easy to organize, and this also had positive influence on family life of many labour migrants.
- Financial expenditures of migrant-dependent households back in Ukraine were very much re-oriented. Previously hypothesized regularity was now confirmed: in the periods of economic underdevelopment private transfers from abroad are mostly spent on the current needs of migrants' households, while in times of better economic environment and observable growth such remittances are mostly spent on real estate, vehicle purchases, university education for children, and also as an initial capital for starting one's own business. Similar conclusions concerning external migration from Poland have been drawn by one of the leading Polish researchers, R. Jończy. This author has studied the external transfers to migrants' households in Opole voivodship and noted that despite significant growth of transfers (at least 2.15 billion zlot during 2004, the year of Poland's entry to the EU), they did not contribute to economic value of the region in question. Members of migrants' families spent these transfers on everyday spending which was often an economic waste, including commodities and services which were actually produced outside the native region. As a result, assets which could have contributed to the economy of the region and stimulate its development,

were at least partially returned to places of their origin (Jończy, 2000).

- The legal status of many migrants also became much better regulated; legal employment and work permits became a more common practice; several intergovernmental agreements concerning legal employment opportunities for Ukrainian citizens in the selected European countries have helped fight human trafficking and criminal victimization of the Ukrainians in the receiving societies.
- Gradual integration of Ukrainian migrants into the receiving communities, transnational families have become quite common
- Gradual deproblemization of external migration presentations in media and mass discourse

Therefore, during these two periods (potentially, the two first periods, since this wave is still ongoing) of the fourth wave of external migration from Ukraine, significant changes already happened in its key features. However, several migration imaginations have remained unchanged throughout the whole period under study. For example, our empirical research records positive stereotyping of European receiving countries overall. The Ukrainians mostly see Europe in a rather sketchy way – as a homogenous well-maintained society with a high quality of all aspects of welfare. Such imaginations absolutely ignore any differences inside the EU, including those in levels of life quality, much like the social stratification of the receiving societies and complex socioeconomic dynamics of these countries' development as such. The additional discursive unit to that is negative stereotyping of their own society in Ukrainian minds, which can be interpreted as a "self-fulfilling prophecy" (Merton, 1968). This, in turn, becomes one of the reasons for low efficiency of reforms in the country and not very impressive results in the fight against corruption in particular.

The political crisis of 2013–2014 and the signing of the Association Agreement between Ukraine and the EU, along with further liberalization of the migration regime for Ukraine, most probably, would lead to another period in the fourth wave of Ukrainian emigration. Today we can already note some of its new features. As with any other forecast, speaking about potential further development of Ukrainian migration we must keep in mind "the tree of opportunities", the most and the least likely directions in its development. Obviously, the most important variable in such forecasts, and this applies not only to migration, but also to more general forecasts (social dynamics, economic development etc.) would be Ukraine's progress in its Eurointegration intentions. Uncertainty of the European Union's future, foreshown by the Brexit, leads us to consider not only moderately optimistic scenarios of further events, but also of problematic, pessimistic ones.

Sound and reasonable analysis of the current situation with Ukrainian external migration allows us assume that in the near future the following its features would strengthen:

- The circular nature of migration: when going abroad for work does not mean the human resource is wasted for good, and this more stable circular migration would allow gradually transforming brain drain into brain gain
- a less dysfunctional social and psychological consequences for migrants' families due to wider use of communications which help establish at least the virtual presence of migrants

- transnational families would become more common, as well as the so-called host families
- gender rebalancing which already started during the early years of the fourth wave would become more obvious
- further shift from economic/materialistic migration motives to more institutional and sociocultural ones (which are mixed materialist/post-materialistic)
- quality changes in the legal status of labour migrants and their legal protection, more guarantees for labour rights due to large-scale recruiting programs initiated at the level of governments and supported by large businesses

There are also reasons to suppose that at the next stage of Ukrainian emigration the diaspora's role would be much less important, for new migrants, first of all. There are many reasons for that, including: growing individualization of cultural, social and economic lives in many countries; fewer discrimination barriers which previously used to force migrants to establish communities for support and protection from a rather unwelcoming society; rapidly developing social segmentation by the lifestyle principle, by values, interests, professional specialization (as opposed to previous segmentation by language, culture, religion and/or ethnicity).

Despite how optimistic the above may sound, there would also be some potential negative trends. Both at home and abroad in the near future the Ukrainians would most probably suffer from the ongoing precarization. Today's neoliberal flexibility of the labour market would further shift the load of risks and uncertainty from employers on employees. And the first "victim" in it would be social guarantees and chances for life-long stable employment. We need to note here that labour precarization is the unavoidable consequence of neoliberal reforms, in any economy, due to lesser influence of the state and retreat from the paternalistic model of public administration. This is exactly the vector of the ongoing reforms in Ukraine today. Note that the advisor to the Minister for Finance of Ukraine is the American economist A. B. Laffer, who indeed is the follower of neoliberalism and also the former advisor to such well-known politicians as M. H. Thatcher and R. W. Reagan. Moreover, Slovak and Polish neoliberal reformers I. Mikloš and L. Balcerowicz are the co-heads of the Group of Strategic Advisors supporting reforms in Ukraine; the latter is also the President's representative in the Cabinet of Ministers of Ukraine. Therefore, we have reasons to state that the Ukrainian state today, at least to some extent, is on its way to Reaganomics and Thatcherism.

Very similar processes are actually observed in many other countries. They totally comply with the interests of the largest employers since such policies minimize their economic risks and enable a more flexible and timely reaction to changes in the market environments, for example, by means of production reorganization and/or staff cuts. In most cases trade unions are excluded from the processes of decision-making (as it is hard to imagine the trade union of freelancers, for example).

At the same time, Ukraine has some local features in this regard. First of all, precarization contrasts itself with the comparatively recent paternalistic past which used to guarantee employment, free education and healthcare, state-owned place of residence etc. In the Soviet times, loss of a job could have only been initiated by an employee, not an employer. Till now, a large share of the Ukrainian population perceives the absence of labour right guarantees as a stress factor, as one of the elements of social deprivation. And this is one of the key reasons behind the popularity and significant social influence of rather leftist and populist political groups (which can be called "Ukrainian" only formally). Secondly, there are objective reasons to state that the welfare level in Ukraine is among the lowest in Europe. The specific feature of the Ukrainian economy is the poverty of working population. Today, just as during the crisis of the 1990s, having a constant place of work does not insure one from poverty. In this context, neoliberal reforms accompanied by the ongoing economic crisis leads the whole country to the situation when labour precarization becomes an important push factor.

Therefore, European fears related to migration risks in case of visa regime abolition become quite understandable. These risks are getting more and more real, considering the combination of push factors on the Ukrainian side and a range of economic, institutional and discursive pull factors on the European side. However, a visa-free regime for Ukraine itself can become a vital innovative factor which may potentially intensify institutional reforms in the country and attract more Western investments into the Ukrainian economy. In the longer term, a visa-free regime may also influence the political elites (by minimizing their authoritarian intentions, still widely popular) and general public (by strengthening the right, more objective perception of democratic models of European governance).

The problem of migration risks as of today is very much understudied, in both theoretical and empirical aspects. Therefore, today there is no predictive model to measure and assess the migration risks which potentially can arise after the introduction of a visa-free regime for Ukrainian citizens crossing the EU borders. Until such predictive models are developed, all related discussions within the administrative, expert and public discourses are very much politically biased. Thus, probably the only way to forecast the migration risks related to visa-free regime between

Ukraine and the EU would be to study the corresponding experience of the countries with similar experiences. For example, back in 2004 Poland became the member of the European Union. As noted by R. Jończy and D. Rokita-Poskart, who studied the empirical materials of the Opole voevodship: "Poland's entry to the EU caused significant changes in the employment of the Pols, especially during the years straight after the EU entry. Then, growth in the number of Pols employed abroad was recorded, however, already after 2008 the dynamics of this indicator became much more stable" (Jończy and Rokita-Poskart, 2014).

Therefore we can predict that in the context of external migration, a visa-free regime in the short term would, most probably, have certain dysfunctional consequences for both sending and receiving societies, primarily due to sharp and significant growth of illegal employment. At the same time, the long-term potential advantages from a visa-free regime concern changes in labour migration as such: from being the factor of constant social, economic and legal destabilization, it will turn into the factor of positive institutional, economic and sociocultural changes at the borders of the European Union. In the opposite case, the continuation for forced ghettoization of Ukraine straight behind "the closed doors" would preserve the destabilizing nature of migration, and most probably, would also have negative impacts on the institutional, political, economic and sociocultural dimensions of further development of Ukrainian society's.

List of References

Adamic, L. (1932) *Laughing in the Jungle: The Autobiography of an Immigrant in America.* New York: Harper & Brothers.

Alt, J. (2003) *Leben in der Schattenwelt. Problem complex illegale migration. Neue erkentnisse zur lebens situation "illegaler" Migranten aus Munchen und anderen Irten Deutchlands.* Karlsruhe: Loeper Literaturverlag. pp. 65–298.

Arango, J. (2000) "Explaining migration: a critical view". *International Social Science Journal,* 52(165):283–296.

Bahryanyi, I. (1946) "Chomy ya ne khochu povertatysya do SSSR". *Ukraiinskyi sukhodolovyi instytut.* 7. Viden.

Balakireva O. M., Shestakovskyi O. P. (2012) "Masshtaby trudovoii mihratsii ukraintsiv: dosvid kilkisnoi otsinky". *Visnyk Kharkivskoho natsionalnoho universytetu im.V. N. Karazina.* 993/29. *Seriya: Sotsiolohichni doslidzhennya suchasnoho suspilistva: metodolohiya, teoriya, metody.* p. 102–106 .

Bauer, T. and K. F. Zimmermann. (1999) *Assessment of Possible Migration Pressure and Its Labour Market Impact Following*

EU Enlargement to Central and Eastern Europe, IZA Research Report No. 3, Bonn.

Baubock, R. (2003) "Towards a political theory of migrant transnationalism". *International Migration Review,* 37(3):700–723.

Beauchemin C., Gonzalez-Ferrer A. (2009) *Multi-Country Surveys on International Migration: An Assessment of Selection Biases in Destination Countries,* MAFE Working Paper 3.

Behdad, A. (1994) *Belated Travelers: Orientalism in the Age of Colonial Dissolution.* Durham, NC: Duke University Press.

Bhagwati, J. N. (ed.) (1976) Taxing the Brain Drain, Vol. 1: A Proposal, Amersterdam: North-Holland.

Bilan, Y. (2014a). Labour Migration of Ukraine's Population: Scientific and Public Discourse. *Transformations in Business & Economics, 13*(1), 196–208.

Bilan, Y. (2014b). Migration Aspirations on the Outskirts of Europe: Social and Economic Dimensions. *Transformations in Business & Economics, 13*(2B), 604–614.

Bilan, Y. (2015). Specifics of EUMAGINE transnational migration project. *Sotsiologicheskie Issledovaniya*(1), 146–147.

Biletskyi, L. (1951) *Ukraiinski pionery v Kanadi 1891–1951.* Vinipeg.

Bilokin, S. (1999) *Masovyi terror yak zasib derzhavnogo upravlinnya v SRSR, 1917–1941 rr.* Dzhereloznavche doslidzhennya. Kyiv.

Bitten, N. (2015) A new gender order and a new media in Russia. http://www.zafeminizm.org/219-a-new-gender-order-and-a-new-media-in-russia.html. Accessed 20 April 2017.

Blunt, A. (2007) "Cultural geographies of migration: mobility, transnationality and diaspora". *Progress in Human Geography,* 31(5):684–694.

Biaszczak, A. Firmy chca Ukraincow (2005) http://www4.rp.pl/Rynek-pracy/309309771-Firmy-chca-Ukraincow.html. Accessed 21 April 2017.

Boeri, T. and Briicker, H. (2001) "Eastern Enlargement and EU-Labour Markets: Perceptions, Challenges and Opportunities". *World Economics,* 2(1):49–68.

Bohning, W. R. (1978) "International Migration and the Western World: Past, Present and Future". *International Migration,* 16: 11–22. doi:10.1111/j.1468-2435.1978.tb00959.x

Boneva, B. S., Frieze, I. H. (2001) "Toward a concept of a migrant personality". *Journal of Social Issues,* 57(3):477–491.

Borshchevska, V. D. (2012) "Analiz faktoriv, shcho vplyvayut na riven emihratsii z Ukraiiny za rehionamy". *Upravlinnya rozvytkom, 13.* pp. 141–145.

Boucher, S., Stark, O., Taylor, J. E. (2005) "A Gain with a Drain: Evidence from Rural Mexico on the New Economics of the Brain Drain". *Invited paper, 14th World Congress of the International Economic Association,* Marrakech, Morocco, August 29–September 2.

Bourdieu , P. (1989) "Social Space and Symbolic Power". *Sociological Theory,* Vol. 7, No. 1: pp. 14–25.

Boyd, M. (1989) "Family and personal networks in international migration: Recent developments and new agenda". *International Migration Review,* 23(3):238–270.

Burawoy, M. (1999) "Transition without Transformation: Russia's Involutionary Road to Capitalism". *East European Politics and Societies,* 15(2):269–290.

Bustamante, J. A. (1979) "Emigration Indocumentada a los Estados Unidos". In *Indocumentados: Mitos y Realidades,* 23–67.

Carling, J. (2002) "Migration in the age of involuntary immobility: theoretical reflections and Cape Verdian experiences". *Journal of Ethnic and Migration Studies,* 28(1):5–42.

Carlson, M., Listhaug, O. (2007) "Citizens perceptions of human rights practices: An analysis of 26 countries". *Journal of Peace Research,* 44(4):465–483.

Cavanagh, C. (2003) "Postkolonialna Polska. Biala plama na mapie wspiiczesnej teorii". *Teksty Drugie.* 64:18–19.

Chirkov, V., Vansteenkiste, M., Tao, R., Lynch, M. (2007) "The role of self-determined motivation and goals for study abroad in the adaptation of international students". *International Journal of Intercultural Relations,* 31(2):199–222.

Chopovskyi, V. (2011) "Chuyesh, brate miy ..." *Do 120-littya ukrajinskogo poselennya v Kanadi. Narodoznavchi zoshyty.* 6:917–932.

Chornovol, I. (2002) *Ukraiinska fraktsiya Halytskoho Krajovoho sejmu. 1861–1901.* Lviv: Instytut Ukraiinoznavstva im I. Krypyakevycha.

Christiansen, T., Duke, S., Kirchner, E. (2012) *Journal of European Integration, special issue: The Maastricht Treaty. Second Thoughts after 20 Years.* 34(7):685–698.

Clemens, M. A., Ogden, T. N. (2014) Migration as a strategy for household finance: A research agenda on remittances, payments, and development. CGD Working Paper #354.

Cohen, E. (2017), Effect of Welfare and Employment Policies on the Correlation between Migration and Unemployment, *Economics and Sociology*, Vol. 10, No 1, pp. 246–264.

Cohen, R. (1987) *The New Helots: Migrants in the International Division of Labour.* Aldershot: Gower Publishers.

Collins, D., Morduch, J., Rutherford, S., Ruthven, O. (2009) *Portfolios of the Poor: How the World's Poor Live on $2 a Day.* Princeton, NJ: Princeton University Press.

Collyer, M. (2006) How does a culture of migration affect motivations for migration. Paper presented at the IMISCOE conference on Poverty, Vulnerability and Migration Choice. Geneva,18–19 May 2006.

Communication from the Commission to the Council and the European Parliament on a Community Immigration Policy (2000). Commission of the European Communities. Brussels. 29.

Communication from the Commission to the European Parliament, the Council, the European Economic and Social Committee and the Committee of the Regions, A Common Immigration Policy for Europe : Principles, actions and tools (2008) Commission of the European Communities.

"Council Directive 2003/109/EC of 25 November 2003 concerning the status of third-country nationals who are long-term residents" (2004). *Official Journal of the European Union.* pp. 44–53.

"Council Directive 2005/71/EC of 12 October 2005 on a specific procedure for admitting third-country nationals for the purposes of scientific research" (2005). *Official Journal of the European Union.* pp. 15–22.

Dahlstedt, M. (2001) "Democracy and national imagination: Assumptions of identity and belonging in studies on democracy." *Sociologisk Forskning,* 38(3–4):40–70.

Danylenko, V. M. (2002) *Borotba z "ukraiinskym burzhuaznym natsionalizmom". Politychnyj teror i teroryzm v Ukrajini. XIX-XX st.* Naukova dumka. pp. 707–724.

de Haas, H. (2007) *The myth of invasion. Irregular migration from West Africa to the Maghreb and the European Union. IMI Research report.* University of Oxford, International Migration Institute.

Desyatky ukraintsev staly zhertvamy obmana na "sezonnykh rabotakh" v Finlyandii. http://news.finance.ua/ru/~/1/0/all/2013/08/06/3067430. Accessed 20 April 2017.

DiMaggio, P. J. (1988) "Interest and agency in institutional theory." *Institutional Patterns and Organizations: Culture and Environment.* Cambridge: Ballinger Publishing Company. pp 3–22.

Dity ne spryimayut zarobitchan za batkiv – dyvitsya povnu versiyu dokumentalnoho filmu "Zhinka-bankomat". http://gazeta.ua/articles/culture/diti-ne-sprijmayut-zarobitchan-za-batkiv-divitsya-povnu-versiyu-dokumentalnogo-f/513453. Accessed 20 April 2017.

Dity zarobitchan ranishe pochynayut pyty i kuryty. http://gazeta.ua/articles/ls-children/_diti-zarobitchan-ranishe-pochinayut-piti-i-kuriti/499360. Accessed 20 April 2017.

Durand, J. Massey, D. S. (2004) "Appendix: The Mexican Migration Project" In: *Crossing the Border: Research from the Mexican Migration Project.* New York: Russell Sage Foundation. pp. 301–336.

Duvell, F. (2006). Ukraine – Europe's Mexico: Research Resource Report 1. Oxford. Compas. https://www.compas.ox.ac.uk/fileadmin/files/Publications/Research_projec... Accessed 21 April 2017.

Duvell, F. (ed.) (2006) *Illegal Immigration in Europe – Beyond Control.* Houudmills: Palgrave Macmillan.

Duvell, F. (2014) "Migration and brain drain vs. return and development: the case of Ukraine". In: *Brain Drain – Brain Gain: svitovyu kontekst ta ukraiinski realii.* Lviv, 2014. pp. 30–41.

Efionayi-Mader, D., Chimienti, M., Dahinden, J. and Piguet, E. (2001) *Asyldestination Europa – Eine Geographie der Asylbewegungen.* Zurich, Seismo.

Ensuring social security benefits for Ukrainian migrant workers (2012) Grupa tehnichnoii pidtrymky z pytan gidnoii pratsi ta bjuro MOP dlya kraiin Tseentralnoii ta Skhidnoii Yevropy. MBP.

ESS Round 6: European Social Survey Round 6 Data (2012). Data file edition 2.1. Norwegian Social Science Data Services, Norway – Data Archive and distributor of ESS data.

Estoniiya sproshchuye vydachu viz ukraintsiyam iz zony ATO. http://www.wz.lviv.ua/news/77152. Accessed 21 April 2017.

Eurostat. Asylum and first time asylum applicants by citizenship, age and sex annual aggregated data. http://ec.europa.eu/eurostat/en/web/products-datasets/-/MIGR_ASYAPPCTZA. Accessed 21 April 2017.

Gallardo, G. D. L., Korneeva, E., & Strielkowski, W. (2016). Integration of Migrants in the EU: Lessons and Implications for the EU Migration Policies. *Journal of International Studies,* 9(2), 244–253.

Fan, C. S., Stark, O. (2011) "A Theory of Migration as a Response to Occupational Stigma." *International Economic Review,* 52(2):549–571.

Farion, I. (2009) Khochesh maty ukrainsku pensiyu? Davai 100 "baksiv"! http://archive.wz.lviv.ua/articles/71265. Accessed 21 April 2017.

Farrell, H., Hiritier, A. (2007). "Introduction: Contested Competences in the European Union". *West European Politics,* 38 (2):227–243.

Favell, A., Guiraudon, V. (2010) *The Sociology of the EU.* Basingstoke: Palgrave.

Fawcett, J. T., Arnold F. (1987) *Explaining Diversity: Asian and Pacific Immigration Systems. Pacific Bridges: The New Immigration from Asia and the Pacific Islands.* Staten Island: Center for Migration Studies.

Fevre, R. (1984) *Cheap Labour and Racial Discrimination.* Aldershot: Gower.

Findlay, A. M., El, L. (1999) "Methodological issues in researching migration." *Professional Geographer,* 51:50–59.

Fischer, S. (2008) Executive Summary. Ukraine: Quo Vadisi Chaillot Paper. 108. European Union Institute for Security Studies. p. 9–24.

Fiut, A. (2007) "In the Shadow of Empires. Postcolonialism in Central and Eastern Europe – Why not?" In: *From Sovietology to Postcoloniality.* pp. 33–40.

Fligstein, N. (2001) "Fields, power, and social skill: a critical analysis of the new institutionalisms". *Ekonomicheskaya sotsiologiya.* 2(1):4–25.

Freeman, G. P. (1979) *Immigration Labor and Racial Conflict in Industrial Society: The French and British Experience 1945–75.* Princeton: Princeton University Press, 1979.

Glaser, B. G., Strauss, A. L. (2006) *The Discovery of Grounded Theory. Strategies for Qualitative Research,* 4th ed. A Division of Transaction Publishers, New Brunswick (USA) and London (UK).

Gorny, A. (2005) „Wybrane zagadnienia podejscia jakosciowego w badaniach nad migracjami miedzynarodowymi", *Przeglad Polonijny.* 31(3):155–170.

Goss, J., Lindquist, B. (1995) "Conceptualizing international labor migration: a structuration perspective." *International Migration Review.* 29:317–351.

Governance indicators by the World bank. http://data.worldbank.org/data-catalog/worldwide-governance-indicators. Accessed 21 April 2017.

Granovetter, M. (1999) "Coase Encounters and Formal Models: Taking Gibbons Seriously." *Administrative Science Quarterly,* 44:158–162.

Gregory, D. (2000) Discourse. In: Johnston, R.J., Gregory, D., Pratt; G. and Watts, M. (eds.). *The Dictionary of Human Geography.* Oxford: Blackwell. pp. 180–181.

Grishnova, E. A., Brintseva, E. G. (2014) Prekarizatsiya kak proyavleniye krizisnyh yavleniy v socialno-trudovoi sfere Ukrainy. Doklad predstavlen v ramkakh sessii "Reaktsiya rynka truda na krizis", XIV Aprelskya mezhdunarodnya nauchnaya konferentsiya "Modernizatsiya ekonomiki obshchestva", 2–5 aprelya, 2013, Moskva.

Haidutisikyi, A. (2014) Skasuvannya vizovoho rezhymu z YeS: mozhlyvosti i ryzyky dlya Ukraiiny. Chomu do naslidkiv potribno hotuvatysya vzhe zaraz. http://gazeta.dt.ua/international/ skasuvannya-vizovogo-rezhimu-z-yes-mozhlivosti-y-riziki-dlya-ukrayini-chomu-do-naslidkiv-potribno-gotuvatisya-vzhe-zaraz-_.html Accessed 21 April 2017.

Hall, P., G. J. Ikenberry (1989) *The State.* Milton Keynes. Open University Press.

Huntington, S. P. (1993) "The Clash of Civilizations." *Foreign Affairs,* 72(3):22–49.

Hanusyk, Yu. B. (2013) "Prychyny ta naslidky inflyatsii: vitchyznyanyi ta zarubizhnyi dosvid" *Zbirnyk naukovykh prats Natsionalnogo universytetu derzhavnoii podatkovoii sluzhby Ukraiiny. 2.* pp. 42–52.

Harris, J., Todaro, M. (1970) "Migration, Unemployment, and Development: A Two-Sector Analysis." *American Economic Review,* 60:126–142.

Herasymchuk, I. "Ya boyalasya, shcho v meni upiznajut' ukrajinku". http://archive.wz.lviv.ua/articles/76615. Accessed 21 April 2017.

Hodovanska, O. (2010) "Ukrajinska trudova mihratsiya: etnolohichnyj aspect" *Svitohlyad. No 6.* pp. 67–71.

Hollifield, J. F. (1998) "Migration, Trade and the Nation-State: The Myth of Globalization." *UCLA Journal of International Law and Foreign Affairs,* 3(2):595–636.

Hrabovych, O. (1992) Do pytannya akulturyzatsii ukraiinskoii emigratsii. Ukraiinska emigraciya. istoriya i suchasnist. pp. 207–215.

Hrytsak, Ya. (1995) "Shifting Identities in Western and Eastern Ukraine." *The East and Central Europe Program Bulletin.* 5(3). pp. 21–32.

Hutsal, P. Z. (2005) *Ukraiinska emihratsiya v Kanadi i SSHA ta natsionalno-vyzvolnyi rukh na zakhidnoukraiinskyh zemlyah (1914–1923).* Natsionalna akademiya nauk Ukraiiny.

Iglicka, K. (2003) "The foreign labour market in Poland", in K. Iglicka (ed.), Migration and labour markets in Poland and Ukraine, 40–50. Warsaw: Institute of Public Affairs.

Iievrosyritstvo po-ukrainskomu (2011) http://www.dua.com.ua/2011/035/arch/9.shtml Accessed 21 April 2017.

Level of corruption perception in Ukraine according to the Transparency International Corruption Perception Index http://cpi.transparency.org/cpi2011/results/. Accessed 21 April 2017.

Inglehart, R. (1977) *The Silent Revolution.* Princeton University Press. Princeton..

Inglehart, R., Norris, P. (2003) "The true clash of civilizations". *Foreign Policy,* (135): pp. 62–70.

Inglehart, R., Welzel, C. (2005) *Modernization, Cultural Change and Democracy: The Human Development Sequence.* New York: Cambridge University Press.

Institute of Sociology of the National Academy of Sciences of Ukraine. http://i-soc.com.ua/institute/smonit_2013.pdf Accessed 21 April 2017.

Intervju z p. I. Shvab, menedzherom Mizhnarodnoho pravozakhysnoho tsentru "La Strada – Ukraina" (2006), Ekspres, # 139.

Yuskiv, B. (2009) *Hlobalizatsiya i trudova mihratsiya v Iievropi.* – Rivne.

Ivankova-Stetsiuk, O., Seleshchuk, H. (2012) "Vyklyky ta adaptatsiyni rezervy polilokalnykh rodyn ukrainskykh trudovykh mihrantiv", in Transnatsionalini simyi yak naslidok ukrainskoi trudovoi emihratsii: problemy ta shlyakhy ikh rozvyazannya: Zbirnyk dopovidei Mizhnarodnoii naukovo-praktychnoi konferentsii, 22 bereznya 2012 r. Vyd-vo NU "Lvivsika politekhnika". pp. 16–24.

Ivankova-Stetsiuk, O. B. (2012) *"Tserkva v prostori migratsii: etnokulturni resursy ta sociointegratyvnyi potentsial religiinykh spilnot ukraiintsiv: monografiya"*, Lviv: Instytut narodoznavstva NAN Ukraiiny; Komisiya UGKC u spravah migrantiv.

Jacobson, D. (1996) *Rights Across Borders: Immigration and the Decline of Citizenship.* Baltimore, Maryland: Johns Hopkins University Press.

Jacoby, A. (1994) "Felt Versus Enacted Stigma. A Concept Revisited". *Social Science & Medicine,* 38:269–74.

Jałowiecki, B., Hryniewicz, J., Mync, A. (1994) *Ucieczka mizgiw z nauki i szkolnictwa wyiszego w Polsce w latach 1992–1993. Raport z badan.* Uniwersytet Warszawski. Europejski instytutrozwoju regionalnego i lokalnegoStudia regionalne i lokalne. 14(47). Warszawa. Str. 7.

Jaźwińska, E. (2000) „Metody iloiciowe w badaniach nad migracjami" *Miidzynarodowymi Seria: prace migracyjne.* 36. Instytut Studiuw Spoiecznych UW.

Jaźwińska, E., Kaczmarczyk I, P., Napierala, P. (2008) „Metodologia badania migracji z Polski – podejicie etnosondaiowe: doiwiadczenia badawcze a projekt MPLM", Wspiiczesne migracje zagraniczne Polakiw. Aspekty lokalne i regionalne. Uniwersytet Warszawski Wydziai Nauk Ekonomicznych Osrodek Badai nad Migracjami.

Jensen, K. B. (1990) "Television futures: A social action methodology for studying interpretive communities". *Critical Studies in Media Communication,* 7(2).129–146.

Jevtukh, V., Kovalchuk, O., Popok, A., Troshchynskyi, V. (2010) "Ukraiinska etnichnist poza mezhamy Ukraiiny". *Narodna tvorchist ta etnografiya,* 1. p. 48–57.

Jończy, R. (2000) „Ekonomiczne konsekwencje i determinanty zagranicznych migracji zarobkowych", *Polityka Społeczna,* nr. 5/6.

Jonczy, R. (2003) *Migracje zarobkowe ludnoici autochtonicznej z wojewidztwa opolskiego. Studium ekonomicznych determinant i konsekwencji.* Opole: Wydawnictwo Uniwersytetu Opolskiego.

Jończy R., Rokita-Poskart D. (2014) *Zmiany w zakresie zatrudnienia w Polsce i za granicą ludności autochtonicznej województwa opolskiego w okresie 2004–2010.* Studia Ekonom-iczne. pp. 145–157,

Jowell, R. (1998) "How comparative is comparative research". *American Behavioral Scientist,* 42:168–177.

Kacharaba, S. (1995) *Ukraiinska emigratsiya. Emigratsiynyi rukh zi Skhidnoii Halychyny ta Pivnichnoii Bukovyny u 1890–1914 rokah.* Lviv, 1995.

Kacharaba, S. (2002) „Emigratsiina polityka Polshchi ta yiyi reali-zatsiya na Zakhidniy Ukraiini (1919–1939)". *Problemy slovya-noznavstva,* 52. pp. 73–85.

Kacharaba, S. (2003) *Emigratsiya z zahidnoii Ukraiiny (1919–1939).* Lviv.

Kandrychyn, S. (2008) „Differentsyatsyya sotsyalnogo pros-transtva Ukrainy i Belorusii kak effect "stolknoveniya tsyvilizatsyj"". *Sotsyologiya: teoriya, metody, marketing.* № 4. – pp. 74–96.

Kannika, A. (2008) Situation and Trends of Vietnamese Labor Export. http://www.asianscholarship.org/asf/ejourn/articles/kannika_a.pdf

Kearney M. (1986) "From the Invisible Hand to Visible Feet: Anthropological Studies of Migration and Development". *Annual Review of Anthropology,* 15(33):1–36.

Kilkist vymushenykh pereselentsiv v Ukraiini perevyshchyla 1,1 milyon osib. http://www.unn.com.ua/uk/news/1447873-minsotspolitiki-v-ukrayini-uzhe-ponad-1-1-mln-osib-vimushenikh-pereselentsiv. Accessed 21 April 2017.

Kizilov A., Nikolaevskyi V., Petrova Ya. (2006) "Osobennosti mihratisionnykh protsessov v ukrainskom pohranichje (po rezulitatam sotsiolohicheskoho issledovaniya v Kharkovskoi i Lvovskoi oblastyakh)", *Metodolohiya, teoriya i praktika sot-siolohicheskoho analiza sovremennoho obshchestva. Sbornik nauchnykh trudov v 2kh tomakh. T.2.* Kharkovskiy natsionnal-nyi universitet im. V. N. Karazina. pp. 57–63.

Klimkin: YeS poboyuyetsya skasuvannya vizovoho rezhymu dlya Ukrainy cherez vidsutnist kontrolyu za kordonom (2015) http://ukranews.com/news/162023.Klimkin-ES-opasaetsyaotmeni-vizovogo-rezhima-dlya-Ukraini-iz-za-otsutstviya-kontrolya-za-granitsey.uk. Accessed on 21 April 2017.

Knapp, M. S. (1979) *Ethnographic contributions to evaluation research. Qualitative and quantitative methods in evaluation research.* Beverly Hills: Sage.

Kolodziej, E. (1982). *Wychodzistwo zarobkowe z Polski 1918–1939: Studia nad politykai emigracyjnai II Rzeczypospolitej.* Warszawa: Ksiaizika i Wiedza.

Kontseptsiya demohraficheskoho razvitiya Rossiskoi Federatsii na period do 2015 hoda (2012) http://demoscope.ru/weekly/knigi/koncepciya/koncepciya.html. Accessed 21 April 2017.

Kontseptisiya hosudarstvennoi mihratsyonnoi politiki Rossiyskoi Federatsii. (2012) http://raspp.ru/about/docs/tematicheskie_dokumenty/koncepciya_gosudarstvennoj_migracionnoj_politiki_rossijskoj_federacii_proekt/. Accessed on 21 April 2017.

Korek, J. (ed.) (2007) *From Sovietology to Postcoloniality: Poland and Ukraine from a Postcolonial Perspective.* Södertörns högskola. Stockholm.

Koser, K., Pinkerton, C. (2004) *The Social Networks of Asylum Seekers and the Dissemination of Information about Countries of Asylum.* London: University College London.

Kowalski, T., Polowczyk, J. (2012) *Comparative Analysis of Economic Transformation in the Ukraine and Selected European Countries.* Poznan: University of Economics.

Kritz M., Lim L. L., Zlotnik H. (eds.) (1992) *International Migration Systems: A Global Approach.* Oxford: Clarendon Press. pp. 263–278.

Kuhn, T. S. (1962) *The Structure of Scientific Revolutions.* Chicago: University of Chicago Press.

Kurunova, Iiu. (2012) "Analiz ekonomichnykh ta sotsialnykh chynnykiv zovnishnyoi mihratsii z Ukrainy" *Visnyk Mizhnarodnoho Sloviyansikoho universytetu. Kharkiv, Seriya «Ekonomichni nauky».* XV(2). pp. 119–125.

Kutsenko, O., Horbachyk, A. (2014) "Postimperskije regiony: assocyirovanaya zavisimost v razvitii Vostochnoj Evropy", *Mir Rosii.* № 1. pp. 60–86.

Ledeneva, A. (1998) *Russia's Economy of Favours: Blat, Networking and Informal Exchange.* Cambridge University Press. Cambridge.

Leontenko, O. (1999) "Problemy stanovlennya i rozvytku trudovoji emigratsii z Ukraiiny", *Ukraiina: aspekty praci. Naukovo-praktychnyi ta sotsialno-politychnyi zhurnal, 5.* pp. 28–32.

Libanova, E. M. (2011) „Mihratsiyni transferty, bidnist i nerivnist v Ukraïni. Sotsialno-ekonomichni ta etnokulturni naslidky mihratsii dlya Ukraïny", Zb. materialiv nauk.-prakt. konf / uporyad. O. A. Malynovska. Kyiv: NISD – 344 s. – S.15–26.

Lindberg, J. S. (1930) *The Background of Swedish Emigration to the United States. An Economic and Sociological Study in the Dynamics of Migration.* University of Minnesota Press. Minneapolis.

Link, B., Phelan, J. (2001) "Conceptualizing Stigma". *Annual Review of Sociology,* 27(3): 363–85.

Luhmann, N. (1995) *Social Systems.* Stanford: Stanford University Press.

Malinovska, O. A. (2006) "Formuvannya spilnoi mihratsiynoi polityky Yevropeiskoho Soyuzu", *Stratehichna panorama, 2.* pp. 142–151.

Malinovska, O. A. (2011) *Trudova mihratisiya: sotsialni naslidky ta shlyakhy reahuvannya. Analitychna dopovid.* – NISD.

Malmborg, M., Strath, B. (2002) *The Meaning of Europe: Variety and Contention Within and Among Nations.* Oxford: Berg.

Markov I., Boiko Yu., Bondarenko M., Ivankova-Stetsiuk O., Seleshchuk H., Yakubyak A. (2009) *Na rozdorizhzhi. Analitychni materialy kompleksnoho doslidzhennya protestiv ukrainskoy trudovoi mihratsii (krainy Yevropeiskoho Soyuzu ta Rosiiska Federatsiya).* Lviv.

Marunchak, M. (1991) *Istoriya ukrajinciv Kanady.* – Vinipeg. pp. 17–18.

Massey, D., Alarcon, R., Gonzalez, H., Durand, J. (1987) *Return to Aztlan: The Social Process of International Migration from Western Mexico.* Berkeley, LA: University of California Press.

Massey, D., Arango, J., Hugo, G., Kouaouci, A., Pellegrino, A., Taylor, E. (1993) "Theories of International Migration: A

Review and Appraisal." *Population and Development Review,* 19 (3): 431–466.

Massey, D. S., Arango, J., Huog, G., Kouaouci, A., Peregrino, A. Taylor, J. E. (1998) *Worlds in Motion: Understanding International Migration at the End of the Millenium.* Oxford: Clarendon Press.

Massey, D. S. (2015) "A Missing Element in Migration Theories", *Migration Letters,* 12(3):279–299.

McLuhan, M. (1962) *The Gutenberg Galaxy: "When Change Becomes the Fate of Man".* Toronto: University of Toronto Press.

Medved, F. (2003) "The end of the European 'zero' immigration policy model: proactive economic migration policy and actors' interests. Razprave in gradivo", *Treatises and Documents: Journal of Ethnic Studies.* Inititut za narodnostna vpraianja (Ljubljana). 42:116–151.

Melles, T., Jaron, R. (2009) Using Tag Clouds to Analyse and Visualise Results of Open Ended Questions. General Online Research Conference (GOR) http://www.websm.org/db/12/13235/rec/. Accessed on 21 April 2017.

Merton, R. K. (1968) *Social Theory and Social Structure.* Free Press. New York.

MID poyasnyl, pochemu ukrayntsam otkazyvayut vo vjezde v Rossiyu (2014) http://korrespondent.net/ukraine/events/3209884-myd-poiasnyl-pochemu-ukrayntsam-otkazyvauit-vo-vezde-v-rossyui-. Accessed on 21 April 2017.

Mihranty z Ukrainy na rynku pratsi. (2015) http://bezpiecznapraca.info.pl/ua/novyny/81-migranti-z-ukraini-na-rinku-praci. Accessed on 21 April 2017.

Mishchuk, H., & Grishnova, O. (2015). Empirical study of the comfort of living and working environment–Ukraine and Europe: comparative assessment. *Journal of International Studies* Vol, 8(1).

Moravcsik, A. (2000) "The Origins of Human Rights Regimes: Democratic Delegation in Postwar Europe", *International Organization 54 (spring):.*pp. 217–227.

Morrison, T. K. (1982) "The Relationship of US Aid, Trade and Investment to Migration Pressures in Major Sending Countries." *International Migration Review,* 16(1):4–26.

Mukomel, V. I. (2005) *Myhratisyonnaya politika Rossii: Postsovetskie konteksty.* Institut sotsiologii RAN, 2005. p. 153–154.

MZS obitsyaye do 2015 roku bezvizovyi rezhym vlasnykam biometrychnykh pasportiv (2014) http://dt.ua/UKRAINE/mzs-obicyaye-do-2015-roku-bezvizoviy-rezhim-vlasnikam-biometrichnih-pasportiv-156228_.html Accessed on 21 April 2017.

MZS poperedzhaje ukraiintsiv pro nebezpeku poiizdok do Rosii (2015) http://ukr.lb.ua/news/2015/03/05/297708_mzs_poperedzhaie_ukraintsiv_pro.html. Accessed on 21 April 2017.

National bank of Ukraine (2015) http://www.bank.gov.ua/control/uk/index. Accessed on 21 April 2017.

Nemetskaya politsiya zaderzhala ukrainskykh turystov za vizy, poluchennye "obmannym putem (2014) http://zn.ua/SOCIETY/nemetskaya_politsiya_zaderzhala_ukrainskih_turistov_za_vizy,_poluchennye_obmannym_putem.html Accessed on 21 April 2017.

No Border Network. (1998) The cooperation process with Ukraine. The migration management programme. http://www.noborder.org/iom/index.php. Accessed on 21 April 2017.

North, D. (1990) *Institutions, Institutional Change and Economic Performance.* Cambridge: Cambridge University Press.

Obshchestvennoye mneniye. (2012) Ed. By N. Zorkaya. Levada Centr. Moscow.

Odynets, S. (2013) Ukraiinski mihranty syohodni chynyat aktyvnyi tysk na nashykh politykiv. http://gazeta.dt.ua/socium/grigoriy-seleschuk-ukrainskie-migranty-segodnya-okazyvayut-aktivnoe-davlenie-na-nashih-politikov-_.html. Accessed on 21 April 2017.

Official site of the State statistical service of Ukraine (2015) http://www.ukrstat.gov.ua/ Accessed on 21 April 2017.

Okólski, M. (1997) *Statystyka imigracji w Polsce. Warunki poprawnoici, ocenastanu obecnego, propozycje nowych rozwiizai.* Working Papers. ISS UW.

Okólski, M. (2004) *Migracje a globalizacja. Globalizacja od A do Z.* E. Czarny (red.); Narodowy Bank Polski, Departament Komunikacji Spoiecznej. – Warszawa : Narodowy Bank Polski, 2004. – S. 199–232. – S. 215–216.

Pang, C. L. (2007) "Chinese Migration to Belgium." In: Van Naerssen, T. (ed.), *Migration in a new Europe: People, borders and trajectories in the enlarged EU.* Rome: International Geographical Union.

Parkhomenko, N. (2012) "Trudova mihratsiya v Ukraini: okremi aspekty ta viddzerkalennya u ZMI", *Visnyk Kyivskoho natsionalnogo universytetu im. T. Shevchenka: Ukrainoznavstvo,* 16. – Pp. 63–65.

Pasichnyk, O. (2012) "Zastosuvannya matematychnykh metodiv dlya analizu chynnykiv vplyvu na naselennya na riznykh stadiyakh mihratsii", *Visnyk Khmelnytskoho natsionalnogo universytetu.* 3(3). – Pp. 209–213.

Petriv, R. V. (1993) *Genezys kapitalizmu u mistah Skhidnoii Halychyny v kintsi XVIII – pershiy polovyni XIX st. (1772–1850).* – Ivano-Frankivsk.

Petrov, V. (1959) *Ukraiinski kulturni diyachi URSR 1920–1940. Zhertvy bilshovytskogo teroru.* – New-York.

Piore, M. J. (1979) *Birds of Passage: Migrant Labor Industrial Societies.* Cambridge University Press.

Pirozhkov, S., Malinovskaya, E., Homra, A. (2003) *Foreign Labour Migration in Ukraine: socio-economic aspect.* NIBM. Kyiv.

Podobed, O. A. (2008) "Sotsialno-pravovi ta moralno-psyhologichni umovy zhyttya ta diyalnosti I. Bahryanoho u Zakhidniy Nimechchyni (1945–1950)", *Naukovi zapysky Vinnytskoho derzhavnoho pedagogichnogo universytetu im. M. Kotsjubynskogo,* #14. pp. 260–266.

Polshcha torik vydala ukraiintsyam na 15% bilshe viz (2015) http://www.pravda.com.ua/news/2015/01/17/7055393/. Accessed on 21 April 2017.

Polsha znachitelno uvelichila vydachu mnoholetnikh viz dlya ukraintsev (2015) http://zn.ua/UKRAINE/polsha-znachitelno-uvelichila-vydachu-mnogoletnih-viz-dlya-ukraincev-192142. html. Accessed on 21 April 2017.

„Polska wiza, ale praca za euro" (2011) *Gazeta Wyborcza* http:// wyborcza.pl/1,76842,10098611,Polska_wiza__ale_praca_za_ euro.html. Accessed on 21 April 2017.

Popov, V. (2006) *Life Cycle of the Centrally Planned Economy: Why Soviet Growth Rates Peaked in the 1950s.* Paper presented at the AEA conference in Boston, January 2006.

Portes, A. (1983) "International Labor Migration and National Development." In: M. M. Kritz, ed., *U.S. Immigration and Refugee Policy. Global and Domestic Issues.* Lexington: Lexington Books.

Portes, A., Sensenbrenner, J. (1993) "Embeddedness and Immigration: Notes on the Social Determinants of Economic Action". *The American Journal of Sociology,* 98(6):1320–1350.

Postanovlenie Sovmina RSFSR # 404 (1988) "O neotlozhnyh merakh po uluchsheniyu torgovogo obsluzhivaniya naseleniya v RSFSR".

Problema sotsialnoho zakhystu ukraiinskykh pratsivnykiv-mihrantiv. Natsionalnyi instytut stratehichnykh doslidzen. Analitychna zapyska (2012) http://www.niss.gov.ua/articles/ 949/. Accessed on 21 April 2017.

Profil gidnoii pratsi v Ukraiini. Mizhnarodna organizatsiya pratsi. (2012) http://www.ilo.org/wcmsp5/groups/public/_dgreports/ _integration/documents/publication/wcms_154571.pdf. Accessed on 21 April 2017.

Prybytkova, Y. (2009) *Myhratsyi i vremya: ukrainskyi variant razvitiya. Postsovetskie transformatsii: otrazhenie v mihratsyyakh.* Adamanti. pp. 63–115.

Prykordonni ukraintsi zmozhut` bez viz yizdyty do Rumunii (2015) http://www.wz.lviv.ua/news/77478. Accessed on 21 April 2017.

Pyrozihkov, S., Malynovsika, O., Marchenko, N. (1997) *Zovnishnya mihratsiya v Ukraiini: prychyny, naslidky, stratehii.* Akadempres. – 128 c.

Raport na temat obywateli Ukrainy. Urząd do spraw cudzoziem-ców. www.udsc.gov.pl/wp-content/.../Ukraina-20.03.2016-r.. pdf. Accessed on 21 April 2017.

Rees, P.. Stillwell, J., Convey, A., Kupiszevski, M.. (eds.) (1996) *Population and Migration in the European Union*. Chichester: John Wiley and Sons. p. 313.

Reichlova, N. (2004) *New Member Countries and Migration Flows*. Institute of Economical Studies, Prague.

Reketyry obkladaly «danynoyu» simyi zarobitchan (2013) http://www.wz.lviv.ua/news/30525. Accessed on 21 April 2017.

Remittances in Ukraine (2013) http://www.bank.gov.ua/doccatalog/documentiid=80651. Accessed on 21 April 2017.

Reporters sans frontières (RSF) dévoile l'édition 2017 du Classement mondial de la liberté de la presse (2016) http://index.rsf.org/#!/index-details. Accessed on 21 April 2017.

Rishko-Porcescu, A. (2015) *Transformatsiya sotsialnoho prostoru velykoho mista u chasovomu ta sotsietalnomu vymirakh*. Dysertatsya na zdobuttya naukovoho stupenya kandydata sotsiolohichnykh nauk 22.00.04 - spetsialni ta haluzevi sotsiologii. Instytut sotsiologii NAN Ukrainy, Kyiv.

Rosiya vidminyaye „liberalizm" shchodo ukrainskykh zarobitchan (2014) http://wz.lviv.ua/news/84537-rosiia-vidminiaie-liberalizm-shchodo-ukrainskykh-zarobitchan. Accessed on 21 April 2017.

Rosiyan v Ukraiinu puskatymut tilky za zakordonnym pasportom. (2014) http://www.ukrinform.ua/ukr/news/rosiyan_v_ukraiinu_puskatimut_tilki_za_zakordonnim_pasportom. Accessed on 21 April 2017.

Rybalichenko V. Zarobitchan peretvoryuyut na boyovykiv (2015) http://www.golos.com.ua/article/17101. Accessed on 21 April 2017.

Said, E. W. (2001) "The Clash of Ignorance." *The Nation*. 273(12): pp. 11–14.

Sandelowski, M. (1991) "Telling Stories: Narrative Approaches in Qualitative Research", *The Journal of Nursing Scholarship*, 23:161–166.

Scharpf, F. W. (2014) After the Crash: A Perspective on Multilevel European Democracy. MPFIG discussion paper 14/21. http://www.mpifg.de/people/fs/publ_en.asp#DiscussionPapers. Accessed on 21 April 2017.

Glick-Schiller, N., Basch L., Blanc-Szanton C. (1992) "Transnationalism: A new analytic framework for understanding migration" In *Towards a transnational perspective on migration: Race, class, ethnicity and nationalism reconsidered*, eds. Nina Glick-Schiller, Linda Basch and Christina Blanc-Szanton. New York: Academy (Annals of the New York Academy of Sciences). pp. 1–24.

Schutz, A. (1962) "On Multiple Realities", in: A. Schutz, Collected Papers, The Hague: Martinus Nijhoff. pp. 207–59.

Shafranosh, O. (2016) Pyata hvylya. Sribna zemlya. http://sz.uz. ua/novini-zakarpattya/ukrajina/3796-p-yata-khvilya.html.

Shekhovtiseva K. V. (2013) Vyyiavlennya holovnykh prychyn pidvyshchennya kilkosti vybulykh osib u strukturi mihrantiv Ukrainy. Upravlinnya rozvytkom, 13. pp. 136–141.

Shestakovskyi O. P. (2010) Poshyrenist ta osoblyvosti spryinyattya etnichnoii dyskryminatsii v Ukraini. Metodolohiya, teoriya ta praktyka sotsiolohichnoho analizu suchasnoho suspilstva: Zbirnyk naukovykh prats, 16. – C. 465–474.

Singleton, A. (1999) Combining quantitative and qualitative research methods in the study of international migration. *Social research methodology*, 2(2):151–157.

Sohlashenie o sotrudnichestve v oblasti trudovoi myhratsii i sotsialnoi zashchity trudyashchikhsya-mihrantov. (2005) http://zakon5.rada.gov.ua/laws/show/997_012. Accessed on 21 April 2017.

Solt, D. (1999) Tekushchie tendentsii v mezhdunarodnoi mihratsii v Evrope. Russkyi arkhypelah: setevoi proekt "Russkoho mira". http://www.archipelag.ru/agenda/povestka/povestka-immigration/europa-dis/tendentsii/. http://zakon5.rada.gov. ua/laws/show/997_012

Sotsialne oblychchya novitnyoi ukrainskoii trudovoi mihratsii (2003) Lviv. – 40 s.

Soysal, Y. N. (1994) *Limits of Citizenship: Migrants and Postnational Membership in Europe.* Chicago: University of Chicago Press.

Speer, M. (2008) *The Ukraine as a Country Used for Transit Migration.* Berlin: SWP.

Standing, G. (2011) *The Precariat: The New Dangerous Class.* New York: Bloomsbury Academic.

Stark, O. (1984) "Migration decision making: a review article". *Journal of Development Economics,* Vol. 14:251–259.

Stark, O. (1991) *The Migration of Labor.* Cambridge: Basil Blackwell.

State migration service of Ukraine (2016) http://dmsu.gov.ua Accessed 21 April 2017.

State statistical service of Ukraine (2016). http://www.ukrstat.gov.ua Accessed 21 April 2017.

Stebelsky, I. (1992) "Ukrainian population migration after World War II", *The refugee experience: Ukrainian displaced persons after World War II* / W.W. Isajiw a.o. (ed.). Edmonton: Canadian Institute of Ukrainian Studies Press, University of Alberta. pp. 21–66.

Steinmo, S., Thelen, K. (1992) *Structuring Politics: Historical Institutionalism in Comparative Analysis.* New York: Cambridge University Press.

Stendig, S. (1935) *Polska a Palestyna.* Warszawa. S.13–15.

Streimikiene, D., Bilan, Y., Jasinskas, E., & Griksaite, R. (2016). Migration Trends in Lithuania and other new EU Member States. *Transformations in Business & Economics, 15*(1), 21–33.

Strielkowski, W., Tumanyan, Y., Kalyugina, S. (2016), Labour Market Inclusion of International Protection Applicants and Beneficiaries, *Economics and Sociology,* Vol. 9, No 2, pp. 293–302

Subtelny, O. (1992) "Ukrainian political refugee: an historical overview" *The refugee experience: Ukrainian displaced persons after World War II.* W.W. Isajiw a.o. (ed.). Edmonton: Canadian Institute of Ukrainian Studies Press, University of Alberta. pp. 3–20.

"Suchasnyi rab koshtuye vid plyashky horilky i do kilikasot dola-riv" (2011) *Viche.*.

Susak, V. (2003) "Ukrainski hostyovi robitnyky ta immihranty v Portuhalii (1997–2002 rr.)". *Ukraintsi v suchasnomu sviti. Konferentsiya ukrainskykh vypusknykiv prohram naukovoho stazhuvannya u SShA*, Yalta, 12–15 veresnya 2002 r., Stylos. – S. 194–207.

Susak, V. (2007) "Samoorganizatsiya vs derzhavnyi paternal-ism: porivnyalnyi analiz ustanovok zhyteliv Lvova i Donet-ska (1994–2004)", *Sotsiologiya: teoriya, metody, marketing, 1.* pp. 63–73.

Susak, V. I. (2009) *Paternalistski ustanovky i praktyky hromadyan Ukrainy v umovakh postkomunistychnykh transformatsiy*: Dys... kand. nauk: 22.00.03.

Sztompka, P. (2002) *Socjologia: analiza spoieczeistwa.* Wydawnictwo Znak.

Tallberg, J. (2006) *Leadership and Negotiation in the European Union.* Cambridge: Cambridge University Press.

Theo, S. Y. (2003) "Dreaming Inside a Walled City: Imagination, Gender and the Roots of Immigration". *Asian Pacific Migration Journal,* Vol. 12:411–438.

Thomas,W. I., Znaniecki, F. (1918) *The Polish Peasant in Europe and America.* Boston, MA: Badger.

Todaro, M. (1976) *Internal Migration in Developing Countries: A Review of Theory, Evidence, Methodology and Research Priori-ties.* International Labour Office.

Trudova mihratsiya yak instrument internatsionalizatsii (2010) Zbirnyk materialiv kompleksnoho doslidzhennya trudovoi mihratsii i rynkiv pratsi (Ispaniya, Italiya, Moldova, Ukraina, Rosiyska Federatsiya). Drukarski kunshty.

Trudovaya mihratsiya bez moshennichestva. http://gazeta.zn.ua/ LAW/trudovaya_migratsii_bez_moshennichestva.html Accessed 22 April 2017.

Tsapenko, Y. P. (1998) „Soyuz "zakrytykh dverei". *Myhratsiya. (3–4).* pp. 38–40.

Tsapenko, Y. P. (2009) *Upravlenye mihratsiey: opyt razvitykh stran.* Institut mirovoi ekonomiki i mezhdunarodnykh otnosheniy RAN. Akademiya.

Ukaz Prezidenta Rossiyskoi Federatsii o privlechenii i ispolzovanii v Rossiiskoi Federatsii inostrannoj rabochei sily (2002) http://www.visas.ru/info/law-ukazrabsila.html. Accessed 21 April 2017.

Jendzjowsky, I. (2011) *Ukrainian Archival Records at the Provincial Archives of Alberta: An Annotated Guide.* Provincial Archives of Alberta, Friends of the Provincial Archives of Alberta Society. Edmonton.

Ukrainska trudova mihratsiya do kraiin Yevropeiskoho Soyuzu u dzerkali sotsiologii: informatsiyno–analitychne vydannya. (2005) Pid red. N. Parkhomenko i A. Staroduba. NVF "Slavutych–Delfin". – 127 c.

Ukrainske suspilstvo 1992–2012. Stan ta dynamika zmin. Sotsiolohichnyi monitoryng. (2012) Instytut sotsiolohii NAN Ukrainy.

Ukraiinski trudovi mihranty lehalizuyutsya v Italii (2010) http://news.bigmir.net/ukraine/192065. Accessed 21 April 2017.

Ukraina stala liderom po urovnyu torhovli lyudmi – MOM. (2013)   http://korrespondent.net/ukraine/events/1503421-ukraina-stala-liderom-po-urovnyu-torgovli-lyudmi-mom. Accessed 21 April 2017.

Ukrainska trudova mihratsiya: realii, vyklyky ta vidpovidi. http://openukraine.org/ua/news/593-fond-open-ukraine-oprilyudnity-pershu-v-ukrajini-dostovirnu-statistiku-shhodo-ukrajinsykih-zarobitchan-za-kordonom. Accessed 21 April 2017.

Ukrainskaya Hretsiya: prychyny, problemy, perspektivy (po rezultatam oprosa trudovykh mihrantov) (2010) Pod red. E. Levchenko. Ahentstvo "Ukraina".

Ukraintsy obmanyvayut Polshu, chtoby probratsya v Zapadnuyu Evropu. http://obozrevatel.com/politics/ukraintsyi-obmanyivayut-polshu-chtobyi-probratsya-v-zapadnuyu-evropu.htm. Accessed 21 April 2017.

Ukraintsy poluchayut polskie vizy dlya nelehalnykh poezdok v drugie strany Shengena. http://korrespondent.net/ukraine/

events/1249832-smi-ukraincy-poluchayut-polskie-vizy-dlya-nelegalnyh-poezdok-v-drugie-strany-shengena. Accessed 21 April 2017.

Uryad rozryvaye ugodu pro malyi prykordonnyi ruh mizh Ukraiinoyu ta RF. http://www.pravda.com.ua/news/2015/03/4/7060446/. Accessed 21 April 2017.

Uzarashvili, O. (2006) Ditei zarobitchan "sadyati na holku". http://archive.wz.lviv.ua/articles/48285. Accessed 21 April 2017.

Varetska, O. (2005) „Socialno-ekonomichne pidgruntya trudovoi migratsii naselennya Ukraiiny", *Aspekty pratsi. 5.* pp. 34–40.

Varvartsev, M. M. (1996) "Atypiy Honcharenko – pioner ukraiinskoii emigratsii v SshA" *Ukraiinskyi istorychnyi zhurnal. – # 6.* pp. 105–116.

Vasylyeva, M. O., Kasko, V. V., Orlean, L. M., Pustova, O. V. (2012) *Ukraiina yak kraiina pryznachennya dlya torgivli lyudmy. Materialy dlya praktychnogo vykorystannya pratsivnykamy prykordonnoi sluzhby, pravoohoronnyh organiv ta suddiv.* Feniks.

Vasylyk, M. (1982) *Ukraiinski poselennya v Argentyni. –* Mjunhen. p. 13.

Verner, N. (2015) Nashi u Warshavi. ukr.lb.ua/news/2015/03/12/298204_nashi_varshavi.html. Accessed 21 April 2017.

Veryga, V. (1996) *Narysy z istorii Ukraiiny.* Svit. Lviv.

Veryga, V. (2002) *Za mezhamy batkivshchyny: zbirnyk naukovyh statej i dopovidej.* Instytut ukraiinoznavstva im. Krypyakevycha.

Vianello, A. F. (2012) „Transnatsionalni simyi mizh Ukrainoyu ta Italieyu" *Transnatsionalni simyi yak naslidok ukrainskoi trudovoi emihratsii: problemy ta shlyakhy ikh rozvyazannya: Zbirnyk dopovidei Mizhnarodnoii naukovo-praktychnoii konferentsii, 22 bereznya 2012 r.* Vyd-vo NU "Lvivska politekhnika". pp. 107–116.

Vidyakina, M. M. (2008) „Perspektyvy formuvannya hlobalnoii modeli rehulyuvannya mizhnarodnoii mihratsii" *Ekonomichnyi prostir: Zbirnyk naukovykh prats. 15.* Dnipropetrovsk: PDABA. pp. 13–24.

Virtis, Ye. (2012) „Stratehii dohlyadu v ukrainsikykh transnatisionalinykh simyakh: pershi vysnovky" *Transnatsionalni simyi yak naslidok ukrainskoi trudovoi emihratsii: problemy ta shlyakhy iikh rozvyazannya: Zbirnyk dopovidei Mizhnarodnoi naukovo-praktychnoi konferentsii,* 22 berezniya 2012 r. Vyd-vo NU "Lvivska politekhnika". pp. 124–132.

Vollmer, B. (2016) *Ukrainian Migration and the European Union – Dynamics, Subjectivity, and Politics.* Basingstoke & New York: Palgrave Macmillan. Volodko, V. (2007) "Vybir kraiiny migratsii ta zhyttyevi traektorii ukraiins`kyh trudovykh migrantiv" *Visnyk Odeskoho nationalnoho universytetu.* 12(6):679–687.

Volodko, V. (2007b) "Osoblyvosti reprezentatsii suchasnykh mihratsiynykh protsesiv v ukrainskiy ta polskiy presi" *Metodolohiya, teoriya i praktyka sotsiolohichnoho doslidzhennya suchasnoho suspilistva:* zb. nauk. pr. - Kh.: Vyd. tsentr Kharkivskogo natsionalnogo universytetu im. V. N. Karazina. p. 376–380.

Volodko, V. (2009) "Deyaki kharakterystyky simei suchasnykh ukrainskykh trudovykh mihrantiv (na prykladi zhinok-mihrantok v Hretsii)" *Sotsiolohiya u (post)suchasnosti: nasolodzhuyuchys` vidpovidalnistyu. Zbirnyk naukovykh tez uchasnykiv VII naukovoi konferentsii studentiv ta aspirantiv,* Kharkiv.

Volodko, V. (2011) *Vplyv trudovoi mihratsii na simeyni roli suchasnykh ukrainskykh zhinok (z dosvidom roboty u Polshchi ta Hretsii).* Dysertatsiya (rukopys). Kyiv: Kyivskyi natsionalnyi universytet imeni T. Shevchenka.

Voronovych, Z. (2011) "Ispanskym" zarobitchanam pensiyu rakhuyut, "italiyskym" – ni. http://archive.wz.lviv.ua/articles/94866. Accessed 21 April 2017.

Voronyanskyj, O. V. (2012) *Ekonomichna polityka derzhavy v suchasniy Ukraiini.* Gileya. 59(4):692–697.

Vovkanych, S. (2004) „Rozbudova innovatsiynogo suspilstva v konteksti demographichnogo rozvytku Ukraiiny", *Aktualni problemy ekonomiky.* 8:115–124.

Weyskrabovi, B. (2012) *Economic Aspects of Remittances and Migration: Case Study of Ukraine and the Czech Republic. Master Thesis.* Charles University in Prague. Faculty of Social Sciences. Institute of Economic Studies.

White, H. C. (1981) "Where Do Markets Come From." *American Journal of Sociology,* 87:517–47.

Whyte, W. F. (1943) *Street Corner Society: The Social Structure of Italian Slum.* Chicago: University of Chicago Press.

Wimmer, A., Glick Schiller, N. (2002) "Methodological nationalism and beyond. Nation state formation, migration and the social sciences. Global Networks", *Journal of Transnational Affairs,* 2(4):301–334.

World Bank. (2011) *Migration and Remittances Factbook 2011.* Washington, DC.

World Bank (2015) http://www.worldbank.org/en/country/ukraine. Accessed 21 April 2017.

World values survey Wave 6 2010–2014 official aggregate v.20150418. World Values Survey Association. Aggregate File Producer: Asep/JDS, Madrid SPAIN http://www.worldvaluessurvey.org/wvs.jsp. Accessed 21 April 2017.

Yeryomin, A. (2010) Italiya – hoduvalnytsya, Italiya – rozluchnytsya... http://archive.wz.lviv.ua/articles/84487. Accessed 21 April 2017.

Yurydychna entsyklopediya. (1999) Red. Y. Shemshuchenko, Ukraiinska entsyklopediya. Kyiv.

Zafirovski, M. (1999) "Probing into the social layers of entrepreneurship: outlines of the sociology of enterprise." *Entrepreneurship & Regional Development,* 11(4):351–371.

Zakharov, B. (2003) Narys istorii dysydentskogo ruhu v Ukrajini (1956–1987). Folio.

Zaremba, H. (2014) "Zovnishnya mihratsiya ukrajintsiv. Stan doslidzhennya", *Sotsialni tehnologiji: aktualni problem teoriji ta praktyky. Vypusk 62.* pp. 44–45.

Zazueta, C. H., Garcia y Griego, M. (1982) Los Trabajadores Mexicanos en Estados Unidos: Resultados de la Encuesta Nacional de Emigraciin a la Frontera Norte del Pais y a los Estados Unidos, Mixico, Secretaria del Trabajo y Previsiin Social, Serie Anilisis 3.

Zovnishni trudovi mihratsii naselennya Ukraiiny (2002) Za red. E.M. Libanovoi, O.V. Poznyaka. – K.: RVPS Ukrainy NAN Ukrainy.

Index

EUMAGINE
    findings   214, 222
  insecurity   67, 81, 86
Philippines, emigration
    experiences   8
Poland, migration to
  extent   78, 81, 82, 83, 85
  favoured destination   195,
    201
  history   56
  management of   58, 71, 127,
    131, 132
  research   148, 149, 157, 163,
    210, 252
Polish external migration,
    studies   35, 36, 147,
    148, 257
political elites   viii, 31, 48, 69,
    190, 228
political events of 2013–2014
  build up to   viii, 31, 190, 221
  consequences   76, 131, 218,
    224, 253
Portes, A.   40, 211
Portugal, migration to   70,
    127, 128, 132, 155, 157
postmaterial values   xv, 34,
    243, 250
precarization   72, 119, 122,
    131, 138, 256
President's Decree (1993),
    on Russian-Ukraine
    migration   120
professional success,
    EUMAGINE project
    factor   188

Prometheism   59
pull factors   xix, 55, 59, 157
push factors
  economy and
    unemployment   xviii, 8,
    49, 55, 71, 72, 126
  socio-political   xiv, 59, 61, 138
push/pull factors
  EUMAGINE findings   224,
    226, 229, 230, 256
  in Ukrainian migration
    waves   49, 63, 85, 87
  theory and research   4, 9, 10
Pylypiv, Ivan (Ukrainian
    migrant)   52

Q

qualifications of migrants
  in various migration
    waves   37, 51, 52, 57
  loss of investment in   7,
    73, 97
  policies and
    agreements   118
qualitative research
  data analysis   151
  sampling   148
  studies using   41, 145, 162,
    193
quality of life
  EUMAGINE findings   217,
    243, 252
  perceptions   92
  political instability   81, 86
  search for better   xviii, xx